A FIELD GUIDE TO
TEXAS SNAKES

SECOND EDITION

A FIELD GUIDE TO
TEXAS SNAKES

ALAN TENNANT

Contributing Authors
John E. Werler, Joseph E. Forks, Gerard T. Salmon,
Andrew Sansom, and L. David Sinclair

Maps
D. Craig McIntyre

GULF PUBLISHING

Lanham • New York • Oxford

Gulf Publishing Field Guide Series:
A Field Guide to Texas Snakes
2nd Edition

Published by Gulf Publishing
An Imprint of the Rowman & Littlefield Publishing Group
4720 Boston Way
Lanham, Maryland 20706
Distributed by National Book Network

Library of Congress Cataloging-in-Publication Data

Tennant, Alan, 1943–
    Gulf publishing field guide to Texas snakes / by Alan Tennant; contributing authors, John E. Werler, Joseph E. Forks, and Gerard T. Salmon. ; maps, D. Craig McIntyre. — 2nd ed.
        p.   cm. — (Gulf publishing field guide series)
    Rev. ed. of: A field guide to Texas snakes. c 1985.
    Includes bibliographical references (p.—   ) and index.
    ISBN 0-88719-277-4 (alk. paper)
    1. Snakes–Texas–Identification.   I. Tennant, Alan, 1943– Field guide to Texas snakes.   II. Title.   III. Series.
QL666.06T464 1998
597.96'09764–dc21   97-44587
                                                                     CIP

Formerly published as *Texas Monthly Field Guide Series: A Field Guide to Texas Snakes.*

For Helen

Contents

Typhlopidae

Blind Snakes

Colubridae

Small Burrowing Snakes

Whipsnakes, Racers, and Indigo Snakes

Brown-Blotched Terrestrial Snakes

Large Kingsnakes

Red- and Black-Banded Snakes

Mildly Venomous Rear-fanged Snakes

Elapidae

Coral Snakes

Viperidae

Moccasins

Rattlesnakes

Acknowledgments

In compiling this book, my debt to mapmaker, editor, consultant, and decades-long buddy Craig McIntyre, cannot be overstated. The same is true for Connie, Jeff, and Jonathan McIntyre.

In addition, contributing authors Joseph E. Forks and Gerard T. Salmon have devoted a major part of their lives to discovering the secret life of the gray-banded kingsnake, *Lampropeltis alterna*—the search for which, every spring and summer, brings hundreds of reptile enthusiasts to West Texas. What Forks and Salmon have learned about this intriguing member of Texas' herpetofauna is offered here for the first time: The intricate color patterns that vary markedly according to its geographically complex occurrence and descriptions of every known collecting site.

Beyond the contributions of this volume's contributing authors, I am indebted to Jim Stout for introducing me to field herpetology, to *Thamnophis* enthusiasts Bill and Donna Marvel, as well as to Damon Salceies and Troy Hibbitts for their careful observations of ophidian natural history, and to my very thorough researcher Melody Lytle. I am also most grateful to Kenny Wray for his enormous enthusiasm in helping in every way I asked; to Dr. Kathryn Vaughan, Dr. Jonathan Campbell, and Dr. Andrew Price for sharing their academic/governmental perspectives with me, and especially to Dick Bartlett for his unwavering support and encouragement.

My sincere thanks, also, to those who graciously and laboriously read, corrected, and commented at length on several of the preliminary manuscripts leading to this volume's predecessor, *The Snakes of Texas* (Texas Monthly Press, 1984): Dr. Neil B. Ford, University of Texas at Tyler; William W. Lamar; Dave Barker; Jim Stout; and A. J. Seippel.

Well before either book came into existence, however, only the generosity of many in the herpetological/medical/natural history community who contributed freely of their time and knowledge made these books possible. In addition to those previously cited they include Joseph M. Abell; Bob Binder; Johnny Binder; W. F. Blair; Bryan Blake; Dave Blody; Hugh Brown; Mark Brown; Jim Bull; Patrick Burchfield; Jim Constabile; Bill Degenhardt; Barbara Dillingham; Dr. James R. Dixon; Jim Dunlap; David Easterla; Rowe Elliott; Richard Etheridge; Mollie and David Francis; Dr. Frederick R. Gehlbach; Dr. Thomas Glass; Jerry Glidewell; Charles Goodrich; Harry Greene; Ed Guidry; David M. Hardy; Terry Hibbitts; Toby Hibbitts; Richard Hix; Erik Holmback; Richard Hudson;

J. P. Jones; John Jones; Tim Jones; Jack Joy; Alan Kardon; Robert E. Kuntz; Greg Lasley; the late wizard of herpetoculture, Jozsef Laszlo; Ray Meckel; Dennie Miller; William B. Montgomery; Susie and S.I. Morris; the late Eileen Morron; Rick Pratt; Hugh Quinn; Gus Renfro; Francis Rose; Dr. Craig Rudolph; Findlay E. Russell; Neils Saustrup; Barbara Scown; Dean Singleton; Larry and Marlene Smitherman; Jeannie Taylor; Luke Thompson; Earl Turner; Thomas Vermersch; Russ Walker; Brett Whitney; Michael A. Williamson; Sherri Williamson; Larry David Wilson; Tom Wood; Richard Worthington; and Jim Yantis.

Visually, this book is indebted both to the fine drawings of artists John Lockman and David Moellendorf; and to photographers Michael Allender, Dave Barker, Richard D. Bartlett, Michael J. Bowerman, T. L. Brown, Paul Freed, D. Craig McIntyre, George O. Miller, William B. Montgomery, Damon Salceies, and Robert Wayne Van Devender.

It is also important to acknowledge my debt to Roger Conant and Joseph T. Collins' *A Field Guide to the Reptiles and Amphibians of Eastern and Central North America* (Boston: Houghton Mifflin, 1991) as the source of several of the record lengths cited in this volume. Beyond the inspiration this volume provided, its co-author, Joe Collins, spent a good deal of time discussing with me speciation theory and ophidian evolution, for which I offer my thanks.

Finally, in the first book we worked on together, *A Field Guide to Snakes of Florida,* I wrote that my editor at Gulf Publishing, Tim Calk, was patient, fair, and supportive. Now he has become a friend.

Alan Tennant
Lexington, Texas

We tried our best to make the second edition of this field guide an accurate, informative, and enjoyable reference to the diverse indigenous snakes of Texas. Friends and family accuse me of spending more time in Texas than in my home in the northeast, and those that have made my frequent trips and study of Texas' herpetofauna a much more enjoyable undertaking deserve mention. There are many, but most importantly: Dave and Tracy Barker, Jeff Barringer, Doug Beckwith, Dave Blody, Steve Boyd, Pat Cherryhomes, Dr. James Dixon, Dave Doherty, Doug Duerre, John Fraser, Joe Forks, Kathy Freeman, David Heckard, Troy Hibbitts, John Hollister, Jim McLean, Dennie Miller, Norm Nunley, Ray Queen, Jeff and Cathy Ross, Damon Salseies, Craig and Linda Trumbower, Russ Walker, and Dr. Kathryn Vaughan.

Gerard T. Salmon
Rhinebeck, New York

Preface

In the end
We will preserve only what we love,
We will love only what we understand,
We will understand only what we have learned.

—Senegalese Conservationist Baba Dioum

Paleontologist Robert T. Bakker once observed that only with considerable difficulty had he been able to gain a perspective from which a thecodont—a stubby little Jurassic reptile—seemed as beautiful as a cheetah. The thecodont just had a different environment. An environment to which it adapted by squatting on the shores of ancient mud pans, gobbling down smaller creatures and living in the same tentative give-and-take with its neighbors that, extrapolated across the great panoply of living beings, reveals an infinitely complex system of delicately counterweighted balances.

The system is so intricate that only a bit of its circuitry is yet available to our understanding, but its essence is clear. Cosmologically intermingled sets of opposing hungers and wills-to-live suspend each life form in a tenuous balance between dominance over its environment and extinction. In this unconscious genetic struggle each species' capacities contribute to the natural forces massed against its prey, its predators, and often, its neighbors. Collectively asserted, the efforts of those neighbor/competitors tend to oppose the species' own drive for biological success just enough for both sides to coexist, balanced in communities ranging from those swarming through a drop of water to others carpeting the continents' great plains.

Although periodically reshuffled by evolutionary changes typically brought about by environmental upheaval, over long spans of time these communities are comparatively stable. During these periods, an ongoing system of opposing interests typically maintains an only slightly-varying stasis, with dropout species quickly being replaced by variations of neighboring organisms, which venture evolutionary tendrils into every newly-vacated environmental space.

As little more than blinking spectators to this most magnificent of mortal processes, we can only respect the contenders. Yet nothing could be further from our historical record: Wildlife of all kinds has always been something for mankind to overcome, to exploit, or to eliminate if it gets in the way.

Shedding the opacity of the cultural biases that have for thousands of years fueled this drive for dominance is the first step toward respecting our fellow beings. But it's not easy because as Bakker recognized, the most difficult step in learning anything meaningful about the natural world is to begin to overcome the slanted human perspectives that determine so many of our biological empathies—especially where snakes are concerned.

In the prevailing cultural context serpents are so scary and repugnant that, even to people who would hesitate to harm any other vertebrate, it has long seemed proper to kill a snake. Yet with the disappearance of so many formerly abundant animals that viewpoint is changing. Gradually, we are starting to see how much we've lost in ridding ourselves of the bears and wolves, mountain lions, and rattlesnakes that threatened first our lives, then our livestock.

Too late, for the most part, awareness is dawning of the fundamental ignorance of seeing such creatures as villains, of filtering their appearances and actions through our provincial human perspectives of good and evil, beauty, and ugliness—as though such narrow criteria could set standards for a system of harmonies that preceded our existence by billions of years and will certainly outlast us by an equivalent span. Culturally ingrained as it is, to choose certain striking beings—cheetahs, swallows, or redwood trees—to grace with our eccentric notion of beauty is to ignore how meager are our recently-acquired cultural concepts when judged against a cosmic order whose structure binds the stately parade of stars and planets, shapes the flow of the tectonic currents that mold the continents, and has wrought the symmetry of serpents no less than that of tigers.

Moreover, assigning malfeasance to creatures we perceive as psychologically alien creates in us an illusion, an illusion that our species is different, a higher sort of creature.

It is this unconsciously arrogant notion that obscures from us our essence. We are but one minuscule thread in the planet's great organic tapestry—a thread, moreover, entirely dependent upon neighboring threads to maintain its place in the weave of life. In this intricate matrix every single species of us is bound to our neighbors by myriad dovetailing pacts of mutual dependency—supremely complex pacts, pacts not of our choice nor over which we exercise control, but mutually dependent pacts, nevertheless, on which our joint survival ultimately depends.

This book is an attempt to bridge, in a single small area of knowledge, the large and growing gap between the data of the professional biological journals and the general, popular awareness of the natural world that largely determines our role in preserving or destroying it.

Snakes and the Law

Andrew Sansom
Executive Director

L. David Sinclair
Director Wildlife Enforcement
Texas Parks and Wildlife Department
Austin, Texas

In Texas, snakes can be categorized into three distinct classes; (1) non-protected non-game, (2) protected or threatened non-game, and (3) endangered. These three classes are governed by statutes enacted by the Texas Legislature and by regulations adopted by the Texas Parks and Wildlife Commission.

Statutes and regulations that affect the collection or hunting of non-protected, non-game snakes in Texas are currently minimal. Section 1.101, *Parks and Wildlife Code,* provides that "hunt" means capture, trap, take, or kill, or an attempt to capture, trap, take, or kill. Chapter 42, *Parks and Wildlife Code,* requires that a person hunting any animal (terrestrial vertebrate) in Texas must possess a hunting license; therefore, a person collecting or hunting snakes is required to possess a hunting license.

There are no restrictions regarding means and methods for hunting snakes, provided a person is hunting on private property. Section 62.003, *Parks and Wildlife Code,* allows a person to hunt an animal from a motor vehicle within the boundaries of private property. No attempt may be made to hunt any wild animal from the vehicle on any part of a public road or public road right-of-way within the state.

If the collecting or hunting of snakes occurs on a public road, there are restrictions regarding the means and methods used. It is lawful for a person to drive a vehicle to any area along a public road, park the vehicle off the road, and walk the road right-of-way to collect or hunt snakes. While collecting or hunting snakes, using a vehicle on a public road in an abnormal, unlawful, or erratic manner—which includes driving slow enough to create a safety hazard, stopping on the pavement or roadbed, shining lights in ditches, or turning crossways in the roadway to spot snakes lying on the opposite ledges of the right-of-way—constitutes probable cause to believe hunting from a vehicle on a public road is occurring in violation of Section 62.003, *Parks and Wildlife Code*. (It may also be a violation of the *Texas Transportation Code*.) An officer may make a determination of whether a person is hunting from a vehicle by observing the driver's use or maneuvering of the vehicle on a public road during the collection or hunting process. A person who violates Section 62.003, *Parks and Wildlife Code*, commits an offense that is punishable as a Class C *Parks and Wildlife Code* misdemeanor ($25–$500 fine). A second or subsequent violation of this statute within 5 years of the first offense is punishable as a Class B *Parks and Wildlife Code* misdemeanor ($200–$2,000 fine and/or a jail term not to exceed 180 days). In either event, each snake unlawfully hunted or collected constitutes a separate offense.

Snake collectors or hunters should know that it is against the law to: (1) discharge a firearm on or across a public road as provided in Section 42.01, *Texas Penal Code*, punishable by a fine not to exceed $500; (2) hunt without landowner's consent as provided in Section 61.022, *Parks and Wildlife Code*, punishable on first offense as a Class C *Parks and Wildlife Code* misdemeanor ($25–$500 fine), on second or subsequent offense as a Class B *Parks and Wildlife Code* misdemeanor ($200–$2,000 fine and/or a jail term not to exceed 180 days)—both offenses result in an automatic loss of hunting license for a period of from 1–5 years—and (3) trespass on the privately-owned property adjacent to the roadway as provided in Section 30.05, *Texas Penal Code*, punishable as a Class B misdemeanor with a fine not to exceed $2,000 and/or 180 days in a jail, unless the person possesses a deadly weapon. Then the offense is a Class A misdemeanor with a fine not to exceed $4,000 and one year in jail.

Snakes that are listed as protected or threatened non-game are regulated by the Texas Parks and Wildlife Department and no person may take, possess, transport, export, sell or offer for sale, or ship any species of snake listed as protected, or possess, transport, export, sell, or offer for sale, goods made from any snake listed as protected. It is not a violation to possess or transport live, mounted, or preserved specimens of species legally collected in another state, except that a copy of a valid out-of-state permit authorizing the possession of the specimens must accompany each specimen during transport within Texas and must be retained by the person or institute possessing the specimen. A person may possess, transport, export, sell, or offer for sale goods made from snakes listed as protected, provided the person possesses proof that the goods were obtained from lawfully taken snakes. A violation of the protected non-game statutes or regulations is a Class C *Parks and Wildlife Code* misdemeanor ($25–$500 fine).

The following species are protected or threatened non-game:

Big Bend Blackhead Snake (Blackhood Snake)	*Tantilla rubra (Tantilla rubra cucullata)*
Black-striped Snake	*Coniophanes imperialis*
Brazos Water Snake	*Nerodia harteri*
Concho Water Snake	*Nerodia paucimaculata*
Indigo Snake	*Drymarchon corais*
Louisiana Pine Snake	*Pituophis melanoleucus ruthveni*
Northern Cat-eyed Snake	*Leptodeira septentrionalis*
Scarlet Snake	*Cemophora coccinea*
Smooth Green Snake	*Liochlorophis vernalis*
Speckled Racer	*Drymobius margaritiferus*
Texas Lyre Snake	*Trimorphodon biscutatus*
Timber Rattlesnake	*Crotalus horridus*

Endangered species statutes are cited in Chapter 68, *Parks and Wildlife Code*. Snakes that are indigenous to Texas are endangered if listed on the United States list of Endangered Native Fish and Wildlife or if they are on the Fish and Wildlife Threatened with Statewide Extinction list as filed by the Executive Director of the Texas Parks and Wildlife Department. Currently, there are no native species listed as endangered in Texas.

Section 68.015, *Parks and Wildlife Code,* is related to prohibited acts regarding endangered species and no person may possess, sell, distribute, or offer or advertise for sale an endangered snake unless the snake has been lawfully born and raised in captivity for commercial purposes under the provisions of Chapter 68, *Parks and Wildlife Code.*

A person may possess endangered snakes for the purpose of propagating them for sale if the person has acquired a commercial propagation permit issued under the authority of Chapter 68, *Parks and Wildlife Code.* A permit may be issued if it is determined that the applicant has acquired initial breeding stock from a person permitted by the Department or otherwise legally acquired. The applicant must not have violated the laws of the United States, Texas, or any state with respect to the acquisition of breeding stock. The original propagation permit is valid for one year and the fee is $300. At the end of one year, a renewal propagation permit may be issued for a period of 3 years at a cost of $550.

No person may possess, sell, distribute, or offer or advertise for sale any goods made from endangered snakes unless: (1) the goods were made from snakes born and raised in captivity for commercial purposes under the provisions of Chapter 68, *Parks and Wildlife Code;* or (2) the goods were made from snakes taken in another state and the person presents documented evidence to the Department to substantiate that fact. No person may sell, advertise, or offer for sale any species of snake not classified as endangered under the name of any endangered snake.

Section 68.006, *Parks and Wildlife Code,* provides that a permit may be issued under the authority of Subchapter C, Chapter 43, *Parks and Wildlife Code,* to possess, take, or transport endangered snakes for zoological gardens, scientific research, or to take or transport endangered snakes from their natural habitat for propagation for commercial purposes and makes it a violation to conduct any of these activities without the permit. A person who violates any provision of Chapter 68, *Parks and Wildlife Code,* commits a Class C *Parks and Wildlife Code* misdemeanor ($25–$500 fine). A person who violates any provision of this chapter and who has been convicted on one previous occasion of a violation of this chapter commits an offense that is a Class B *Parks and Wildlife Code* misdemeanor ($200–$2,000 fine and/or a jail term not to exceed 180 days). It is a Class A *Parks and Wildlife Code* misdemeanor ($500–$4,000 fine and/or a jail term not to exceed one year) if a person commits an offense of this chapter and has two or more previous convictions.

Public land under the control of the Texas Parks and Wildlife Department is also regulated for hunting. It is an offense to harm, harass, disturb, trap, confine, possess, or remove any wildlife from a unit of the state park system except by a permit issued by the Director or as provided by Subchapter D, Chapter 62, *Parks and Wildlife Code.* Additionally, no person may take or attempt to take or possess wildlife from a wildlife management area except in the manner and during the times permitted by the Department under Subchapter E, Chapter 81. A violation of these statutes or rules is a Class C *Parks and Wildlife Code* misdemeanor ($25–$500 fine).

In addition to criminal fines that may be imposed, a person may be assessed a civil recovery fee for snakes unlawfully killed, caught, possessed, or injured in violation of the *Parks and Wildlife Code* or regulation adopted under the authority of the *Parks and Wildlife Code.* The recovery value for each non-protected non-game snake is the commercial value of the species at the time it was illegally killed, caught, taken, possessed, or injured. The recovery value for each individual protected or threatened snake equals $500, plus the commercial value of the species at the time it was illegally killed, caught, possessed, or injured.

Examples of fees that may be assessed are as follows:

Non-protected non-game snakes:

Trans-Pecos Copperhead	*Agkistrodon contortrix pictigaster*	$63.00
Trans-Pecos Rat Snake	*Bogertophis subocularis*	$63.00
Diamondback Rattlesnake	*Crotalus atrox*	$8.00

Protected or threatened non-game snakes:

Concho Water Snake	*Nerodia paucimaculata*	$515.50
Indigo Snake	*Drymarchon corais*	$515.50
Texas Lyre Snake	*Trimorphodon biscutatus*	$503.00

A game warden or other peace officer commissioned by the Department may search a game bag, receptacle, or vehicle if the game warden or peace officer has a reasonable suspicion that it contains a wildlife resource that has been unlawfully taken. A wildlife resource includes animal, bird, reptile, amphibian, fish, or other aquatic life, the taking or possession of which is regulated in any manner by the *Parks and Wildlife Code,* and a game warden or other peace officer commissioned by the Department may inspect a wildlife resource that is discovered during a lawful search. In addition, to enforce the game and fish laws of Texas, a game warden may enter on any land or water where wild game or fish are known to range, and no action may be sustained against a game warden of the Department to prevent his entering when acting in his official capacity.

Information provided in this section may change due to state or federal legislation or Texas Parks and Wildlife Commission action. Any questions regarding these regulations may be directed to the Texas Parks and Wildlife Department Law Enforcement Division at (512) 389-4800.

As of February 1998, it seems likely that a Commercial Collecting Permit may soon be needed necessary for anyone possessing more than 6 species/subspecies in the field, and a Non-Game Animal Dealer Permit required of anyone selling, or buying for resale, any non-game animal not protected by law in Texas.

A. T.

Introduction

This field guide describes every species and subspecies that is known to occur in Texas. The number assigned to each animal in the text is also used in the photograph captions and the index.

The common and scientific names used here follow, for the most part, the nomenclature established by the Society for the Study of Amphibians and Reptiles in *Standard Common and Current Scientific Names for North American Amphibians and Reptiles,* third edition, Joseph T. Collins et al. Lawrence, Kansas: University of Kansas Museum of Natural History (1990).

The *species accounts* groups the snakes into sections that reflect (a) a snake's resemblance to other similarly patterned serpents; (b) its occupancy of similar habitat—aquatic snakes, for example; and/or (c) its taxonomic relationship to other members of the same section.

The *range maps* accompanying the text define the distribution of these animals. Even in well-studied areas the geographical range of many species and subspecies has not been determined with precision, however, and range demarcations are necessarily generalizations. Moreover, because the environmental conditions determining reptiles' presence in an area are in perpetual flux, range maps are best thought of as constantly altering cartographic kaleidoscopes, with the dark-shaded portion of each map representing only the temporary distribution of a particular species or subspecies.

The more lightly shaded regions on some of the maps indicate zones of intergradation—areas where the ranges of two or more subspecies overlap. Genetic crosses found in these areas often exhibit characteristics of each of the neighboring subspecies, but because the boundaries of intergradation zones between adjacently ranging subspecies are even more variable than the boundaries between full species, specimens occurring in intergradation zones may (a) exhibit any combination of the characteristics of either of the subspecies involved, or (b) closely resemble the non-intergrade form of either race.

Moreover, snakes are likely to occur only where proper environmental conditions exist. An animal may be quite common in some places, yet very rare in other areas well within its overall geographical distribution, because reptiles in general and snakes in particular are not found everywhere within their geographic ranges. This means habitats that can support a significant population are likely to occur only in certain parts of their range. Elsewhere, less favorable conditions often mean that the species or subspecies may be rare or entirely absent throughout much of its overall range.

Human intervention is also now so rapidly changing Texas' natural ecosystems that as habitat alteration causes extirpation of many animal and plant populations, other species and subspecies may expand their territories to occupy areas where they are currently unrecorded. It is far more likely that large numbers of species and subspecies will simply not be replaced, however.

Despite many snakes' rapid replacement rates, most varieties are now in decline. In my more than forty years' observations of Texas herpetofauna it has become clear that the numbers of all reptiles, and particularly those of terrestrial snakes, have dramatically diminished. This is largely due to two factors:

1. The vastly increased presence of man. Most important is the conversion of thousands of square miles of natural terrain to residential and commercial human usage—territory where few snakes are able to survive. Also significant is the enormously increased traffic on the state's ever-expanding highway system. On these lethal networks of pavement, the constant passage of vehicles creates a 24-hour, year-round web of death to reptiles too unwary of cars to do much besides look up at the last moment.

2. The invasion of South American fire ants, which have devastated populations of both small fossorial and larger egg-laying snakes in the eastern half of the state.

Because none of these increased-mortality factors show any sign of abating, one can expect the formerly rich herpetofauna of Texas to continue to decline, and while no species or even subspecies is likely to become extinct in the near future, many fewer reptiles of all kinds will be out there fulfilling the roles they would have played in a healthier ecosystem.

Published material used in compiling the distribution areas of the maps includes G. G. Raun and F. R. Gehlbach, *Amphibians and Reptiles in Texas* (Dallas: Dallas Museum of Natural History, 1972); *Herpetological Review*, vols. 3–13; J. Glidewell, *Southwestern Naturalist* 19 (2):213–23, 1974; D. Miller, "A Life History Study of the Gray-banded Kingsnake, *Lampropeltis mexicana alterna*, in Texas" (master's thesis, Sul Ross State University, 1979); John E. Werler, *Poisonous Snakes of Texas and the First Aid Treatment of Their Bites* (Austin: Texas Parks and Wildlife, 1978); Roger Conant/Joseph T. Collins, *A Field Guide to*

Reptiles and Amphibians of Eastern and Central North America (Boston: Houghton-Mifflin, 1991); *Journal of Herpetology 11* (2):217–20, 1977); C. J. Cole and L. M. Hardy, *Bulletin of the American Museum of Natural History,* vol. 171 (New York, 1981); and J. S. Mecham, *Copeia* (1956:51–52).

Those who assisted with advice, field records, and additional distribution data include Connie, Jeff, and Jonathan McIntyre; Earl Turner; Dr. Neil Ford; Dr. Craig Rudolph; Terry Hibbitts, Jr.; Troy Hibbitts; Toby Hibbitts; Dr. Jonathan Campbell; Jim Stout; Jack Joy; Johnny Binder; Michael Allender; Bill and Donna Marvel; Thomas Vermersch; and Dr. Frederick R. Gehlbach.

Texas Snake Habitats*

Benjamin Tharp's *The Vegetation of Texas* (1939), W. Frank Blair's *The Biotic Provinces of Texas* (1950), and a synthesis of modern distributional data suggest that Texas has six primary natural regions:

1. The **Forest Region** of East Texas, principally composed of a pine/hardwood forest, fringed on the west by the oak-hickory forest called the Cross Timbers in North Central Texas.

2. The **Prairie Region,** of both North Central and Coastal Texas, defined by its original tall- or short-grass prairie, known as blackland prairie in Central Texas or, near the coast, salt grass prairie.

3. The **Tamaulipan Region** of South Texas, comprising both tall-grass and short-grass prairie interspersed with clumps of woody plants that form thorn woodland, locally called chaparral or, more often, simply brush.

4. The **Edwards Plateau Region** of West Central Texas, containing both short-grass prairie and oak-juniper evergreen woodland, locally called cedar brakes.

5. The **High Plains Region** of the Texas Panhandle, covered for the most part with short-grass prairie but broken by mesas and canyons occupied by evergreen woodland.

6. The **Chihuahuan Desert Region** of Trans-Pecos Texas, which includes shrub desert in low basins, short-grass prairie on the rolling plains above, succulent desert and evergreen woodland on the lower and upper mountain slopes, respectively, and coniferous forest on a few high peaks.

Riparian or **Deciduous Woodland** follows creeks and rivers through all natural community types of the state.

Thirty-six percent of the 105 species and subspecies of snakes living in Texas are of eastern derivation. These animals range widely in eastern or southeastern North America but reach their western limits in Texas, where most are stopped by either the arid western plateaus or the short-

 *Contributions by Frederick R. Gehlbach, Baylor University.

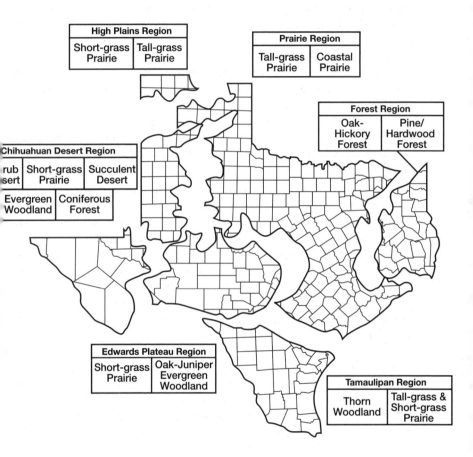

High Plains Region

Short-grass Prairie	Tall-grass Prairie

Prairie Region

Tall-grass Prairie	Coastal Prairie

Forest Region

Oak-Hickory Forest	Pine/ Hardwood Forest

Chihuahuan Desert Region

rub sert	Short-grass Prairie	Succulent Desert
Evergreen Woodland	Coniferous Forest	

Edwards Plateau Region

Short-grass Prairie	Oak-Juniper Evergreen Woodland

Tamaulipan Region

Thorn Woodland	Tall-grass & Short-grass Prairie

5

grass prairie of the High Plains. The eastern hognose snake, the Texas rat snake, and the timber rattlesnake are examples.

The second important group of snakes (23% of the state's species) is basically western or southwestern, with eastern limits in Texas set by the central tall grass prairie. The ground snake, the longnose snake, and the prairie rattlesnake are among this group. Additionally, there exists a small number (14%) of central North American or Great Plains species, such as the Texas blind snake, the Texas lined snake, and the western hognose snake. A yet smaller group (9%) is of Chihuahuan regional derivation, among which are the Trans-Pecos rat snake, the western hooknose snake, and the rock rattlesnakes. A few (9%) transcontinental species also range across Texas, including ringneck snakes, desert and speckled kingsnakes, and several garter snakes, while some essentially tropical snakes, such as the indigo, cat-eyed, and black-striped snakes, reach the northern limits of their range in the state's Tamaulipan Region. A single endemic, the Harter's water snake, is found entirely within Texas.

James Rogers (1976) analyzed these distributions and found that vertical landscape diversity and the number of coexisting small-mammal species were the chief positive influences on the number of local snake species. High altitude has a significant negative effect, however. The diverse ophidian population of the eastern and central portions of the state is, of course, the result of the strong eastern faunal element, but Texas' overall diversity is due to the addition of numerous western serpents plus the mix of important specialties from the Great Plains, Chihuahuan Desert, and Tamaulipan regions; no other state has as many snake species.

The following table is only an approximation of the probable frequency, as best as is known, with which a snake species or subspecies makes use of or is able to inhabit a particular type of habitat. Various microhabitats within these large geographic/geologic/vegetation areas are preferred by most snakes, and only a few species and subspecies such as racers, Texas rat snakes, bullsnakes, and western diamondback rattlesnakes occur throughout most of the terrain—*even in the Habitat Types where they are listed as* **C**, or **Common**.

Therefore, a species or subspecies designated as C in a given habitat means it is generally **Common** in that specific geographic area. That is, in a particular habitat type, this species or subspecies can be expected to occur—*somewhere*—on most sizeable rural tracts of land containing both unaltered or minimally-altered habitat and a variety of vegetation and terrain typical of the area, including lakes, ponds, or waterways. (The animal is unlikely to occur *everywhere* on such tracts of land for, even in areas where it may be listed as **Common**, most snake species and subspecies are found only in specific localities. Water snakes and ribbon snakes are found almost exclusively in and around bodies of water, for example, although most of this species' range is made up of dry land, and many other species and subspecies are usually restricted to such riparian corridors.)

Further, snake populations are notoriously unstable, with some species and subspecies being locally abundant in some locales, in some years, and nearly absent in the same areas at other times. Moreover, reptiles in general and snakes in particular are extremely seasonally-oriented, weather-sensitive creatures. Many species and subspecies spend much, or all, of the year in hiding below the surface, and their movements abroad are subject to a huge range of seasonal and atmospheric conditions. Therefore, at any given time—even on tracts of land where a species or subspecies is abundant—one cannot necessarily expect to find the animal, for the subterranean lives of many snakes mean they can be abundant in an area but only rarely be seen by humans. (Complicating this situation, snakes' population fluctuations can make them seem more abundant in an area—or, in years of prolonged drought for example, much more rare—than that species or subspecies may prove to be over many years' observation.)

A U, or **Uncommon** species would occur on only a few such tracts of land, even within the Habitat Types it normally occupies.

An **R** designation means a **Rare** species, or one that infrequently occurs even on large tracts of natural land within a particular habitat type.

A * symbol means that a species' or subspecies' occurrence in a given habitat type is not yet known. No habitat chart such as this has previously been published for Texas snakes, and as with all natural history studies, its data are still incomplete and subject to revision. We welcome information to this end.

Although Texas snakes are about equally divided between prey specialists/habitat generalists (eastern hognose, the crayfish snakes, Texas coral snake), habitat specialists/prey generalists (*Nerodia*-genus water snakes, western cottonmouth, the rock rattlesnakes), and prey-and-habitat generalists (western diamondback rattlesnake, bullsnake, Texas rat snake), the *prey*—invertebrate and vertebrate—of most native snakes tends to be habitat-specialized, so that most species and subspecies occur more often in certain biotic communities than in others.

	Chihuahuan Desert Region				
	Shrub Desert	*Short-grass Prairie*	*Succulent Desert*	*Evergreen Woodland*	*Coniferous Forest*
1. Plains Blind Snake *Leptotyphlops dulcis dulcis*					
2. New Mexico Blind Snake *Leptotyphlops dulcis dissectus*	*	*	*	C	*
3. Trans-Pecos Blind Snake *Leptotyphlops humilis segregus*	C	*	C	*	*
4. Flathead Snake *Tantilla gracilis*					
5. Plains Blackhead Snake *Tantilla nigriceps*	*	U	U	*	*
6. Southwestern Blackhead Snake *Tantilla hobartsmithi*	C	C	C	*	*
7. Mexican Blackhead Snake *Tantilla atriceps*					
8. Blackhood Snake *Tantilla rubra cucullata*	*	*	R	*	*
9. Texas Brown Snake *Storeria dekayi texana*					
10. Marsh Brown Snake *Storeria dekayi limnetes*					
11. Florida Redbelly Snake *Storeria occipitomaculata obscura*					
12. Rough Earth Snake *Virginia striatula*					
13. Western Smooth Earth Snake *Virginia valeriae elegans*					
14. Mississippi Ringneck Snake *Diadophis punctatus stictogenys*					
15. Prairie Ringneck Snake *Diadophis punctatus arnyi*					
16. Regal Ringneck Snake *Diadophis punctatus regalis*	U	U/R	U/R	U	U
17. Ground Snake *Sonora semiannulata*	C	C	C/U	U	*
18. Western Worm Snake *Carphophis amoenus vermis*					

	High Plains Region		Edwards Plateau Region		Tamaulipan Region		Prairie Region		Forest Region	
	Short-grass Prairie	Tall-grass Prairie	Short-grass Prairie	Oak-Juniper Evergreen Woodland	Thorn Woodland	Tall-grass and Short-grass Prairie	Tall-grass Prairie	Coastal Prairie	Oak-Hickory Forest	Pine/Hardwood Forest
		C	C	C	*	U	C	*		
	*	*								
	U	U	C	C	*	*	C	*	C/U	C
	C	C	C	*	*	R	U			
			C	*		*				
						R				
			U	C/U	C	*	C		C	C
								C		
									U	U
			*	C/U		U	C	U	C	C
			*	C			C/U	U	C/U	C/U
									U	U/R
	U	U	U	U			U	*		
	C	C	C	C	U	U	C/U			
									*	*

(table continued on next page)

	Shrub Desert	Shortgrass Prairie	Succulent Desert	Evergreen Woodland	Coniferous Forest	
19. Lined Snake *Tropidoclonion lineatum*						
20. Eastern Garter Snake *Thamnophis sirtalis sirtalis*						
21. Texas Garter Snake *Thamnophis sirtalis annecteans*						
22. Checkered Garter Snake *Thamnophis marcianus marcianus*	U	C/U	R	C	*	
23. Western Plains Garter Snake *Thamnophis radix haydenii*						
24. Eastern Blackneck Garter Snake *Thamnophis cyrtopsis ocellatus*	U	U	U	C	*	
25. Western Blackneck Garter Snake *Thamnophis cyrtopsis cyrtopsis*	U	U	U/R	C	C/U	
26. Western Ribbon Snake *Thamnophis proximus proximus*						
27. Redstripe Ribbon Snake *Thamnophis proximus rubrilineatus*						
28. Gulf Coast Ribbon Snake *Thamnophis proximus orarius*						
29. Arid Land Ribbon Snake *Thamnophis proximus diabolicus*	U	U	R	U	*	
30. Diamondback Water Snake *Nerodia rhombifer rhombifer*			C/U			
31. Yellowbelly Water Snake *Nerodia erythrogaster flavigaster*						
32. Blotched Water Snake *Nerodia erythrogaster transversa*	U/R	U/R	U/R	U		
33. Broad-banded Water Snake *Nerodia fasciata confluens*						
34. Florida Water Snake *Nerodia fasciata pictiventris*						
35. Mississippi Green Water Snake *Nerodia cyclopion*						

	High Plains Region		Edwards Plateau Region		Tamaulipan Region		Prairie Region		Forest Region	
Short-grass Prairie	Short-grass Prairie	Short-grass Prairie	Oak-Juniper Evergreen Woodland	Thorn Woodland	Tallgrass and Shortgrass Prairie	Tallgrass Prairie	Coastal Prairie	Oak-Hickory Forest	Pine/Hardwood Forest
---	---	---	---	---	---	---	---	---	---
*		C/U	U	*	U/R	C	C/U		.
							R	R	R
		U	R	R	U/R	*			
U	C	C/U	C/U	C	C	C	*		
C	U								
		C/U	C						
C/U									
						C		C	C
		C	C			C			
				C	C		C		
C	C								
		C/U	C/U	C	C	C	C	C	C
								C	C
C	C	C	C	C	C	C	C		
							C/U	C	C
					C Brownsville Daly				
							R	R	R

11

(*table continued on next page*)

	Chihuahuan Desert Region				
	Shrub Desert	Shortgrass Prairie	Succulent Desert	Evergreen Woodland	Coniferous Forest
36. Gulf Salt Marsh Snake *Nerodia clarkii clarkii*					
37. Brazos Water Snake *Nerodia harteri harteri*					
38. Concho Water Snake *Nerodia harteri paucimaculata*					
39. Graham's Crayfish Snake *Regina grahamii*					
40. Gulf Crayfish Snake *Regina rigida sinicola*					
41. Western Mud Snake *Farancia abacura reinwardtii*					
42. Texas Patchnose Snake *Salvadora grahamiae lineata*					
43. Mountain Patchnose Snake *Salvadora grahamiae grahamiae*	*	C/U	C/U	C	*
44. Big Bend Patchnose Snake *Salvadora deserticola*	C	U	C	*	*
45. Rough Green Snake *Opheodrys aestivus*					
46. Smooth Green Snake *Liochlorophis vernalis*					
47. Eastern Coachwhip *Masticophis flagellum flagellum*					
48. Western Coachwhip *Masticophis flagellum testaceus*	C	C	C	C	C
49. Central Texas Whipsnake *Masticophis taeniatus girardi*	U	U	C/U	C	*
50. Desert Striped Whipsnake *Masticophis taeniatus taeniatus*	U		C/U	C	C/U
51. Schott's Whipsnake *Masticophis schotti*					
52. Ruthven's whipsnake *Masticophis ruthveni*					
53. Southern Black Racer *Coluber constrictor priapus*					

| Shortgrass Prairie | High Plains Region | | Edwards Plateau Region | | Tamaulipan Region | | Prairie Region | | Forest Region | |
	Shortgrass Prairie	Shortgrass Prairie	Oak-Juniper Evergreen Woodland	Thorn Woodland	Tall-grass and Short-grass Prairie	Tall-grass Prairie	Coastal Prairie	Oak-Hickory Forest	Pine/Hardwood Forest
							C/U		
		C	C						
		C	C						
		U	*	R	R	U	C	U	U/R
							C	U	U
							U	C/U	C/U
		C	C	U	U	C	U		
		C	C	*	U	C	C	C	C
							R		
							U	C	C
C	C	C	C	C	C	C			
		C/U	C						
				C	C		C		
				C	U				
								C	C

(table continued on next page)

13

	Shrub Desert	Short-grass Prairie	Succulent Desert	Evergreen Woodland	Coniferous Forest
Chihuahuan Desert Region					
54. Buttermilk Racer *Coluber constrictor anthicus*					
55. Tan Racer *Coluber constrictor etheridgei*					
56. Eastern Yellowbelly Racer *Coluber constrictor flaviventris*	R	R	R	R	
57. Mexican Racer *Coluber constrictor oaxaca*					
58. Central American Speckled Racer *Drymobius margaritiferus margaritiferus*					
59. Texas Indigo Snake *Drymarchon corais erebennus*	R		R		
60. Eastern Hognose Snake *Heterodon platirhinos*					
61. Dusty Hognose Snake *Heterodon nasicus gloydi*					
62. Plains Hognose Snake *Heterodon nasicus nasicus*					
63. Mexican Hognose Snake *Heterodon nasicus kennerlyi*	U	C/U	U		
64. Western Hooknose Snake *Gyalopion canum*	U	C/U	U	C/U	
65. Mexican Hooknose Snake *Ficimia streckeri*					
66. Louisiana Pine Snake *Pituophis ruthveni*					
67. Bullsnake *Pituophis catenifer sayi*					
68. Sonoran Gopher Snake *Pituophis catenifer affinis*	C/U	C	C/U	C	C
69. Texas Glossy Snake *Arizona elegans arenicola*					
70. Kansas Glossy Snake *Arizona elegans elegans*	C/U	C/U	C/U		
71. Painted Desert Glossy Snake *Arizona elegans philipi*	*		*		

High Plains Region		Edwards Plateau Region		Tamaulipan Region		Prairie Region		Forest Region	
Short-grass Prairie	Short-grass Prairie	Short-grass Prairie	Oak-Juniper Evergreen Woodland	Thorn Woodland	Tall-grass and Short-grass Prairie	Tall-grass Prairie	Coastal Prairie	Oak-Hickory Forest	Pine/Hardwood Forest
								C	C
								C/U	C/U
C/U	C/U	C/U	C/U	U	U	C	C	C	C
				U	U				
				R					
				C/U	U				
U	U	U	U		U/R		C/U	C	C
		U	U			R	R	R	*
C	C								
				U	C/U				
		U							
				U	U				
								R	R
C	C	C	C/U	C	C	C	R		
				C	C	R		*	
*	*	R				*			

	Shrub Desert	Short-grass Prairie	Succulent Desert	Evergreen Woodland	Coniferous Forest
72. Texas Rat Snake *Elaphe obsoleta lindheimerii*					
73. Baird's Rat Snake *Elaphe bairdi*	U	U	C/U	C/U	C/U
74. Great Plains Rat Snake *Elaphe guttata emoryi*	U	C/U	U	C/U	U
75. Trans-Pecos Rat Snake *Bogertophis subocularis*	C/U	R	C/U	U	*
76. Prairie Kingsnake *Lampropeltis calligaster calligaster*					
77. Speckled Kingsnake *Lampropeltis getula holbrooki*					
78. Desert Kingsnake *Lampropeltis getula splendida*	U	C/U	U	U/R	
79. Louisiana Milk Snake *Lampropeltis triangulum amaura*					
80. Mexican Milk Snake *Lampropeltis triangulum annulata*					
81. New Mexico Milk Snake *Lampropeltis triangulum celaenops*	U/R	R	U/R	R	R
82. Central Plains Milk Snake *Lampropeltis triangulum gentilis*					
83. Gray-banded Kingsnake *Lampropeltis alterna*	R	R	U	U	R
84. Northern Scarlet Snake *Cemophora coccinea copei*					
85. Texas Scarlet Snake *Cemophora coccinea lineri*					
86. Texas Longnose Snake *Rhinocheilus lecontei tessellatus*	C/U	C/U	C/U		
87. Texas Night Snake *Hypsiglena torquata jani*	C	C/U	C	U	*
88. Black-striped Snake *Coniophanes imperialis imperialis*					

	High Plains Region		Edwards Plateau Region		Tamaulipan Region		Prairie Region		Forest Region	
	Short-grass Prairie	Short-grass Prairie	Short-grass Prairie	Oak-Juniper Evergreen Woodland	Thorn Woodland	Tall-grass and Short-grass Prairie	Tall-grass Prairie	Coastal Prairie	Oak-Hickory Forest	Pine/Hardwood Forest
			C	C	R	R	C	C	C	C
			U	C/U						
	C/U	C/U	C	C	C	C	C	C	U	U/R
			*			R	C/U	C/U	C	U
	U/R	U/R					C	C	C	C
			U	U	C/U	C/U	C/U			
							U	U	C/U	U
			R	R	C/U	C/U		C/U		
		*								
		R								
			*	R						
									C/U	C/U
					R	*		R		
	U	C/U	U	U	C	C				
		*	U	U	C/U	C/U	*			
					U	U				

(table continued on next page)

	Shrub Desert	Short-grass Prairie	Succulent Desert	Evergreen Woodland	Coniferous Forest
				Chihuahuan Desert Region	
89. Northern Cat-eyed Snake *Leptodeira septentrionalis septentrionalis*					
90. Texas Lyre Snake *Trimorphodon biscutatus vilkinsonii*	R		U/R	*	*
91. Texas Coral Snake *Micrurus fulvius tener*			R		
92. Southern Copperhead *Agkistrodon contortrix contortrix*					
93. Broad-banded Copperhead *Agkistrodon contortrix laticinctus*					
94. Trans-Pecos Copperhead *Agkistrodon contortrix pictigaster*	U		U	C/U	*
95. Western Cottonmouth *Agkistrodon piscivorus leucostoma*					
96. Western Pigmy Rattlesnake *Sistrurus miliarius streckeri*					
97. Western Massasauga *Sistrurus catenatus tergeminus*					
98. Desert Massasauga *Sistrurus catenatus edwardsii*		U			
99. Timber Rattlesnake *Crotalus horridus*					
100. Western Diamondback Rattlesnake *Crotalus atrox*	C	C	C	C	U
101. Blacktail Rattlesnake *Crotalus molossus molossus*	U	U/R	C	C	C
102. Prairie Rattlesnake *Crotalus viridis viridis*		U			
103. Mojave Rattlesnake *Crotalus scutulatus scutulatus*	U	U/R	C/U	U	*
104. Mottled Rock Rattlesnake *Crotalus lepidus lepidus*		R	C/U	C/U	C/U
105. Banded Rock Rattlesnake *Crotalus lepidus klauberi*			C/U	R	*

High Plains Region		Edwards Plateau Region		Tamaulipan Region		Prairie Region		Forest Region	
Short-grass Prairie	Short-grass Prairie	Short-grass Prairie	Oak-Juniper Evergreen Woodland	Thorn Woodland	Tall-grass and Short-grass Prairie	Tall-grass Prairie	Coastal Prairie	Oak-Hickory Forest	Pine/Hardwood Forest
				R					
		C/U	C/U	C/U	C/U	U	C/U	C/U	C/U
						U	*	C	C
		C/U	C/U			C	C		
		U	U			U	C	C	C
							U/R	U/R	U/R
C/U	C/U	R					U	R	
				*	U/R				
						U	U/R	C/U	U
C	C	C	C	C	C	C	C		
			U						
C	C								

Venom Poisoning

With their bright, unblinking eyes that reflect an apparently preternatural serenity, an ability to seemingly rejuvenate themselves by casting off their aged skins, and uncanny agility—"the way of the serpent upon the rock"—snakes are clearly different from other animals. For millennia, men have perceived in them beguiling intimations of immortality, the serpent that tempted Eve being the archetype, but more often these animals have fascinated men because of their power.

No culture placed more emphasis on serpents' ability to kill than the Toltec-Aztec-Maya civilizations of Middle America, where the early rattlesnake god, which ultimately evolved into the feathered serpent Quetzacuatal, became the deity whose potency sanctified the priesthood's control over every aspect of the peoples' daily lives. The same, seemingly transcendent power of venomous snakes was called upon by the Egyptian priesthood, and by the earliest years of the dynasties the serpent's ability to kill with a pinprick was taken as such a sign of celestial potency that the serpent-god, Uraeus, personified by the Egyptian cobra, Naja haje, rose among the celestial pantheon to a position second only to that of Ra, the sun king. Naja haje thus became the symbol of imperial authority, and the bejeweled face of a cobra glared from the brow of every royal headdress—the flared neckpiece of which was itself designed to emulate the snake's spreading hood.

The priesthood, maintaining that the lethal virulence of mortal cobras derived from Uraeus himself, sometimes cut open the limbs of bitten individuals to release the "supernatural vapors" thought to have been implanted by the reptile's fangs, which did no therapeutic good but probably served to further terrorize the populace. Because there was simply no other reasonable explanation for the destructive power of venomous snakebite, however, this supernatural-vapors-theory held sway for hundreds of years after the demise of the last pharaoh, and characterized even the logical Roman approach to medicine. The belief was not challenged until, in one of the lesser-known scientific confrontations of the Renaissance, Francesco Redi opposed the physicians of seventeenth-century Florence. They believed that the virulent symptoms of envenomation were caused by the *rage* of the serpent, somehow passed, like the madness of a rabid dog, into its victim by the otherwise innocuous saliva; but Redi maintained that the "direful effects" of snakebite were the result of a lethal poison held in the snake's "great glands."

There was little to support this point of view, though, for even with the advent of chemical analysis, researchers found that those reptilian glands did not hold poison—at least not any substance, such as the toxic alkaloids or burning acids, known to poison. Snake venom, it turned out, was an apparently commonplace protein, so nearly indistinguishable from egg white in structure that in 1886 R. Norris Wolfenden, speaking for the Commission on Indian and Australian Snake Poisoning reported:

"It is quite impossible to draw any deductions as to the nature of the poison. It is merely a mixture of albuminous principles."

The first real clue to how this particular assemblage of reptilian body fluids could bring about the immediate incapacitation and rapid physical deterioration of other animals came six years later, with French physician John de Lacerda's conceptualization of the tissue-disintegrating biological catalysts he termed enzymes.

Much like the enzymes of stomach acid, harmless in the gut but able to break down devoured flesh into its constituent amino acids, the venom of North American pitvipers—rattlesnakes, copperheads, and cottonmouth—kills by enzymatically disintegrating its victim. For victims of venom poisoning this can be a major problem because only a few toxicologists have gotten far into unraveling these complex biological sequences, mostly because snake venom poisoning is a rare injury even in Texas—where more bites occur than in any other state.[1]

Treatment and Toxicology

W. C. Fields liked to tell people he always kept some whiskey handy in case he saw a snake—which he also kept handy. Some people are still drawn to Fields' remedy, but almost no one is aware that following conventional first-aid practices is just about as dangerous. Without question, trying to cut open a snakebite wound in the field is far more dangerous than doing nothing at all. Even under the best of circumstances, attempting to suck out the venom from an open wound causes harm and bestows no benefits.

Fortunately, as a practical matter it's also usually out of the question because getting bitten by a venomous snake is such a terrifying experience that subsequently being able to execute this classically prescribed

---

[1] The vast majority of the several thousand snakebites that occur annually in the United States involve nonvenomous serpents and require nothing more than reassurance and a tetanus shot. Of the few true envenomations, most occur in the southwestern states, and less than a dozen a year are fatal. In Texas, one or two fatalities from envenomation occur in an average year.

quasi-surgical procedure is simply impossible for most people. It's much better to spend one's efforts getting proper medical management than to try and fumble through ill-advised therapy in the field. All you need remember is to immobilize the envenomated extremity, remove rings or shoes before swelling makes that difficult, then wrap the limb firmly but not tightly in a splinted elastic bandage. The most important part is promptly getting the victim to a good hospital.

Binding the limb with thin, circulation-cutting cords, packing it in ice for long periods, or cutting open the punctures are dangerous procedures that go awry because they are founded on a basic misunderstanding of the complex process that begins when a venomous snake bites a human being. The scariest misconception is that a strike by one of these animals results in the injection of a dollop of lethal fluid, which then oozes through the veins toward the heart. If this were the case one would probably do whatever possible to arrest its progress, but that isn't what happens at all.[2] Once venom enters the body it almost instantly incorporates itself into the body's tissues, where it is no more removable than is ink dripped on a wet sponge. The "good" part to this scenario is that this immediate bonding to tissues doesn't leave venom free to go anywhere else in the body very rapidly, either, which means that temporarily localizing it in one area is easily accomplished with the mild pressure of an elastic bandage. This simply doesn't call for the radical, invasive techniques of most traditionally-espoused therapies, whose goal is either to drain the venom away or prevent its transit through the circulatory system, neither of which is possible in the hospital, much less in the field.

Why it is not possible—a thought at great odds with the popular concept of snakebite poisoning—is the result of the predatory role venom plays in a serpent's life. The venom of North American pitvipers is not designed kill large animals, for example; its primary function is to digest small, mostly rodent prey. Therefore, pitviper venom only gradually disperses through the body, methodically digesting tissues as it goes, using most of its 12 to 30 separate peptides and enzymes for various digestive functions.

Like all digestive processes, this one is complicated, because most of venom's diverse proteases and kinases have a separate metabolic function, often a different target organ, and frequently a different way of

---

[2]Envenomation doesn't always accompany either a coral snake or pitviper bite, and superficial punctures by pitvipers are free of toxins about 15% of the time, while no more than 40% of coral snake bites result in severe poisoning. Superficial envenomation is also much more common than severe poisoning, and unless heavy poisoning has been established, it is irresponsible to destroy irreplaceable nerve and muscle tissue by following invasive first-aid measures.

getting there. These toxins include hyaluronidase, collagenase, thrombin-like enzymes, L-amino oxidase (which gives venom its amber tint), phosphomonoesterase, phosphodiesterase, two kinds of kinases (which are both similar to pancreatic secretions and which prepare soft tissue for more extensive breakdown by analogous solutions in the reptile's stomach), nucleotidase, at least one phospholipase, arginine ester hydrolase, and various proteolytic enzymes.[3]

Within the bodies of human beings bitten by pitvipers, these enzymes simply disintegrate the living tissues just as in the snakes' rodent prey, where this sort of pre-ingestion enzymatic breakdown of the prey's internal structure renders large lumpy bodies into softer, more easily swallowed bites. Hyaluronidase, for example, breaks down connective fibers in the muscle matrix, allowing various proteases and trypsin-like enzymes to penetrate the limbs directly.[4]

In concert with several endothelial cell-specific thrombin-like enzymes, other peptides simultaneously perforate the vascular capillary walls, allowing the seepage of plasma thinned by the simultaneous assault of another set of venom enzymes—phospholipase A combines with lipids in the blood to inhibit their coagulatory function; toxic fibrinolytic and thrombin-like enzymes disintegrate the hematic fibrinogen also required

---

[3]Many of these venom enzymes operate most powerfully in complementary combinations.

[4]Quite different are the deadliest venom fractions, the neurotoxically-active polypeptides. These are the primary venom components of Elapids, such as the Texas coral snake, *Micrurus fulvius tener,* which paralyzes other snakes it feeds on. Similar neurotoxically-destructive proteins are present in smaller proportions in all snake venom, even that of ostensibly hematoxic, or blood-targeted venoms, but in the peptide-based venom of Elapids these enzymes are targeted toward the neural membranes branching from the upper spinal cord. Here, such peptides block acetylcholine receptor sites in the junctions between adjoining nuchal ganglia, impairing neuromuscular transmission and, by shutting down the autonomic triggering of respiration, can sometimes cause death by suffocation.

Other components of Elapid venom are hemolytic, or blood- and circulatory-system directed. While generally less potent than its neurotoxic elements, these cardiotoxic venom components can be lethal in high doses. Wyeth's equine-derived coral snake antivenin (Antivenin, *Micrurus fulvius,* Drug Circular, Wyeth, 1983) does not neutralize these hemolytic elements, however.

Only in fairly high doses does it have any effect against the neuroxtic components of coral snake venom, either, with a median dose 6.5 vials. At this level, 35% of patients experience side effects; in 50% of those cases, side effects are severe, resulting in anaphylactic shock or serum sickness.

Another coral snake antivenin, with about the same dosage requirement, effectiveness, and problematic side effects, is manufactured by the Instituto Butantan in Sao Paulo, Brazil, from antibodies generated by a mixture of the venom of two South American coral snake species, *M. corallinus* and *M. frontalis.* Only the new, ovine-based *Micrurus* antivenin currently under development at St. Bartholomew's Hospital, Medical College, London, and the Liverpool School of Tropical Medicine, Liverpool, U.K., neutralizes both neurotoxic and cardiotoxic components of *Micrurus* venom. In preliminary trials during 1993, it has done so with a fourfold reduction in dosage, and because this antivenin is derived from sheep antibodies, the negative side effects of prior sensitization to equine-based serums used in previous inoculations are largely absent.

for clotting; and a pair of related hemolysins, specifically keyed to the destruction of red blood cells, attack the erythrocytes directly.[5]

All this begins to occur very quickly because venom's proteins are so structurally similar to those of its victim that within seconds of injection its toxic enzymes have thoroughly incorporated themselves into the blood and tissues of their recipient.[6]

This affinity of snake venom for living protoplasm was widely recognized among primitive peoples, and stood as the rationale behind the most common American Indian antidote for snakebite, which was to slice through the fang marks and press the freshly opened body of a bird against the wound in the hope that some of the still un-bonded serum within might be drawn up into the unsaturated avian tissues. Although venom was never actually sucked out in this way, the approach seemed rational enough for variations to have been recommended by frontier medical officers looking for a better means of extraction than the dangerous and ineffective cut-and-suck regimen. Except for the inclusion in some army snakebite kits of thin sheets of latex to place between mouth and wound, however, no improvement on the old method was developed until the 1920s, when Dudley Jackson (1929) slightly refined the extraction approach by placing a series of heat-transfer suction cups over incisions both across the fang marks and around the perimeter of the expanding mound of edema that surrounds most serious pitviper envenomations.[7]

---

[5]Circulating lymphatic fluid is the major dispersive medium of most venom components, but the neurotoxically-targeted peptide components of Elapid venoms, including those of the Texas coral snake, disperse primarily through the bloodstream, where they are not subject to any mechanical constraint short of a total tourniquet.

Only antivenin is effective in treating this sort of envenomation, and only in poisoning by such peptide-based venoms is employing a temporary total arterial tourniquet appropriate because, cinched down for more than few minutes a tourniquet is likely to cause permanent injury to the limb, sometimes severe enough to require amputation. This is such a dangerous procedure that binding tourniquets around any pitviper envenomation except that of a certain severe coral snake envenomation or a toddler deeply poisoned by a big rattlesnake, is now decried by almost everyone involved in treating snakebite.

[6]The relative proportion of these elements in the venom mix varies considerably. Determined by the varying output cycles of each of more than a dozen secretory cells that release their separate toxins into a viper's paired storage bladders, or lumens, the venom's composition varies from day to day. This makes venom one of the most complex of biological substances and to some extent accounts for the disparity in potency observed between similarly sized snakes of the same species taken from the wild at the same time. (Because different venom ingredients are present in variable concentrations at any given time, their relative effect on each of a victim's organs may also be somewhat different.)

Outside the lumen, venom will even digest itself, for catalytic agents pumped into the serum from secondary secretory glands located downstream from the primary storage bladder metabolically break down venom's peptide components—which are themselves easily digested proteins.

[7]Although probably the best of the incision therapies, Jackson's approach was unable to prevent the disabling tissue necrosis associated with severe crotalid envenomation and was entirely useless against the peptide-based venom of the coral snake.

Recently, sophisticated surgical techniques for dealing with the most pernicious type of deep pitviper envenomation have been developed by Dr. Thomas G. Glass, professor of surgery at the University of Texas Medical School in San Antonio. Although most pitviper toxins reach only subcutaneous levels, occasionally a large rattlesnake accomplishes a much deeper penetration, sinking its fangs through skin, subcutaneous fatty layers, and the outer muscle fascia to deposit an infusion of venom within the muscle belly. While a rattler's toxins are much more destructive here, even a large amount of venom this far below the surface may produce few external symptoms because such areas are poorly supplied with nerve endings. (In subcutaneous tissues great pain, swelling, and discoloration accompany venom poisoning, but at great depth the venom's proteolytic enzymes may be temporarily encapsulated within the underlying layers of muscle, and give few symptomatic indications of how severe the bite actually is. The trick, of course, is being able to tell a real subfascial poisoning of this sort from the far more common, largely symptomless superficial snakebite in which little or no envenomation has occurred, and being able to do it in a hurry. If such a bite is diagnosed, a considerable amount of the infusion can sometimes be removed by deep incision and debridement, although only in this unusual sort of poisoning is a major surgical campaign generally advisable—and then only if it is executed by one of the handful of those experienced in the delicate excision of this sort of deep-lying lacunae.)

Most of the time, however, even under ideal laboratory conditions, there is not much to be gained from surgery. In experiments with cats and rabbits, F. M. Allen (1939) demonstrated that no benefit resulted even from removing within five minutes a large volume of tissue surrounding an injection of either western diamondback rattlesnake or eastern cottonmouth venom. Because during this brief time the animals had already absorbed the venom's most lethal peptide components, all the victims that received a large enough dose to kill a surgically untreated control also died, leading Allen to conclude that large infusions of crotalid venom spread so quickly throughout a large mass of tissue that even when a large excision follows, the seemingly normal tissue outside the excised area still contains enough venom to cause the animal's death.

Other properties of snake venom also weigh heavily against cutting into the fang marks after a bite. One of these is the tendency of reptilian toxins to suppress the body's bactericidal and immune responses, particularly the action of its white blood cells, for without the leukocytes' prophylactic intervention, an exceptionally receptive environment awaits the host of pathogens introduced by every deep incision. Moreover, the rapid dispersal of these infective agents is ensured by the seepage of contaminated plasma and lymphatic fluid that, following envenomation, is suffused through tissues made more permeable by the fiber-dissolving effect of hyaluronidase. It is also almost unbearable to be cut open after a pitviper bite because the digestive dissolution of blood within the subcutaneous tissue releases bradykinin from its disintegrating plasma and serotonin from its serum platelets, and both substances produce burning pain that makes the skin so sensitive that the prospect of crude pocketknife incisions becomes nearly unthinkable.[8]

An even more pressing reason to avoid incision is that the anticoagulant effect of pitviper venom on plasma fibrinogen so impairs the blood's ability to clot that opening an envenomated limb is likely to produce much more profuse bleeding than one would expect. It is always dangerous to risk bleeding in patients with low levels of fibrinogen, and following severe envenomation this is particularly chancy because when people die of snakebite (which happens in less than 1% of poisonings inflicted by native species) loss of circulating blood volume is what kills them.[8] Therefore, maintaining sufficient circulating blood volume is the key to initial management of critical snakebite poisoning, and cutting open a limb that may bleed profusely is not the way to go about maintaining blood volume.

After severe envenomation, internal bleeding always occurs but, except for the most severe poisonings, it takes hours to lose much blood internally because leakage through enzyme-perforated arterioles and venules only very gradually allows the vascular fluids to pool in the interstitial spaces of an envenomated limb. (Eventually, however, a seemingly minimal amount of such swelling—Findlay E. Russell, the country's leading authority on the subject, estimates as little as a two-centimeter increase in the circumference of a thigh—can account for the loss into the tissue spaces of nearly a third of the body's circulating blood volume, dropping vascular pressure enough to put the patient into shock.)

Ironically, though, the swelling of edema seldom threatens the limb itself. Though huge serosanguinous blisters may bulge up around pitviper bites, the distension is usually soft and limited to the epidermal and outer cutaneous layers. As this fact has become widely known, the common practice of surgically opening such swollen limbs—a technique formerly thought to relieve hydraulic pressure built up by the swelling

---

[8]In poisoning by most pitvipers (although envenomations by western—Type A venom—populations of the Mojave rattlesnake, *Crotalus scutulatus,* may entail a large complement of neurotoxically-active peptides), the venom's ultimate target is not the heart, which almost invariably performs perfectly throughout the ordeal, but the lungs. Among snakebite's few fatalities, pulmonary embolism is a nearly universal finding postmortem, but congestive pooling of blood in the lungs seldom has time to accumulate enough fluid to interfere with respiration before fatal shock from loss of circulating blood volume has occurred.

that might cause necrosis due to restricted circulation—is rarely employed, even in the most severe envenomations.[9] (What may help, however, is a mild cooling of the limb, which can offer a slight numbing of the pain. An icepack on the forehead can also mitigate the intense nausea often associated with venom poisoning, and because toxin-induced intestinal spasms have sometimes been violent enough to provoke hemorrhage of the trachea, any reduction in their severity is of importance.)

Severely chilling a bitten limb, however, is deadly to it. While the cell-disintegrating action of enzymes *is* slowed by extreme cold, it would take freezing a limb to achieve sufficient chilling to deactivate its infused venom enzymes.[10]

The conservative approach of simply wrapping the bitten limb or digit in an elastic bandage, splinting it to keep it immobile, then rewrapping the entire area, allows essential oxygen exchange while the broad pressure of the elastic bandage (which gently compresses the lymph vessels) slows the largely muscular-contraction-pumped flow of venom-saturated lymphatic fluid (and enzymatic venom fractions, the most numerous components of pitviper toxins, are dispersed primarily through the lymph system).

This singularly safe and effective field treatment dovetails with the medical consensus that now prevails concerning subsequent hospital management of severe reptile envenomation—an approach that relies heavily on the intravenous administration of antivenin combined with antihistamines to stifle allergic reaction. Proponents of this approach maintain that not only are the life-threatening systemic failures that may

---

[9]In treating some 200 venomous snakebites, Ken Mattox and his team at Houston's Ben Taub Hospital have used fasciotomy to relieve hydraulic tourniqueting less that a half-dozen times, while Russell, in treating more ophidian envenomations than anyone in North America, has never had to perform a fasciotomy due to excessive intra-compartmental pressure. In the occasional case where this procedure is necessary, exceptional circumstances generally prevail: Because unusually tight cartilaginous bands across his wrist prevented the spread of the extravasating fluids being pumped into the hand of a Central Texas farm worker bitten by a large diamondback rattler, Austin orthopedic surgeon Joseph M. Abell was forced to open the man's wrist—the only time he has ever had to resort to this measure.

[10]The worst of the cold-treatment therapies was ligature-cryotherapy. This regimen received popular attention during the 1950s as a way to avoid the obvious perils of incision and suction, but it instead combined two extremely destructive procedures—putting tourniquets around a limb or extremity, then radically chilling the constricted part by immersing it in ice, sometimes for hours. As might be expected, tissue deprived of the oxygen exchange and waste dispersal of normal blood flow and subjected to the cell membrane-cracking effect of lengthy chilling—while simultaneously being exposed to a concentrated dose of corrosive venom enzymes—died so frequently that amputations following ligature-cryotherapy became almost routine.

Though this procedure is no longer followed in medical circles, a legacy of its erroneous concepts remains, and some public service print materials as well as television commercials still refer to packing envenomated limbs in ice.

follow heavy ophidian envenomation best offset by antivenin antibodies, but that the serum offers the only significant means of mitigating the often extensive local necrosis caused by pitviper toxins.

Antivenin

Nearly as biologically complex as the venom it is cultured to neutralize, antivenin is still viewed with suspicion by both doctors and laymen, largely as a result of the poor reputation of earlier, less well-prepared serums. (In particular, the old Institute Pasteur globulin often caused adverse responses because so much was asked of it by European doctors using it under primitive conditions in the bush to treat the devastatingly toxic bites of African cobras, mambas, and vipers.) Administered by an experienced physician with immediate access to intensive care facilities, however, Wyeth's current North American *Crotalinae* and *Elapid* antivenins are fairly safe, although they must be administered with extreme care. Because antivenin can trigger allergic histamine shock, or anaphylaxis—a much more serious manifestation of the ordinary allergic response elicited by sensitizing agents from feathers to pollen—it should never be used outside a hospital.

This is because, like any other immunization, antivenin therapy depends on establishing a protective titer of antibodies in the entire bloodstream.[11] But, unlike other immunizations, to help the victim of snake venom poisoning, antivenin therapy must establish this titer in a very short time. That calls for the rapid, massive infusion of the foreign proteins that make up antivenin, but which heavily impact the chemistry of the body's blood supply. (Moreover, if a severe allergic reaction such as serum anaphylaxis occurs, the offending substance obviously cannot be removed. Unmoderated, this allergic response can result in enough swelling to obstruct the respiratory passages and even coronary attacks have occurred.)[12]

---

[11]This is why antivenin must never be injected directly into an envenomated extremity—you can't build up immunity in a finger alone.

[12]Anaphylaxis could probably be avoided altogether if animals other than horses were used to make antivenin, but historically only horses—the traditional source animals for all types of immunization vaccines—have been bled for the serum antibodies they produce in response to small, periodic injections of snake venom. These antibodies are so nearly the same for all North American pitvipers that Wyeth distributes a single antivenin, *Crotalinae,* for use against the bites of copperheads, cottonmouths, and all indigenous rattlesnake species; for coral snake envenomation, Wyeth has a separate antivenin, *Micrurus.*

The problem is that horses have been used to produce so many antigen-bearing vaccines that people who have been inoculated against typhoid, tetanus, and diphtheria bacilli have often become sensitized to equine cellular matter. This does not create a problem when they receive the very small dose of foreign protein involved in subsequent immunizations, but when a large volume of equine proteins is suddenly dumped into their systems (as happens during emergency antivenin therapy), they sometimes experience allergic anaphylaxis.

Other experimental animals have also been used to produce plasma antigens, but only on a small scale. Pitviper antivenin prepared from both sheep and goat blood has produced milder reactions

Yet administered by an experienced physician with immediate access to intensive care facilities, both Wyeth's current North American *Crotalinae* and *Elapid* antivenins can save lives. The most critical aspect of their use lies in the need for immediate intervention, usually with antihistamines, to offset the coronary or respiratory difficulties that may be provoked. (Before antivenin can be administered each patient's sensitivity to equine proteins must be determined, which is done by a standard allergic-reaction skin test trial.)

Individuals vary so widely in their sensitivity to antivenin infusion that some people need nearly twice as long as others to build up the same blood level of antibodies, but if it can be tolerated, several vials of the vaccine may be given during the first hour. Infusion is then maintained at two or three vials per hour until an adequate plasma titer is established, after which a marked decrease in the discomfort of the poisoning is normally evident.

The reason for this dramatic improvement lies in the way antivenin acts to prevent the proteolytic, fibrinolytic, and hemolytic action of snake venom. Introduced into the bloodstream, its equine antibody clusters are drawn to the venom's large, variably-shaped toxic peptides and enzymes. (Enzymes are usually spherical; peptides may be tubular, coiled, or globular, but all are spiked externally with sharp-edged, key-like protuberances that penetrate the venom's target cells and disintegrate their structure.) Antivenin antibodies physically encrust these protrusions so thickly that the toxins can no longer penetrate their target cells, eventually building up enough protective frosting to attract the body's particle-devouring macrophagocytes—cleaner cells that, like giant amoebas, eventually engulf and digest most of the conglomerate specks of alien protein.

But they don't do it without problems. As the last of the deactivated antibody-antigen complexes precipitate out of the blood 6 to 10 days after treatment, they may lodge in vascular vessel walls throughout the body, causing the skin rashes, hives, and temporary kidney impairment that collectively are known as serum sickness. Moreover, long after recovery a small cadre of the body's own antigens (spawned both by the

than the equine vaccines because few people have been sensitized to sheep and goat proteins. Antivenin has even been derived from western diamondback rattlesnake blood—to which no one is pre-sensitized. This antivenin has afforded laboratory animals a high level of protection from the effects of pitviper envenomation, especially when combined with goat antibodies.

Human beings could also generate reaction-free antibodies if anyone were willing to undergo the misery of periodic minimal venom poisoning. Understandably, no commercial human-globulin antivenin has ever been produced, but William E. Haast, who for many years operated the Miami Serpentarium, has injected small, antigen-producing amounts of elapid venom into himself for decades. As a probable result, he has survived a number of what in all likelihood would otherwise have been fatal cobra bites, and has even transfused his own presumably antigen-bearing blood into other victims of elapid poisoning, perhaps mitigating the effects of their envenomations. (Haast, incidentally, is now in his mid-eighties and remains amazingly vigorous.)

venom and by the antivenin's equally foreign horse serum antibodies) typically remains in the bloodstream, sensitizing the individual to any subsequently encountered equine globulins—or to another snakebite.

Although *Crotalinae* and *Micrurus* antivenin are kept by major hospitals, an emergency source is the producer, Wyeth Laboratories of Philadelphia (610 688-4400). Another option is to contact the Antivenin Index, compiled by the Arizona Poison Center, which offers a comprehensive array of data on venomous snakebite and a list of all the antivenins currently stored in the United States, including those for foreign species. Their 24-hour emergency number is 602 626-6016.

Finally, some authorities on envenomation by both native and exotic reptiles are:

David L. Hardy, M.D.
Arizona Poison Control System
Coagulation Research Laboratory
Department of Pediatrics,
University of Arizona Health Sciences Center
Tucson, Arizona

Sherman A. Minton, M.D.
Department of Biology,
Indiana University Medical Center
Bloomington, Indiana

James L. Glenn, M.D.
Western Institute for Biomedical Research
Salt Lake City, Utah

L.H.S. Van Mierop, M.D.
Department of Pediatrics (Cardiology)
University of Florida Medical School
Gainesville, Florida 32611

Damon C. Smith
Therapeutic Antibodies, Inc.
St. Bartholomew's Hospital Medical College
Charterhouse Square
London, EC1, U.K.
(New Coral Snake Antivenin)

Joseph M. Abell, M.D., Austin

David Feliciano, M.D., Ben Taub Hospital, Houston

Thomas C. Glass, Jr., M.D., Clinical Associate Professor of Surgery, University of Texas Medical School, San Antonio

Ronald Jones, M.D., Parkland Hospital, Dallas

George Jordan, M.D., Ben Taub Hospital, Houston

Ken Mattox, M.D., Ben Taub Hospital, Houston

Venom Potency Table

The following comparative values for the relative venom toxicities of Texas' venomous snakes are based on the widely accepted standard known as the LD50. This stands for the Lethal Dosage, or amount of venom required to kill, within 24 hours, 50% of the laboratory mice injected with it. Used in slightly varying interpretations since the 1930s, it is the standard set (using the Spearman-Karber injection method and employing genetically-uniform Swiss-Webster laboratory mice) by the World Health Organization in 1981.

As a comparative measure of venom potency, the numbers used here are a compilation of 13 major studies of venom potency conducted over the last 63 years on snakes from many different parts of the U.S.[13]

Such collective averaging is valid only as an approximation of the general relative toxicity of the venoms of these species because of the great variability that exists in the make-up and potency of toxins taken from the same snake species. (Venom samples obtained from adult individuals of the same species, taken at the same time of year, are often found to be radically different in the relative proportions of their various hematoxic/neurotoxic venom components.) This variability is compounded by the slightly to highly variable differences between regional snake populations.

The venom potency numbers cited here therefore include the highest and lowest potency values (*0 being the most toxic*) recorded by any of these studies, as well as the mean.

Species	High	Low	Mean
Western Diamondback Rattlesnake, *Crotalus atrox*	4.07	8.42	6.25
Western (Prairie) Rattlesnake, *Crotalus viridis*	2.0	2.37	2.19
Mojave Rattlesnake, *Crotalus scutulatus* (type A) Yuma, Arizona	0.13	0.54	0.34
Mojave Rattlesnake, *Crotalus scutulatus* (type B) unknown	2.29	3.8	3.05
Timber Rattlesnake, *Crotalus horridus*	2.69	3.80	3.25
Pigmy Rattlesnake, *Sistrurus miliarius*	6.0	10.29	8.15
Copperhead, *Agkistrodon contortrix*	7.8	16.71	12.26
Cottonmouth, *Agkistrodon piscivorus*	4.88	5.82	5.35
Coral Snake, *Micrurus fulvius*	0.53	0.73	0.63

[13]Compiled from Githens and Wolff (1939), Gingrich and Hohenadel (1956), Minton (1956), Russell and Emery (1959), Hall and Genarro (1961), Weinstein et al. (1962), Russell (1967), Cohen et al. (1971), Kocholaty (1971), Minton (1974), Glenn and Straight (1977), Glenn and Straight (1978), Russell (1980).

Scalation

Head Scales: Nonvenomous Snake

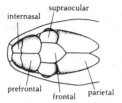

Head Scales: Pitviper

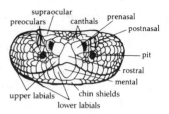

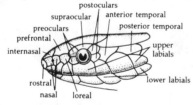

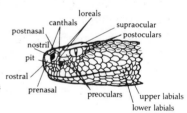

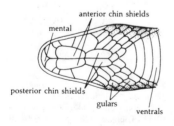

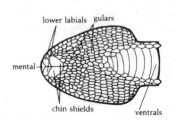

Undertail:
Nonvenomous Snake

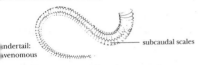

undertail:
venomous — subcaudal scales

Note: The nonvenomous Texas longnose snake
has a single row of subcaudal scales.

Undertail:
Pitviper

*undertail: copperhead
and cottonmouth — subcaudal scales

Note: The venomous coral snake has a double
row of subcaudal scales.

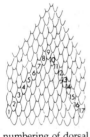

numbering of dorsal
scale rows

smooth scales

divided anal plate

keeled scales

single anal plate

33

Identification Key

People who do a lot of looking at plants or animals develop a seemingly amazing ability to identify them from the merest glance. Typically, rather than instantly picking out the specimen's specific, subtle identifying characteristics, these people are recognizing the unique group of static and kinetic attributes that together make up what might be thought of as the creature's visual gestalt. This skill comes only after seeing a great many similar plants or animals, however, and until it is acquired, about the only way to distinguish difficult species is through the use of a taxonomic key.

This one is a tool to aid in the identification of most snakes found in the state. (It is, of course, possible to encounter the rare serpent not typical of its genus, such as an albino.) All numbered questions should be answered in sequence: a *Yes* answer to the first question leads to question 2. Where more than one question is asked, all answers must be *Yes* to take the *Yes* option. A magnifying glass may be helpful in picking out details of scalation, particularly when identifying small snakes.

If it is difficult to answer a question, assume the answer is *Yes* and continue to the end. If the snake is not the one described in the text, return to the doubtful question and take the *No* option, continuing through the key until the correct genus can be established. Beyond genus level, the photographs, text, and distribution maps will establish a particular animal's species and subspecies.

1. Is the body covered with small dry scales? Does the animal lack legs, fins, movable eyelids, and external ear openings?

yes. 2

no . . . . Not a snake.

2. Is there a pit (depression) on the side of the head, between the eye and the nostril?

nostril

vertical pupil (cat eye)

pit

yes. 3

no 10

3. Does the snake have a single row of scales under the tail? Does it have vertical pupils, like a cat's eyes?

single row   anal plate

yes. 4

no . . . . You have reached this point in error; return to question 2

4. Are there rattles at the end of the tail?

rattles

yes. 5

no 9

5. Are there 8 or fewer large scales and many small granular scales on the top of the head?

yes. 6

no 7

6. This is a rattlesnake of the genus *Crotalus* (99–105).

7. Are there 9 large scales on top of the head?

    yes..8
    no .... You have reached this point in error; return to question 4

8. This is a rattlesnake of the genus *Sistrurus* (96–98).

9. This is a copperhead or cottonmouth of the genus *Agkistrodon* (92–95).

10. Is the snake red, yellow, and black, with the colors arranged in bands that completely encircle the body? Are the red and black bands noticeably wider than the yellow bands, with the red and yellow bands touching?

    yes...11
    no 12

11. This is a Texas coral snake, genus *Micrurus* (91).

12. Does the snake resemble a worm: tiny, pinkish or flesh-colored, with a blunt tail and eyes that appear to be small, almost invisible dots? Are the scales on the belly not much wider than those on the back?

    yes...13
    no 14

13. This is a blind snake of the genus *Leptotyphlops* (1–3).

14. Are all the dorsal (back) scales entirely smooth (not keeled or ridged)?

smooth scales   keeled scales

    yes...15
    no 61

15. Is the snake quite small, and is the tip of its snout upturned? Are there 17 rows of dorsal scales at midbody?

upturned snout   numbering of dorsal scale rows

    yes...16
    no 19

16. Is the top of the head patterned with 1 or 2 prominent blackish bands?

   yes 17
   no 18

17. This is a western hooknose snake, genus *Gyalopion* (64).

18. This is a Mexican hooknose snake, genus *Ficimia* (65).

19. Turn the animal over to locate the anal plate, which covers the vent and is located about two thirds of the way to the tail tip. Is the anal plate single (undivided)?

single anal plate   divided anal plate

   yes 20
   no 30

20. Is the snake uniformly black above, with 17 rows of dorsal scales at midbody?

   yes 21
   no 22

21. This is a Texas indigo snake, genus *Drymarchon* (59).

22. Does the animal have a single row of scales under the tail and 23 rows of dorsal scales at midbody?

single row   anal plate

   yes 23
   no 24

23. This is a Texas longnose snake, genus *Rhinocheilus* (86).

24. Is the belly white or yellowish without any brown or other dark markings?

   yes 25
   no 29

25. Are there 8 lower labial scales, and are the back and sides colored red, black, and off-white?

   yes 26
   no 27 37

26. This is a scarlet snake of the genus *Cemophora* (84, 85).

27. Is the dorsal color off-white blotched with brown? Is there a pale longitudinal line along the spine just behind the head? Are there 12 to 15 lower labial scales?

yes. 28
no . . . . You have reached this point in error; return to question 2

28. This is a glossy snake of the genus *Arizona* (69–71).

29. This is a kingsnake or milk snake of the genus *Lampropeltis* (77–83).

30. Are there 17 or fewer rows of dorsal scales at midbody?

yes. 31
no 50

31. Is the snake longitudinally striped, and does it have an enlarged, triangular-shaped rostral scale that curves back over the snout and has free edges?

rostral scale

yes. 32
no 33

32. This is a patchnose snake of the genus *Salvadora* (42–44).

33. Is the snake small, with a slender body, a tiny head, a solid brown back, and 15 rows of dorsal scales at midbody? Does it lack a loreal scale?

loreal scale   loreal scale absent

yes. 34
no 35

34. This is a blackhead, blackhood, or flathead snake of the genus *Tantilla* (4–8).

35. Are there 2 or more preocular scales?

preocular scales

yes. 36
no 45

36. Are the lower and upper preocular scales about the same size?

yes 37
no 40

37. Is the nasal plate divided? Is the animal slate gray above, with a darker head and a black-speckled orangish belly?

divided nasal plate

yes 38
no 39

38. This is a ringneck snake of the genus *Diadophis* (14–16).

39. This is a western smooth green snake, genus *Opheodrys* (45).

40. Is the animal quite slender for its length, and are there 15 rows of dorsal (back) scales counted at midbody?

yes 41
no 42

41. This is a whipsnake of the genus *Masticophis* (47–52).

42. Are there 17 rows of dorsal scales at midbody, and 13 rows just ahead of the anal plate?

yes 43
no 44

43. This is a coachwhip of the genus *Masticophis* (47–48).

44. This is a racer of the genus *Coluber* (53–57).

45. Is the loreal scale in direct contact with the eye?

loreal scale

yes 46
no 49

46. Is the back black, the lower sides pinkish? Are there fewer than 15 rows of dorsal scales at midbody?

yes 47
no 48

47. This is a western worm snake, genus *Carphophis* (18).

48. This is a western smooth earth snake, genus *Virginia* (13).

49. This is a ground snake, genus *Sonora* (17).

50. Is the animal shiny black above and pink below, with a horny point on the tip of its tail?

yes 51
no 52

51. This is a western mud snake, genus *Farancia* (41).

52. Is the snake quite slender, and are its eyes proportionately very large, with vertical (cat-eyed) pupils?

yes 53
no 58

53. Are the back and sides light brown or buff narrowly banded with darker brown, and are 2 or more loreal scales present?

yes 54
no 55

54. This is a Texas lyre snake, genus *Trimorphodon* (90).

55. Are the back and sides yellowish, with wide, blackish-brown bands? Is the undertail orange or salmon?

yes 56
no 57

56. This is a northern cat-eyed snake, genus *Leptodeira* (89).

57. This is a night snake of the genus *Hypsiglena* (87).

58. Is the snake small and slender, its back and sides longitudinally striped with black and brown? Are there 19 rows of dorsal scales at midbody?

yes 59
no 60

59. This is a black-striped snake, genus *Coniophanes* (88).

60. This is a rat snake of the genus *Elaphe* (72–74).

61. Is the snake comparatively plump, with a snout whose tip is distinctly upturned? Are there 23 to 25 rows of dorsal (back) scales counted at midbody?

upturned snout   numbering of dorsal scale rows

yes 62
no 63

62. This is a hognose snake of the genus *Heterodon* (60–63).

63. Is the anal plate single (undivided)?

single anal plate   divided anal plate

yes. 64
no 71

64. Are there fewer than 19 rows of dorsal scales at midbody?

yes. 65
no 66

65. This is a rough earth snake, genus *Virginia* (12).

66. Is there a distinct, evenly spaced double row of dark brown or black-ish half-moon-shaped markings down the belly scales?

yes. 67
no 68

67. This is a lined snake of the genus *Tropidoclonion* (19).

68. Is there a pale yellowish or reddish stripe along the entire length of the spine? Are there fewer than 27 rows of dorsal scales at midbody?

yes. 69
no 70

69. This is a garter or ribbon snake of the genus *Thamnophis* (20–29).

70. This is a bullsnake, Louisiana pine snake, or Sonoran gopher snake, genus *Pituophis* (66–68).

71. Are there 21 or more rows of dorsal scales at midbody?

yes. 72
no 75

72. Are at least the scales along the spine weakly keeled, and does the flat belly meet the rather vertical (rather than laterally bulging) sides of the slender body at an abrupt angle (like a loaf of bread in cross-section)?

yes. 73
no 74

73. This is a rat snake of the genus *Elaphe* (72–74).

74. This is a water snake of the genus *Nerodia* (30–38).

75. Are there 19 rows of dorsal scales at midbody?

yes 76
no 77

76. This is a crayfish snake of the genus *Regina* (39–40).

77. Are there 17 rows of dark, weakly keeled dorsal scales, each bearing a dart-shaped yellow spot in its center?

yes 78
no 79

78. This is a Central American speckled racer, genus *Drymobius* (58).

79. Are the back and sides bright green?

yes 80
no 81

80. This is a rough green snake, genus *Opheodrys* (45).

81. Is there a prominent brown spot beneath the eye? Is the loreal scale absent?

loreal scale   loreal scale absent

yes 82
no 83

82. This is a brown or redbelly snake of the genus *Storeria* (9–11).

83. This is a rough earth snake, genus *Virginia* (12).

84. Is the animal mustard-brown above, with a thin, black H-shaped dorsal pattern?

yes 85

85. This is a Trans-Pecos rat snake, genus *Bogertophis* (75).

Typhlopidae

Blind Snakes

1 Plains Blind Snake
2 New Mexico Blind Snake
3 Trans-Pecos Blind Snake

1 Plains Blind Snake
Leptotyphlops dulcis dulcis

Nonvenomous   This tiny, primitive reptile, reminiscent of the subterranean, late Cretaceous snakes from which all modern serpents are descended, is much too small to bite humans.

Abundance   Common. The plains blind snake was formerly abundant in areas of soft, loamy soil, especially in early spring before summer's drying and hardening of the ground's upper layers forced it deeper into the earth. Now it is far less numerous due to the recent invasion of South American fire ants.

Size   Slender, and only 2½ to 11 inches in length, *L. d. dulcis* looks much like a large earthworm.

Habitat   This predominantly subterranean snake is sometimes found at the surface beneath leaf and plant litter or under decaying logs. Plains blind snakes also often inhabit the well-watered sod and rich garden humus of residential neighborhoods where it is turned up by those weeding or planting gardens and flower beds.

Prey   Blind snakes feed primarily on the eggs, larvae, and pupae of ants and termites. The adults of soft-bodied insects are reportedly taken as well.

Reproduction   Egg-laying. During late June and early July, female blind snakes deposit 3 or 4 thin-shelled, ½-inch-long eggs (sometimes in a nest cavity used by more than one female) hollowed from decaying vegetation or loose sandy soil.

Coloring/scale form   *Leptotyphlops dulcis dulcis* is much the same shape, size, and color as a large earthworm. It seemingly has no facial features, and its vestigial eyes are no more than dots of non-functional pigment barely visible beneath its enlarged, translucent ocular scales—each of which extends to the mouth, and in the plains subspecies, is preceded by a single upper labial scale. Unlike those of other native snakes, blind snakes' ventral scales are not transversely widened into long plates (14 rows of smooth scales encircle the whole trunk), and the tail is tipped with a tiny spur.

Similar snakes   The **New Mexico blind snake (2)** is found west of the Cap Rock on the High Plains, where it is distinguished by the 2 upper labial scales that occur just forward of the lower portion of each of its ocular scales.

Behavior   If they are recognized as reptiles at all, blind snakes are usually taken to be the newborns of larger snakes. Where soil conditions are ideal, several *L. d. dulcis,* which are often found in close proximity, are invariably mistaken for a "nest of baby snakes."

The specialized spur on the blind snake's tail tip is dug into its tunnel walls to obtain purchase in pressing through the soil, while on open ground (where these animals never cease wriggling in apparent anxiety over being without cover) it may be brought forward, planted, and used to lever the rest of the body ahead.

2 New Mexico Blind Snake
Leptotyphlops dulcis dissectus

Like other *Leptotyphlops*, the New Mexico blind snake resembles a pale, shiny earthworm (like worms, these little reptiles are washed onto the pavement by heavy rains), particularly because adult specimens are no more than 6½ inches long and not much thicker than coat-hanger wire. Blind snakes also resemble earthworms because they lack the distinctly serpentine belly-wide ventral scales of other snakes (on blind snakes' venters, the same size scales as those of the dorsum occur all the way around the blind snake's body, while there is no anal plate because the vent is surrounded by minuscule scales).

There is no narrowing of the neck, so blind snakes' blunt heads and tails seem nearly identical, especially because their vestigial eyes are almost invisible. Their mouths are equally indistinct: Only under a dissecting microscope are a few miniature teeth discernable in the tiny lower jaw. The blind snake's non-tapering posterior end is distinguished, however, by its minuscule tailtip spur.

The New Mexico Blind Snake, *Leptotyphlops dulcis dissectus,* differs from the **Trans-Pecos blind snake (3),** which shares most of its High Plains and Northern Chihuahuan Desert range, by the 3 small scales—the Trans-Pecos has only 1—that separate the tops of the ocular plates that cap its crown.

The New Mexico race is, in turn, distinguished from its subspecies, the **plains blind snake (1),** by the presence of 2 narrow upper labial scales—*dissectus* means "cleft," in reference to their shared central suture—between the lower extension of the ocular plate and the nasal scale; the plains blind snake has but 1 such intervening scale. In other respects the New Mexico blind snake is identical to its subspecies the plains blind snake, and intergrades between the 2 races are common.

Moreover, because *Leptotyphlops dulcis dissectus* so closely resembles its subspecies, *Leptotyphlops dulcis dulcis,* no distinguishing characteristics are visible in a photograph; the New Mexico blind snake's two narrow upper labial scales are so small as to be visible only in an enlarged drawing.

Trans-Pecos blind snake
(L. h. segregus)

Plains and New Mexico
blind snakes
(L. dulcis)

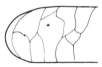

Plains blind snake
(L. d. dulcis)

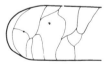

New Mexico blind snake
(L. d. dissectus)

Behavior The New Mexico blind snake's life history is probably identical to that of its subspecies the plains blind snake—including its inclination for several females to deposit their egg clutches in the same nest cavity. Of necessity, in arid country *L. d. dissectus* burrows quite deeply to avoid desiccation; individuals have been unearthed from several feet below the surface by road-grading machinery working the extremely dry, sandy terrain near Castolon on the Rio Grande.

3 Trans-Pecos Blind Snake
Leptotyphlops humilis segregus

Nonvenomous   This animal is much too small to bite humans.

Abundance   Fairly common. Well dispersed over its range, *Leptotyphlops humilis segregus* is, nevertheless, such an inconspicuous little reptile that it is seldom noticed.

Size   Slightly larger than the plains and New Mexico blind snakes, *L. h. segregus* reaches a maximum length of 13 inches.

Habitat   Trans-Pecos blind snakes are recorded from a wide variety of dry terrestrial communities, but are seldom if ever found in severe desert terrain. Their preferred habitat is the slightly more mesic, richer-soiled conditions of the Trans-Pecos grasslands such as those in Presidio Co. south of the Davis Mountains.

Prey   *Leptotyphlops humilis segregus* apparently feeds almost exclusively on the eggs and pupae of ants and termites.

Reproduction   Egg-laying. See **Plains Blind Snake (1).**

Coloring/scale form   The shiny, flesh-colored back may have a brown tinge on 5 to 7 of its vertebral scale rows; the venter is pale pink. Along with 95 other species and subspecies of *Leptotyphlopidae* (many of them abundant in the American tropics), the Trans-Pecos blind snake has a cylindrical head and a tail almost the same diameter as its midsection, so that both its ends look remarkably alike. The head has tiny dots of vestigial ocular pigment, however, while the tail is distinguished by the tiny spur at its tip and by its tendency to wriggle back and forth when the animal is disturbed, smearing musky cloacal fluid over the rest of the body. (Enhancing the protection afforded by the blind snakes' small, tightly overlapping scales, this musk functions as an olfactory armor by discouraging the bites and stings of ants, whose nests blind snakes must enter for food.)

Fourteen rows of these scales encircle the entire trunk, for the elongation of the ventral scales into the transverse plates of most serpents is absent, as is the anal plate.

Similar snakes   Only other *Leptotyphlopidae* are similar. The **plains (1)** and the **New Mexico (2) blind snakes** are distinguished by the 3 small scales present in the center of the crown between the right and left ocular plates; a single mid-crown scale separates the oculars of the Trans-Pecos blind snake. See **New Mexico Blind Snake (2).**

Behavior   L. M. Klauber (1940) noted that this little serpent "progressed with less lateral undulation than other snakes. On smooth surfaces it employed the tail spine to aid in its motion. When placed in loose or sandy soil it burrowed immediately. It is never peaceful or quiet when above ground, but continually searches for something in which to burrow."

Colubridae

Small Burrowing Snakes

4 Flathead Snake
5 Plains Blackhead Snake
6 Southwestern Blackhead Snake
7 Mexican Blackhead Snake
8 Blackhood Snake
9 Texas Brown Snake
10 Marsh Brown Snake
11 Florida Redbelly Snake
12 Rough Earth Snake
13 Western Smooth Earth Snake
14 Mississippi Ringneck Snake
15 Prairie Ringneck Snake
16 Regal Ringneck Snake
17 Ground Snake
18 Western Worm Snake

Lined, Garter, and Ribbon Snakes

19 Lined Snake
20 Eastern Garter Snake
21 Texas Garter Snake
22 Checkered Garter Snake
23 Western Plains Garter Snake
24 Eastern Blackneck Garter Snake
25 Western Blackneck Garter Snake
26 Western Ribbon Snake
27 Redstripe Ribbon Snake
28 Gulf Coast Ribbon Snake
29 Arid Land Ribbon Snake

Aquatic Snakes

30 Diamondback Water Snake
31 Yellowbelly Water Snake
32 Blotched Water Snake

33 Broad-banded Water Snake
34 Florida Water Snake
35 Gulf Salt Marsh Snake
36 Mississippi Green Water Snake
37 Brazos Water Snake
38 Concho Water Snake
39 Graham's Crayfish Snake
40 Gulf Crayfish Snake
41 Western Mud Snake

Patchnose Snakes

42 Texas Patchnose Snake
43 Mountain Patchnose Snake
44 Big Bend Patchnose Snake

Green Snakes

45 Rough Green Snake
46 Smooth Green Snake

Whipsnakes, Racers, and Indigo Snakes

47 Eastern Coachwhip
48 Western Coachwhip
49 Central Texas Whipsnake
50 Desert Striped Whipsnake
51 Schott's Whipsnake
52 Ruthven's Whipsnake
53 Southern Black Racer
54 Buttermilk Racer
55 Tan Racer
56 Eastern Yellowbelly Racer
57 Mexican Racer
58 Central American Speckled Racer
59 Texas Indigo Snake

47

Brown-blotched Terrestrial Snakes

60 Eastern Hognose Snake
61 Dusty Hognose Snake
62 Plains Hognose Snake
63 Mexican Hognose Snake
64 Western Hooknose Snake
65 Mexican Hooknose Snake
66 Louisiana Pine Snake
67 Bullsnake
68 Sonoran Gopher Snake
69 Texas Glossy Snake
70 Kansas Glossy Snake
71 Painted Desert Glossy Snake
72 Texas Rat Snake
73 Baird's Rat Snake
74 Great Plains Rat Snake
75 Trans-Pecos Rat Snake
76 Prairie Kingsnake

Large Kingsnakes

77 Speckled Kingsnake
78 Desert Kingsnake

Red-and-black-banded Snakes

79 Louisiana Milk Snake
80 Mexican Milk Snake
81 New Mexico Milk Snake
82 Central Plains Milk Snake
83 Gray-banded Kingsnake
84 Northern Scarlet Snake
85 Texas Scarlet Snake
86 Texas Longnose Snake

Mildly Venomous Rear-fanged Snakes

87 Texas Night Snake
88 Black-striped Snake
89 Northern Cat-eyed Snake
90 Texas Lyre Snake

4 Flathead Snake
Tantilla gracilis

Nonvenomous   Although technically a rear-fanged opisthoglyph serpent with very mild salivary toxins that presumably help to immobilize its diminutive prey, the flathead snake is far too small to harm humans.

Abundance   Formerly common. Historically among the most abundant of the little soil-colored serpents turned up in flower beds and gardens throughout the eastern two-thirds of the state, *Tantilla gracilis* has now become uncommon in much of its old range. Their decline seems to be largely a result of the devastating impact of invading South American fire ants. In the last few years these hyper-aggressive insects have proliferated in Texas to the extent that, like most other small, egg-laying terrestrial reptiles, whose nests are decimated by the ants, even a solitary flathead snake is now unusual in the same microenvironments where, until recently, several specimens were often found together.

Size   Adult *T. gracilis* reach a length of 10 inches; hatchlings measure only 3 inches, with a girth not much thicker than coat-hanger wire.

Habitat   The flathead snake prefers loose, slightly damp soil in which to burrow; it consequently occurs most often in well-watered deciduous woods and grass/brushland communities.

Prey   The flathead snake's primarily arthropod and annelid prey seems to be, at least in part, partitioned through species-specific predation among the several other small fossorial serpents that successfully share its semi-subterranean microhabitat. Edith R. Force (1935) found the stomach contents of 63 *Tantilla gracilis* "consisted of centipedes and earth-dwelling insect larvae such as cutworms and wireworms; while ground snakes eat mainly . . . arachnids, ringnecks, earthworms."

Reproduction   Egg-laying. Reproduction among *Tantilla* requires a long period of maturation for a small reptile, with females reaching sexual maturity only in the spring of their third year. Studies indicate that both males and females store sperm—an unusual situation made necessary because males' autumn spermatogenesis occurs asynchronously with females' vernal ovulation. In order for viable sperm to be present at the time of ovulation it must, therefore, remain active in the males' vas deferens throughout the winter, then continue to remain viable in seminal receptacles within the female's oviduct for several additional weeks. (Delayed fertilization is also reflected in the morphology of *Tantilla,* whose slender body lets it slip through minuscule spaces in the soil. This genus also lacks an active left oviduct, which serves as an auxiliary sperm storage receptacle.)

Force found copulation to occur during the first half of May, with clutches of 1 to 4 oblong eggs being deposited in either shallow subsurface hollows or within decaying vegetation during the latter part of June. Depending on the temperature, the eggs hatch after about 60 days into neonates no more than 3 inches long, which exactly resemble their parents.

Coloring/scale form   Dorsolateral color is uniformly grayish tan except for the darker crown, whose rear border is slightly concave. Flattened from top and bottom, the snout appears rounded from above; the venter is salmon. Although too small to note easily with the naked eye, there is a single postocular scale and no loreal (the second of the 6 upper labial scales touches, or almost touches, the pre-

SMALL BURROWING SNAKES

49

frontal); the smooth dorsal scales are arranged in 15 rows at midbody and the anal plate is divided.

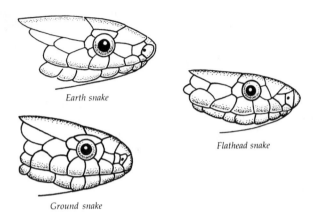

Earth snake

Flathead snake

Ground snake

Similar snakes   The **plains blackhead snake (5)** has 7 upper labial scales, a distinct black skullcap that stretches back 3 to 5 scale rows behind its crown to a point on its nape, and a whitish-edged pink venter. The **earth snakes (12—13)** have a loreal scale and 17 rows of dorsal scales, with faint keels on the scales of at least the middorsal rows. (The rough earth snake also has 5 upper labial scales and more grayish coloration.) **Ground snakes (17)** living in the flathead's range usually have a yellowish or reddish-tan ground color as well as a partially crossbanded back and undertail; there is also both a loreal and paired postocular scales.

Behavior   Secretive and nocturnal, *T. gracilis* is active mainly between April and early November, withdrawing well below ground during the winter by insinuating itself through tiny crevices in the earth. To facilitate this, its skull is no wider than its neck and is compressed from above and below into a penetrating wedge. This enables the flathead snake to vanish in an instant among dense roots, or (as anyone knows who has taken one of these little reptiles inside, only to have it slip out of his fingers) almost magically disappear down through both the pile and woven backing of floor carpeting, searching for its subterranean home.

Plains Blackhead Snake
Tantilla nigriceps fumiceps

Nonvenomous   See **Flathead Snake (4).**

Abundance   Moderately abundant in places such as the thorn brush of the Rio Grande plain and the shortgrass prairie of the Panhandle, *Tantilla nigriceps fumiceps* is seldom noticed because its small size and cryptic microenvironment beneath thick grass usually enable it to escape human attention.

Size   Adults are 7 to 14¾ inches in length.

Habitat   This snake's microhabitat is the subsurface layer where grass roots and fallen vegetative litter meets the harder substrate below; it is most often found at the surface on the slightly damp soil beneath rocks and debris, or on roadways after rain.

Prey   Prey is primarily tenebrionid beetle larvae; also snails, centipedes, worms, spiders, and insect larvae taken in semi-subterranean locations.

Reproduction   Egg-laying. See **Flathead Snake (4).**

Coloring/scale form   The plains blackhead snake's dark skullcap is longer than that of Texas' other *Tantillas,* stretching back 3 to 5 vertebral scale rows to end in a point on the nape; there is a ruddy flush along its midventral line. Arranged in 15 rows at midbody, the dorsal scales are smooth. There is a single postocular and 7 upper labial scales, the second of which, due to the absence of a loreal, touches the prefrontal plate just ahead of the eye. The anterior lower labials generally touch beneath the chin and the anal plate is divided.

Underchin: plains blackhead snake   *Underchin: southwestern blackhead snake*

Similar snakes   The **flathead snake (4)** has 6 upper labial scales and a short brown skullcap whose slightly concave rear border extends rearward no more than 2 scale rows beyond its parietal plates. The straight rear-bordered skullcap of the Trans-Pecos' **southwestern blackhead snake (6)** reaches no more than a single dorsal scale row onto its nape (where it may be edged with a faint pale line), its rostral scale is a bit more pointed, and its first pair of lower labials do not touch under the chin. The **ground snake (17)** has a loreal scale and a pair of postocular scales.

Behavior   Blackhead snakes typically fare poorly in captivity, in part because their small bodies, which are adapted to the comparatively constant temperature below ground, have little resistance to the more pronounced fluctuations of atmospheric temperature. Unless captive *Tantilla* are given soil in which to burrow they will often die from overheating, but these shy burrowers will survive in a natural terrarium matrix of sandy soil if given beetle and termite larvae, small brown centipedes, and small slugs as prey.

6 Southwestern Blackhead Snake
Tantilla hobartsmithi

Nonvenomous   See **Flathead Snake (4).**

Abundance   Probably moderately abundant. Named for venerable herpetologist Hobart M. Smith, this fossorial reptile is seldom noted because its range is sparsely populated by human beings and its underground microenvironment enables it to escape their attention.

Size   Maximum adult length is no more than 9¼ inches.

Habitat   *Tantilla hobartsmithi* is a burrowing snake usually found on the surface only where moisture has condensed under flat stones.

Prey   The stomachs of 37 individuals contained only butterfly, moth, and beetle larvae even though many other suitably-sized invertebrates were to be found in the immediate vicinity.

Reproduction   Egg-laying. One Big Bend female carrying a single egg ready to be deposited was discovered on the first of June.

Coloring/scale form   Basing their studies on the morphology of the tiny spines covering their subjects' hemipenes, Charles J. Cole and Lawrence M. Hardy (1981) revised the classification of the animal formerly known as the **Mexican Blackhead Snake,** *Tantilla atriceps,* into two different species. These authors believe the Mexican blackhead to be confined to a small range in South Texas, while the western part of the population (which inhabits all of the state northwest of Kinney, Edwards, and Sutton counties) is now thought to represent a separate species, the **Southwestern Blackhead Snake,** *Tantilla hobartsmithi.*

This large area contains animals that display several crown configurations, which were once carefully charted because they were thought to define different species. Now it is thought that local populations of *Tantilla hobartsmithi* include individuals with both short black cephalic caps and long ones—caps either bordered or not bordered with a pale nuchal collar—as well as specimens with either all-black or white-spotted snouts.

The shiny brown back and sides of the southwestern blackhead snake are slightly more reddish above than other *Tantilla,* an orangish streak lines the center of its forebelly, and beneath the tail the venter is salmon. The 15 midbody rows of dorsal scales are smooth, there are 7 upper labial scales, and the anterior lower labials usually do not meet beneath the chin. There is no loreal, and the anal plate is divided. See **Plains Blackhead Snake (5),** illustration.

Similar snakes   The black cap of the **plains blackhead snake (5)** tapers to a point on the nape 3 to 5 scale rows behind the parietal scales, while the first pair of lower labial scales meets under its chin.

Behavior   Where *Tantilla hobartsmithi* lives below ground during most of the year is not known, but it is so adept at prying its way through the tiniest soil crevice with its hard, flattened snout that it is able to live an almost entirely subterranean existence. Only during spring and summer does it appear at the surface, and then only in the shadiest, dampest microhabitats beneath rocks. Moderate temperature and moist soil seem to be the main factors that encourage it to ascend to these hiding places, for dry summer heat induces its withdrawal farther below the surface—as well as probable aestivation—while low winter temperatures presumably force these animals to withdraw several feet into the ground.

7 Mexican Blackhead Snake
Tantilla atriceps

Nonvenomous   See **Flathead Snake (4).**

Abundance   Writing in the *Bulletin of the American Museum of Natural History* (1981), and basing their studies primarily on the morphology of the spines covering their subjects' hemipenes, Charles J. Cole and Lawrence M. Hardy revised the classification of the Mexican blackhead snake, *Tantilla atriceps,* into 2 separate species.

The *Tantilla* population found west and northwest of Kinney, Edwards, and Sutton counties, which was formerly included in the species *Tantilla atriceps,* the Mexican blackhead snake, is now defined as a different species, the southwestern blackhead snake, *Tantilla hobartsmithi.*

In contrast, the Mexican blackhead snake, *Tantilla atriceps,* is thought to be a very rare, predominantly subtropical reptile whose range lies primarily in the northern Mexican state of Tamaulipas. It is known in Texas only from a pair of specimens collected over 100 years ago in Duval and Kleberg counties; whether it still occurs north of the Rio Grande is unknown. Little is known of its natural history, and no photograph of a Texas specimen exists.

Size   Maximum adult length is probably no more than 11 inches.

Habitat   In Mexico, *Tantilla atriceps* reportedly occupies both wooded and grassland/thorn brush communities.

Prey   This animal's food preferences are unknown, but like other *Tantilla,* the Mexican blackhead snake probably preys on subterranean insects and their larvae.

Reproduction   Egg-laying. It is likely that one to 3 eggs are deposited in early summer; reproduction is otherwise unknown.

Coloring/scale form   Based on specimens from Tamaulipas, the Mexican blackhead snake displays the typical brownish or grayish dorsolateral hue, slightly darker along the mid-dorsal line, of other *Tantilla.* Its black crown (members of the genus *Tantilla* are also known as crowned snakes) reaches no further rearward than the posterior border of its parietal scutes and does not touch the posterior corner of the mouth. The orangish venter reddens beneath the tail. There are 7 upper labial scales, the 15 rows of midbody scales are smooth, and the anal plate is divided.

Similar snakes   The **flathead snake (4)** has a brown skullcap with a slightly concave rear border and 6 upper labial scales.

Behavior   Texas' *Tantilla* are part of the northeastern branch of a family of predominantly tropical serpents that extends as far south as western South America. All five of this state's species are former members of an ancient, xeric-adapted fauna that once occupied a dry corridor, which joined the desert Southwest to the Florida peninsula. After this community of desert plants and animals was separated into eastern and western segments by the cooler, wetter climate that prevailed along the Gulf Coast during the late Pleistocene, the *Tantilla* genus survived in relict populations in Florida and the Southeast, as well as among those remaining in Texas, which were never cut off from their relatives to the south.

SMALL BURROWING SNAKES

8 Blackhood Snake
Tantilla rubra cucullata

Nonvenomous   The blackhood snake is the only *Tantilla* large and assertive enough to nip a human being. Although technically a rear-fanged opisthoglyph snake (all *Tantilla* have enlarged, though still minuscule, grooved teeth in the rear of their upper jaws), and bearing mild salivary toxins to help immobilize its small prey, the blackhood snake is entirely harmless to humans.

Abundance   Threatened. Protected by the State of Texas as the Big Bend Blackhead Snake, *Tantilla rubra*. This very rare fossorial serpent—until recently known only from relatively few specimens—seldom emerges from its subterranean microenvironment in the Trans-Pecos uplands, although as many as eight individuals have been found in a single area within a few days when weather and soil-moisture conditions were optimal.

Size   Sizable compared to other *Tantillas:* the few recorded blackhood snakes have measured 8½ to 17¼ inches in length.

Habitat   Known from two principal habitats: 1. Elevations between 1,300 and 5,000 feet in the Chisos and Davis mountains; 2. Both broken and flat terrain in the low desert of Terrell and Val Verde counties. (This easterly, desert-living population was formerly known as the Devil's River blackhead snake, *Tantilla rubra diabola.*)

Prey   According to Trans-Pecos *Tantilla* expert Troy Hibbitts, of the University of Texas at Arlington, the blackhood snake's prey is primarily centipedes, particularly members of the genus *Scolependra.* These formidable arthropods— which reach 10 inches in length and, using the prominent fangs for which centipedes are noted, prey regularly on small lizards—are powerful adversaries for snakes barely longer than themselves.

A series of photographs shot by Hibbitts south of Alpine shows how these diminutive predators manage. After seizing a centipede at midbody, *T. r. cucullata* hangs on with determination, chewing on the arthropod's midsection as it twists around to counterattack. (The blackhood's comparatively heavy skull, armored with rimmed eye sockets, evidently enables it to withstand the centipede's fangs, but adult *T. r. cucullata* tend to be scarred on the head and neck from encounters of this kind.) Eventually the *Tantilla*'s mildly paralytic saliva—worked into the chilopode's body by its grooved rear teeth—overcomes the centipede, allowing the blackhood snake to swallow it.

Reproduction   Egg-laying. The single captive-laid clutch, of 3 elongate eggs, recorded for *T. r. cucullata* was deposited June 13, while a female found dead in Big Bend National Park on July 16 contained a pair of eggs whose stage of development suggests that they would have been laid before August. Like those of many small serpents, the eggs are typically quite large for the size of the parent: David Hillis and Stephen Campbell (1982) report finding, in a large, road-killed Presidio Co. female, "a nearly mature egg, .31 by 1.77 inch, [that] accounted for 8.9% of the weight of the specimen."

Coloring/scale form   The most distinctive marking of *T. r. cucullata* is its generally uniformly black head and anterior neck. There are several different nuchal-cephalic patterns, however. In one, except for some pale spots on the lower jaw, the head and neck are wrapped in a solid black hood; in another, the dark hood is inter-

54

rupted across the nape by a light collar sometimes split with blackish pigment over the spine, with white spots occurring on the snout and upper labial scales. (*T. r. cucullata* from the Chisos Mountains often have light collars, while most of those from northern Brewster, Jeff Davis, and Presidio counties have solid dark hoods.)

Among the more easterly population there is often a prominent white collar, a white-tipped snout, and a pronounced oval or irregularly-shaped white spot just below and behind the eye. For 40 years this difference in coloring caused this population to be classified as the Devil's River blackhead snake, *Tantilla rubra diabola,* until it was found that color morphs typical of both populations also occur together in the same area. Both Damon Salceies and I have found disparate color phases in close proximity in Terrell Co. road cuts and in small canyons near Sanderson, and a 1997 paper by James Dixon, Kathryn Vaughan, and Larry David Wilson proposes the blackhood snake be accorded full species status as *Tantilla cucullata* while reserving *Tantilla rubra* for a more southerly-ranging group of exclusively Mexican *Tantilla.*

The venter of all color patterns is off-white. Arranged in 15 rows at midbody, the dorsal scales are smooth; the anal plate is divided.

Similar snakes   The dark crown of the **plains blackhead snake (5)** is pointed or convex along its rear edge, is not followed by a light collar, and does not extend onto the lower jaw. The **southwestern blackhead snake (6)** has an abbreviated dark skullcap that extends laterally only as far as the middle of its upper labial scales; its lower labials and chin are whitish. Although a narrow pale line is occasionally evident just behind the black cap, this area is not followed by a black band. Both these animals also have pinkish venters.

Behavior   Little is known of the subterranean habits of West Texas' predominantly fossorial snakes. Among them are the *Tantillas,* several of which were discovered only recently—Sherman Minton first described the blackhood snake in 1956—and whose taxonomic relationships are still in question. Typical of the genus is *T. r. cucullata,* which evidently makes only sporadic forays above ground, mostly in June and July and almost always during the humid conditions following recent precipitation: each of 6 individuals found on the roads, as well as 2 specimens collected in the field, appeared following rainy periods.

9 Texas Brown Snake
Storeria dekayi texana

Nonvenomous See **Marsh Brown Snake (10)**.

Abundance Common. As live-bearers, brown snakes are somewhat less susceptible than small egg-laying serpents to attacks by South American fire ants because their newborns seem to be sufficiently vigorous to slip away from these newly-introduced insect predators.

Size Most adults are 9 to 12 inches in length; the record is 18 inches.

Habitat In Texas, macrohabitat includes riparian bottomland in the Hill Country, as well as almost every terrestrial milieu in the open deciduous woodland of the Cross Timbers. Texas brown snakes are also found in overgrown pastures, but not as commonly as in places where leaf litter offers cover.

Prey Because their primary prey is slugs, brown snakes are drawn to the planks and sheets of corrugated iron that litter abandoned rural outbuildings because these moisture-conserving shelters provide optimal habitat for desiccation-prone slugs. Earthworms are a secondary food source, and arthropods, salamanders, minnows, and newly metamorphosed frogs are also occasionally taken.

Reproduction Live-bearing. Breeding may occur in spring and fall, with spermatozoa from autumn pairings remaining in the female's oviducts until her spring ovulation. Most births occur between mid-June and the first week in August: One Lee Co. female found in late April fed on slugs and small earthworms until late May, by which time she was obviously gravid and stopped feeding. (Brown snakes provide placental nourishment of the young during the latter stages of fetal development.)

On June 12 this female gave birth to 11 very active young, all about 3¾ inches long. The neonates had dark-speckled gray-brown backs and sides, dark brown heads with little white on their cheeks, and a pale band across the napes of their necks.

After their first shed at about 10 days of age, they were offered Q-tips swabbed with the scents of fish, tadpoles, and worms, but only the scent of slugs and snails elicited a feeding response. Other litters have contained 3 to 27 young, measuring from 3½ to 4½ inches.

Coloring/scale form Dark-speckled reddish brown above, with a pale vertebral stripe, adult Texas brown snakes have bold white posterior labial scales. Below and behind the eye the fifth through seventh upper labials are blotched with one or more big brown spots; another large brown marking occupies the side of the neck. The creamy venter has a few black dots along its sides, there are 17 midbody rows of strongly keeled dorsal scales, no loreal, and a divided anal plate.

Similar snakes The subspecies **marsh brown snake (10)** has a small, dark horizontal bar that lines its light-hued temporal and postocular scales and generally unmarked pale labial scales. The **Florida redbelly snake (11)** has 15 dorsal scale rows, pale areas on its nape, and (in Texas) a red to ocher to blue-black venter.

Behavior Brown snakes favor the soft soil of suburban gardens and flower beds. During cool, damp weather they may move about in the open, even in daylight, but in the hottest months brown snakes are nocturnal. Although not popular as captive animals, they thrive in terrariums (where they are seldom seen), living as long as 7 years.

0 Marsh Brown Snake
Storeria dekayi limnetes

Nonvenomous   When threatened, this little reptile can present a fierce coil-and-strike demeanor, bravely pulling its neck into the same threatening, pre-strike S-curve as larger serpents, then lunging forward. Despite its lack of size, the abruptness of this snake's vigorous strikes is sometimes enough to deter a large, if not very determined, predator. All *Storeria dekayi* subspecies, moreover, also sometimes employ the unusual threat gesture of partially baring their tiny front teeth while laterally flattening their necks.

Abundance   Common. Throughout a 60- to 80-mile-wide strip of the upper coastal plain adjacent to the Gulf, the Texas brown snake is replaced by its subspecies, the marsh brown snake. Here, *S. d. limnetes* inhabits marshy estuarine grasslands and inland prairie communities, where it hides in grassy hummocks.

Size   Adult size is 9 to 13 inches; the record is 16 inches.

Habitat   Marsh brown snakes also shelter in the high-tide flotsam of Texas' coastal barrier islands—the type specimen from which this subspecies' description is drawn was collected under driftwood on Galveston Island, where *S. d. limnetes* is the predominant small "garden snake" found around houses.

Prey   Away from the coast, the marsh brown snake feeds mostly on slugs. On the saline barrier islands *S. d. limnetes* presumably feeds on the earthworms, arthropods, small salamanders, minnows, and newly metamorphosed frogs that also constitute part of the diet of inland-living populations.

Reproduction   Live-bearing. See **Texas Brown Snake (9).**

Coloring/scale form   Both the marsh and the Texas brown snakes are alternatively called DeKay's snakes because their Latin name honors James Ellsworth DeKay, who in the early nineteenth century recorded the northern race along the Atlantic seaboard. (The marsh brown snake's subspecies designation, *limnetes*, refers to the slim horizontal bar or line marking its temporal and postocular scales.) Its faintly dark-speckled back is brown, usually with a paler vertebral stripe. The dorsal scales are keeled, arranged in 15 to 17 midbody rows, and the anal plate is divided.

Similar snakes   The **Texas brown snake (9)** has dark-blotched upper and lower labial scales and lacks the marsh brown snake's dark horizontal bar on otherwise pale temporal and postocular scales.

Texas brown snake

Marsh brown snake

Behavior   Like its close relatives the garter and water snakes, *Storeria* excretes musk from anal glands located in the cloaca, squirms about to smear musk and feces over the source of its distress, and finally flattens its body and rolls over, mouth agape, as if injured.

57

11 Florida Redbelly Snake
Storeria occipitomaculata obscura

Nonvenomous   Like its brown snake relatives, *S. o. obscura* is a shy little woodland animal that does not bite humans.

Abundance   Uncommon. This is a snake of damp forest milieus, and although it is common in much of the southeastern U.S., in Texas *Storeria occipitomaculata* is at the western boundary of its range and is nowhere abundant. Here, the Florida redbelly snake is both rare and restricted in distribution, having been recorded only in Anderson, Bowie, Hardin, Harrison, Houston, Jefferson, Orange, San Jacinto, Smith, and Wood counties.

Size   Most adults are 8 to 10 inches in length, with a maximum of 16 inches.

Habitat   *Storeria occipitomaculata obscura* occurs sporadically in moist, forested parts of East Texas, where it apparently lives mainly beneath decaying logs in pine forest and riparian woodland.

Prey   Slugs are the primary prey of *S. o. obscura:* Richard D. Bartlett reports feeding newborns on "suitably-sized bits" of both common garden slugs and snails. Earthworms are also taken, and as the soil dries during summer this reptile follows its mollusk and annelid prey deeper into the earth along a soil-moisture gradient.

Reproduction   Live-bearing. Small serpents are so short-lived that they must reproduce rapidly. Litters of *S. o. obscura* thus number up to 23, with the 2¾-to 4-inch-long young being born between June and September. Grayer than adults and usually lacking their dark dorsal spots, neonates are patterned with a pale band across the nape.

Coloring/scale form   Three prominent pale spots behind the head are characteristic, as is a double row of dark flecks along both sides of the spine. A prominent, black lower-bordered white spot occurs beneath the eye and, as this animals' name suggests, its venter is red sometimes.

Actually, in Texas *S. o. obscura* varies considerably in coloring: several Anderson Co. individuals were uniformly yellowish brown above with yellow venters and barely discernible nuchal spots; the only markings on their backs were a faint row of dark dots on either side of the spine. The white spot marking the upper labial scales beneath the eye—to which this species' Latin name, *occipitomaculata,* refers—was present, but there was no black border below it. Another individual, found on the southwest edge of Beaumont, had a solid dark brown back and blackish lower sides whose color extended onto the outer edges of its reddish-orange ventral scales—a pattern similar to that of a brown-bellied Bowie County specimen that also had no black border below its white subocular spot. The keeled dorsal scales occur in 15 midbody rows, there is no loreal scale (though a postnasal scale touches the preocular), and the anal plate is divided.

Similar snakes   The **Texas brown snake (9)** has a dark subocular spot; the **marsh brown snake (10)** has a dark horizontal line behind its eye. Both have 17 rows of dorsal scales.

Behavior   Harmless to larger animals, like other *Storeria* the Florida redbelly snake employs an injury- and death-feigning display. After rolling over, mouth agape and tongue hanging loosely, it may flatten its body in several places as though it has been partially crushed.

2 Rough Earth Snake
Virginia striatula

Nonvenomous   This little snake is not big enough to bite humans.

Abundance   Until recently the rough earth snake was the most common serpent in the Cross Timbers, the long strip of intermingled oak-hickory woodland and blackland prairie that stretches northward from the coastal plain into Oklahoma. In the early 1990s, during early spring I was accustomed to recording as many as 80 *Virginia striatula* wherever sheets of fallen metal siding littered abandoned farms. Now most of these sheltered sites harbor only huge nests containing millions of South American fire ants. These voracious predatory insects have so invaded the leaf litter microenvironments inhabited by small fossorial serpents that much of the diverse herpetofaunal community of the eastern third of the state has been wiped out.

Size   *Virginia striatula* may reach 12½ inches in length, at which size its trunk is about as thick as a pencil.

Habitat   See **Western Smooth Earth Snake (13).**

Prey   The stomachs of 45 *V. striatula* contained only earthworms.

Reproduction   Live-bearing. According to James R. Stewart (1989), "*Virginia striatula* represents a stage in . . . evolution in which placental nourishment supplements yolk nutrition (with a consequent) enhancement of newborn quality." Sixteen litters ranged in number from 3 to 8 young, measuring 3 to 4½ inches in length; all the neonates were marked with a pale band across the back of the head and nape.

Coloring/scale form   Rough earth snakes are uniformly grayish brown above, with darker pigmentation around the eyes and on the upper labial scales. The venter is creamy white. There are 17 midbody rows of dorsal scales (several of the vertebral rows are keeled, hence the "rough" of this animal's common name). A horizontally-elongate loreal touches the front of the eye, there are 2 small postocular scales, typically 5 upper labials, and, almost always, a divided anal plate.

Similar snakes   The **western smooth earth snake (13)** is reddish-tan, usually with 6 upper labials and smooth dorsal scales. The **flathead snake (4)** has a compressed head, a tan dorsum, no loreal, a single postocular, and smooth dorsal scales. The **ground snake (17)** has 15 or fewer rows of scales; its loreal does not touch its eye. **Ringneck snakes (14–16)** have smooth scales and black-speckled yellow bellies.

Behavior   Although its lightly shielded head is less effective in rooting through rocky soil than the armored snouts of larger burrowing serpents, *Virginia striatula*'s pointed skull is adequate for penetrating the moist loam where its annelid prey is most plentiful. This type of soil is typical of residential lawns where, because there are few predators, earth snakes are sometimes numerous.

Virginia striatula is most evident at the surface when the soil is moist from recent rains, but as a shallow burrower, even a few warm midwinter days bring this animal to the surface. On one Caldwell Co. hillside I found nine on Dec. 19–a date by which larger serpents had long ceased to be active. The first rough earth snakes to appear at this site in spring emerged during the last week in February.

13 Western Smooth Earth Snake

Virginia valeriae elegans

Nonvenomous   Western smooth earth snakes are too small to bite humans.

Abundance   Common. In both the oak/juniper savannah of the eastern Edwards Plateau and in the residential neighborhoods of cities such as Austin and San Antonio which border the region, *V. v. elegans* is locally abundant. Smooth earth snakes are less common in the eastern part of the range, however.

Size   Most adults measure 7 to 13 inches in length.

Habitat   Microhabitat is most often the damp soil beneath tree litter, the underside of logs, and the humid layer of topsoil and detritus often found beneath human debris.

Prey   Western smooth earth snakes feed mainly on earthworms, but small snails and insects also sometimes constitute prey.

Reproduction   Live-bearing. One 11-inch-long North Texas female gave birth on August 20 to seven 4-inch, charcoal gray neonates.

Coloring/scale form   The uniformly reddish-tan dorsum is unmarked except for the dark hairline seams (that resemble keels) found in the centers of some of the scales adjacent to the faintly keeled vertebral scales found on the posterior portion of the back. The venter is unmarked white, sometimes with a yellowish wash; except as mentioned, the 17 midbody rows of dorsal scales are smooth, the forward edge of the eye is touched by a horizontally lengthened loreal scale, and a pair of small postoculars borders the rear of the eye. There are usually 6 upper labial scales and the anal plate is divided.

Ground snake

Flathead snake

Earth snake

Similar snakes   The **rough earth snake (12)** is grayer, without a russet cast; it has 5 supralabial scales and several rows of lightly-keeled vertebral scales. The **flathead snake (4)** has a slimmer body with a flattened, dark-capped head, a salmon pink venter, no loreal scale, a single postocular, and 15 rows of smooth dorsal scales. The **ground snake (17)** has 15 or fewer rows of smooth dorsal scales, a small preocular separating its eye from its loreal scale, and a faintly braided appearance due to its lighter-hued scale borders.

Behavior   Western smooth earth snakes appear at the surface primarily when the soil is cool and moist. (Among sumac-covered limestone ledges in eastern Kansas, Abilene Zoo director Jack Joy found *Virginia valeriae* on only two or three April days, when they appeared under nearly every large stone. During the summer he turned up numerous worm and ringneck snakes but never another western smooth earth snake.) In hot weather the lack of moisture in surface soil brings about aestivation, and *V. valeria* is more likely to emerge during the cooler months. As late as December in Travis Co., these animals may be active beneath boards and sun-warmed sheets of fallen metal siding.

4 Mississippi Ringneck Snake
Diadophis punctatus stictogenys

Nonvenomous   Ringneck snakes are members of the uneven-toothed subfamily *Xenodontinae,* and all three Texas races of *D. punctatus* have slightly longer (although still minuscule) posterior teeth. These are used to prick the ringnecks' tiny prey, introducing its mildly paralytic salivary enzymes. Ringnecks are not dangerous to humans, however, and almost never bite even when first handled in the field.

Abundance   Uncommon. Abundant in much of the southeastern U.S., the Mississippi ringneck snake is less numerous in Texas, although several individuals may share the same microenvironment in the lower layers of a rotting log or beneath discarded lumber. Many of these optimal microhabitats are now infested with South American fire ants, however, exotic predators that threaten to extirpate much of the state's small herpetofauna . . . especially oviparous species like the ringnecks, whose eggs are especially vulnerable to their depredations.

Size   Adult *D. p. stictogenys* are 10 to 12 inches in length.

Habitat   Throughout its range the Mississippi ringneck is primarily a woodland animal, though it is often found along the forested borders of damp meadows and overgrown fields near water. As with most semi-fossorial snakes, the principal factor determining its presence is the availability of cover—either human debris like discarded sheets of siding or the natural shelter of fallen logs.

Prey   Ringneck snakes are scent hunters that search woodland ground cover for smaller snakes as well as for tiny frogs, salamanders, skinks, earthworms, slugs, and insect larvae. The Mississippi ringneck is itself a mid-level predator in the ophiophagous predatory pyramid, however, for it has been found in the stomach of larger leaf litter scent hunters, such as the coral snake, and in captivity most kingsnakes feed readily on small serpents like the ringneck.

Reproduction   Egg-laying. Two to 8 proportionately large, ¾-inch-long eggs are deposited (sometimes in a common site used by several females) within rotting wood or vegetation. The 4-to 5-inch-long young emerge in as little as 5 weeks.

Coloring/scale form   The Mississippi ringneck's slate-gray dorsum, separated by a bright yellow neck ring from its black head, is unmistakable. The venter, cream beneath the snout, shades to yellow at midbody and darkens to orange under the tail. In Louisiana specimens it is patterned with a double row of tiny black scallops along its centerline; in Texas, most individuals have scattered black ventral crescents. There are usually 15 forebody rows of smooth dorsal scales, a loreal scale is present, and the anal plate is divided.

Similar snakes   The Mississippi ringneck snake is poorly differentiated from both its easterly subspecies, the southern ringneck, *D. p. punctatus,* and its western race, the prairie ringneck, *D. p. arnyi.* In fact, the Mississippi ringneck may be only an intergrade form between these two subspecies, although the **prairie ringneck snake (15)** usually has 17 forebody rows of dorsal scales.

Behavior   Like other *Diadophis,* the Mississippi ringneck snake has evolved a defensive combination of color and posture that includes hiding its head under a body coil, twisting its tail upside down to expose its bright orange-red underside, and voiding musk and feces.

15 Prairie Ringneck Snake
Diadophis punctatus arnyi

Nonvenomous   See **Mississippi Ringneck Snake (14).**

Abundance   Uncommon in the southern part of its Texas range, *Diadophis punctatus arnyi* can outnumber all other serpents in places on the High Plains (H. S. Fitch [1975] captured 279 prairie ringnecks beneath two dozen pieces of sheet metal in a single hilltop field in eastern Kansas). Ringneck snakes apparently follow one another to such communal shelters using the scents left by their musky dermal pheromones; when 40 individuals were released in an enclosure containing 12 evenly-spaced plates, the 4 plates under which the first 5 snakes hid subsequently attracted the whole group, leaving the other but non-scented shelters unoccupied (Dundee and Miller, 1968).

Size   Most adults are 10 to 14 inches long; the record is 16½ inches.

Habitat   Generally subterranean. Despite its name, the prairie ringneck occurs most often in Texas beneath an open sylvan canopy.

Prey   See **Mississippi Ringneck Snake (14).**

Reproduction   Egg-laying. See **Mississippi Ringneck Snake (14).**

Coloring/scale form   Separating the black head from the dark-gray back is a golden neck ring which, in 17 of the 220 individuals examined by Troy Hibbitts, of the University of Texas at Arlington, was interrupted over the spine by dark pigment. The gray lips, chin, and throat are speckled with black, while both the yellow venter and the orange-red undertail are randomly marked with little black half-moons. The dorsal scales are smooth, and occur in either 15 or 17 forebody rows (half the population has 15 rows, the other half, 17). A loreal scale is present between the ocular and nasal scales, and the anal plate is divided.

Similar snakes   The **Mississippi ringneck snake (14)** has 15 anterior rows of dorsal scales. According to Hibbitts, an expert on *D. punctatus,* throughout the Trans-Pecos the prairie ringneck intergrades with its western subspecies, the **regal ringneck snake (16),** a slightly larger, lighter gray western race that often entirely lacks a pale neck ring; it has 17 dorsal forebody scale rows and orange ventral color that extends 1 or 2 scale rows beyond the venter up onto its lower sides. (In the Guadalupe Mountains some ringnecks are the prairie type, some are intermediate between it and the western regal ringneck, and some are the western subspecies.)

Behavior   Prairie ringneck snakes marked during field studies have been recaptured, a year or more later, so close to the same place that this animal's usual range is thought to be no more than 400 feet in diameter, and travel beyond this distance probably represents a seasonal movement between winter brumation and summer egg-laying sites.

If adequate refuge from low winter temperatures is not available within their small summer range, however, some individuals may venture several hundred yards in search of stony hilltops where deep crevices provide the well-drained subsurface refuge necessary for successful brumation. (Flooded dens cause considerable mortality among snakes which, due to cold weather, are unable to relocate to drier quarters.)

In contrast to the activity pattern of most serpents, where only the males move about widely, female *Diadophis punctatus,* which are also larger than males, travel farthest beyond their home territory on journeys to their (sometimes communally-used) nesting sites.

Regal Ringneck Snake
Diadophis punctatus regalis

Nonvenomous   The saliva of *Diadophis punctatus* is toxic to its small prey. Yet when threatened, rather than bite humans even the largest ringneck snakes do no more than evert the brightly colored undertail.

Abundance   Common. Locally abundant throughout West Texas (where the fire ants that prey so heavily on the regal ringneck snake's eastern relatives are unable to survive), *D. p. regalis* is seldom seen because it keeps to the cover of shrub or cactus roots and rock crevices.

Size   *Diadophis punctatus regalis* is named for its comparatively statuesque proportions. Troy Hibbitts, who has studied these animals in depth, has recorded 9 specimens from the Trans-Pecos that measured more than 19½ inches in length.

Habitat   The regal ringneck snake inhabits a variety of Trans-Pecos environments ranging from the evergreen-covered upper slopes of the Davis and Guadalupe mountains to the arid, limestone-floored low-lying desert of Terrell and Val Verde counties. Microhabitat includes the sheltered spaces beneath large rocks, fallen yucca logs, and within shrivelled roots of dead agaves, often those situated near the region's sporadically-flowing rocky streambeds.

Prey   *Diadophis punctatus regalis* reportedly feeds almost entirely on reptiles, principally smaller snakes. This prey is grasped and chewed vigorously until it is immobilized by the salivary toxins introduced by repeated punctures of the slightly enlarged upper rear teeth.

Reproduction   Egg-laying. Two to 5 proportionately large, elongate eggs are laid in early summer.

Coloring/scale form   Regal ringneck snakes vary in dorsal coloring. Some are entirely pale gray above, while others exhibit a full (or partial) pale nuchal band. Hibbitts has found that pale-collared *D. p. regalis* are most likely to be found in Texas near the contact zone with the golden neck-ringed prairie subspecies, although individuals with light-hued nuchal bands occur throughout areas where solid-hued individuals predominate. (Collared forms are more common in southern New Mexico; uncollared morphs predominate in northern Arizona, Utah and Nevada.)

The yellowish lower labial scales are marked with tiny black spots that extend rearward within the band of yellowish-orange ventral pigment that extends 1 or 2 scale rows upward from the venter onto the lower sides. Randomly placed black half-moons spot the yellow to dark gray forebelly; posteriorly, the venter is less heavily spotted as it darkens to red under the tail. There are usually 17 rows of smooth dorsal scales on the forebody; the anal plate is divided.

Similar snakes   An intergrade with the regal race throughout West Texas, the **prairie ringneck snake (15)** is slightly smaller and darker, with a prominent yellow neck band and a black crown. Its yellowish-orange ventral coloring does not extend as far up its sides (only ½ scale row) as that of the regal ringneck.

Behavior   If frightened, a newly captured ringneck snake is likely to twist the red underside of its tail into view (perhaps diverting a predator's attention from its head) while, sometimes, exuding a drop of saliva from the corners of its mouth. See **Ground Snake (17)**.

SMALL BURROWING SNAKES

17 Ground Snake

Sonora semiannulata

Nonvenomous *Sonora semiannulata* does not bite humans.

Abundance Common and widely distributed over all but the eastern quarter of the state.

Size Most adults are less than 12 inches. The record is 16⅜ inches.

Habitat Ground snakes inhabit a wide range of terrestrial milieus, from mountain slopes to low-lying desert, to juniper brakes to High Plains grassland. *Sonora semiannulata* may be locally abundant in both the oak-juniper savannah of the Edwards Plateau and in the succulent- and shrub-desert of the Trans-Pecos, but it is less numerous in both the Panhandle and the thorn woodland of the Rio Grande plain. In addition to these natural habitats, ground snakes are found in suburban areas in disturbed sites such as dumps or empty lots piled with debris.

Prey *Sonora semiannulata* preys principally on invertebrates, reportedly mainly spiders, as well as on centipedes and scorpions.

Reproduction Egg-laying. In Texas, most female ground snakes deposit their clutches of 4 or 5 eggs during early summer.

Coloring/scale form *Sonora semiannulata* is characterized by such a variety of dorsolateral color and pattern that several different combinations may be found among the small population inhabiting a single rocky bluff. Specimens from Central Texas are often uniformly yellowish tan above, however, with a small dark band across the nape. West of the Hill Country, most ground snakes exhibit up to 35 dark vertebral crossbars that may completely encircle the tail and are the source of this reptile's Latin species name; *semiannulata* means "partially-ringed." Individuals from the Trans-Pecos are often a beige/salmon above, with a more intense orange-red vertebral stripe broken by dark crossbars. Their lower sides are a lighter pinkish or yellowish tan, with tiny blocks forming a dashed lateral line.

All *Sonora* have light-hued venters, often boldly crossbarred beneath the tail, but usually without markings forward of the vent. There are 13 to 15 midbody rows of slightly darker-centered smooth dorsal scales—scalation that gives ground snakes' backs a woven-textured appearance. The head is blunt and rounded, with a loreal scale that does not touch the eye, 2 postoculars, and either 6 or 7 upper labial scales; the anal plate is divided.

Similar snakes Flathead (4) and blackhead (5—7) snakes have smaller, ventrodorsally flattened dark-crowned heads, unmarked backs, salmon-colored midbellies, and no loreal scale. Earth snakes (12—13) have 17 rows of dorsal scales that lack the ground snake's two-toned pigmentation; the loreal scale touches the eye.

Behavior Like most small serpents, *S. semiannulata* has little tolerance for surface-temperature variations: even in deep shade the author has seen these animals die after only a few minutes on the surface when the air temperature was above 100°F. This means that during late spring and summer, ground snakes' metabolisms can function above ground only at night. Some *S. semiannulata* exhibit a head-hiding, tail-waving defensive posture called a flash display because it suddenly displays the ground snake's bold subcaudal patterning, a posture similar to the defensive display of the similarly subcaudally-banded coral snake.

Western Worm Snake

Carphophis amoenus vermis

Nonvenomous   The western worm snake is completely harmless to humans.

Abundance   Rare. Known only from Bowie, Red River, and Titus counties in northeast Texas, *C. a. vermis* is apparently one of the state's least numerous serpents. Yet, because of its small size and secretive behavior, this reptile may simply be very difficult to find, for in the Midwest it is abundant enough to occur in small colonies.

Size   Adults are 7½ to 11 inches long.

Habitat   As a western race of an eastern forest serpent, *C. a. vermis* is restricted to damp areas similar to its species' primary habitat of mesic woodland, well-vegetated stream banks, brushy meadows, and overgrown farmland. Usually discovered in spring beneath stones, rotting logs, debris, or leaf mold, worm snakes seek moisture during the drier months by withdrawing to depths of as much as six feet.

Prey   Worm snakes feed primarily on earthworms, slugs, grubs, and soft-bodied invertebrates. Their predators include larger serpents: having found milk snakes near *Carphophis* colonies in Ohio, Roger Conant (1940) suggested that these small kingsnakes may be a major predator.

Reproduction   Egg-laying. In late summer, about 7 weeks after they are deposited in an earthen cavity, the 1 to 8 eggs (which measure about 1¼ by ⅝ inch) hatch into 3-to 4-inch-long young.

Coloring/scale form   The distinctive dorsolateral coloring of *Carphophis amoenus vermis* is a result of the striking longitudinal demarcation that separates this reptile's salmon-hued venter and lower sides from its iridescent, purplish-black back. Like that of other burrowing snakes, the western worm snake's head is no wider than its neck, while its hard, sharply pointed terminal caudal scute is similar to the pointed tailtip of the unrelated *Leptotyphlopidae,* which also use the tailtip as an anchoring pin to press through the soil. The western worm snake's smooth dorsal scales are arranged in only 13 midbody rows; its anal plate is divided.

Similar snakes   None; *Carphophis amoenus vermis* is the only small burrowing snake in Texas with a black-and-salmon horizontal split in pigmentation along its sides.

Behavior   The seasonal activity cycle of the western worm snake is largely a function of both temperature and the moisture level in the earth. In spring, when the organic foodstuff of decomposing leaves draws earthworms to the surface, *Carphophis* is active in the upper layers of the soil, and provided that both air and ground temperature are between 58°F and 78°F and the soil is damp, these animals may even forage abroad during the day. Later in the year, as midday heat dries the surface mulch, annelids retreat deeper into the earth and worm snakes go down with them.

In defense, *C. a. vermis* employs a two-part strategy that, at least with human captors, tends to be effective. When frightened, it expels a yellowish musk from its anal glands, spreading the unpleasant-smelling mucus about in its efforts to escape. In addition, as it tries to thrust itself forward it may suddenly press its hard, pointed tail tip against a tender part of its captor's hand, producing a startling sensation so much like the prick of a tooth that one's reflexive response is to instantly drop the snake.

¹⁹ Lined Snake
Tropidoclonion lineatum

Nonvenomous   Lined snakes do not bite human beings, but if threatened a large specimen may flatten its neck and engage in bluffing strikes.

Abundance   Common. Throughout Texas' coastal plain, central prairies, and the eastern Edwards Plateau, *T. lineatum* is a familiar snake often seen in areas of altered and softened soil near rural houses.

Size   Most adults are between 8 and 15 inches, but J. P. Jones, former reptile director of the Fort Worth Zoo, recorded one gravid Tarrant Co. female of 21½ inches. (Former Dallas Zoo director Jack Joy reports having seen specimens at least an inch longer in Dallas Co.)

Habitat   Lined snakes are semi-fossorial inhabitants of grassland—even in wooded northeast Texas, where *T. lineatum* is seen as road kills on country lanes, it lives mostly in open meadows; primary surface microhabitat is the narrow spaces found beneath rocks.

Prey   Lined snakes feed primarily on earthworms, but *T. lineatum* is one of the few vertebrates to also prey on the little toxic crustaceans, known as sow bugs, which frequent lined snakes' damp retreats.

Reproduction   Live-bearing. Twenty-three Oklahoma broods of 4- to 5-inch-long newborns were deposited between August 9 and August 31.

Coloring/scale form   The lined snake is a little serpent whose dull, gray to olive ground-colored dorsum is lined with a pale vertebral stripe. Each of its sides also has a pale stripe, often ill-defined, and bordered both above and below by dark checks that resemble another pair of stripes. The throat and venter are creamy (the midventral region may have a yellowish cast) with a double row of rearward-arched black half-moons; the pointed head, no wider than the neck, is adapted for burrowing. The lined snake's keeled dorsal scales occur in 19 rows at midbody, in 17 rows just anterior to the vent. There are 5 or 6 upper labial scales and the anal plate is undivided.

Similar snakes   Lined snakes from Texas' northeastern woodland, and another group from the Panhandle were, in 1964, differentiated by Don Tinkle and G.N. Knopf into a pair of separate subspecies: respectively, the central lined snake, *Tropidoclonion lineatum annectens,* and the New Mexico lined snake, *Tropidoclonion lineatum mertensi.* Now, in a pattern of taxonomic reclassification—as more data from the field and newly-developed scientific tools such as DNA relationship-typing alter traditional kinship connections—these two races have been rejoined with the race formerly called the Texas lined snake, *Tropidoclonion lineatum texanum,* to form a single species, the lined snake, *Tropidoclonion lineatum.* (This is a familiar pattern to those engaged in biological research, where colleagues speak of species "splitters" versus their academic opposites, the subspecies "lumpers.")

Lined snakes' close relatives, the **garter snakes (20—25)** have heads twice the width of their necks when seen from above and 8 upper labial scales vertically edged with black along their sutures; none has a double row of black ventral half-moons.

Behavior   Lined snakes are seldom seen in the open, typically remaining coiled beneath cover during the day. Among this animals' favored hiding places in suburban areas are the sunken concrete cylinders that house residential water meters, and meter readers surely see more *T. lineatum* than any herpetologist.

LINED, GARTER, RIBBON SNAKES

Eastern Garter Snake
Thamnophis sirtalis sirtalis

Nonvenomous   If handled, eastern garter snakes may emit musk, flatten their necks and sometimes bite. Individuals that choose to do so can hang on tenaciously.

Abundance   Uncommon in Texas, though still observed periodically in Harris County.

Size   Average adult length is 18 to 26 inches, with a maximum size in Texas of 32½ inches; the largest recorded eastern garter snake measured 49 inches.

Habitat   Eastern garter snakes favor open or semi-open marshy lowlands such as permanently wet meadows, stream banks, and the heavily-vegetated banks of ditches containing water.

Prey   *Thamnophis sirtalis* will prey on almost any smaller creature, but most of its diet consists of aquatic or semi-aquatic life: small fish, frogs, and salamanders. Terrestrial food animals such as toads and earthworms are sought by scent and seized with the aid of sight, but aquatic prey is often taken without using either sense. For example, eastern garter snakes often move along the margins of shallow ponds periodically thrusting their foreparts below the surface and wagging their open mouths from side to side groping for minnows or tadpoles.

Reproduction   Live-bearing. Most eastern garter snake litters are born between May and late July. The 9- to 11-inch-long offspring, which closely resemble their parents, vary enormously in number: based mostly on the size of the mother, litters range from 6 to 60 (large females give birth to many more young).

Coloring/scale form   Garter snakes are named for their resemblance to men's old-time striped sock garters: a distinct pale vertebral stripe is always evident, while a similarly-colored lateral stripe occupies the 2nd and 3rd scale rows above the belly. *T. s. sirtalis* is quite variable in color, however, and unlike eastern garters found in other parts of the country, most individuals found along the upper Gulf Coast have red markings amid the dark pigment separating their straw-colored vertebral and lateral stripes. The venter is white. The 19 midbody rows of dorsal scales are keeled and the anal plate is undivided.

Similar snakes   Western (26) and Gulf Coast (28) ribbon snakes are slimmer, have proportionately longer tails, and a distinct white spot in front of the eye; their pale side stripe occupies the 3rd and 4th scale rows above the belly. The **checkered garter snake (22)** usually has 21 rows of dorsal scales and, behind the jaw, a distinctive pale yellow crescent that separates the black patch on its neck from the rear-

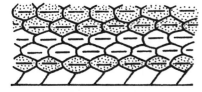

Lateral stripe marking: garter snake

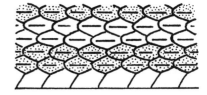

Lateral stripe marking: ribbon snakes

most of its olive upper labial scales; there is no red coloring between the double row of black squares lining each side of its back. The **lined snake (19)** has a smaller head and a double row of black ventral half-moons.

Behavior   Eastern garter snakes are erratic foragers that frequently change direction after hesitating with their heads raised for a better view. In favorable habitat, individual ranges seem to be restricted to about 2 acres, with the activity areas measured in one 3-year study averaging 600 by 150 feet; the greatest distance traveled by any of the project's subject snakes was less than ⅛ mile. Few snakes reach old age in the wild but, as the most-studied snake in confinement, captive *T. s. sirtalis* have lived as long as 14 years.

Texas Garter Snake
Thamnophis sirtalis annectens

Nonvenomous   Texas garter snakes generally choose to emit musk and bump aggressively with the snout rather than bite; a large one can nip with determination, however.

Abundance   Uncommon, but still fairly numerous in scattered locales. According to Frederick R. Gehlbach of Baylor University, Texas garter snake populations were historically highest in the state's tall grass prairies. Over 95% of this blackland ecosystem—has now been cleared for agriculture. But before tractors scraped that prairie into cotton and sorghum fields, its tall grass concealed a million pothole ponds, each harboring its own springtime complement of frantically breeding anurans . . . and the *T. s. annectens* that fed on them.

Size   Adult Texas garter snakes average 18 to 30 inches.

Habitat   Besides tall-grass prairie, Texas garter snakes are usually found in riparian meadowland and juniper-wooded canyons along the eastern edge of the Edwards Plateau. Watery microhabitats include flooded pastures.

Prey   Garter snakes will take any moving prey small enough to swallow, but earthworms, minnows, tadpoles, frogs and small toads are most often reported as food animals of *T. s. annectens*. See **Eastern Garter Snake (20)**.

Reproduction   Live-bearing. See **Eastern Garter Snake (20)**.

Coloring/scale form   With its dark back split by a broad orange stripe that occupies the vertebral scale row as well as more than half of each adjacent row, *T. s. annectens* is a visually striking reptile (when threatened, by spreading its ribs the Texas garter snake can splay its lateral scales to reveal the bright red skin hidden along its sides).

On the forward third of its trunk, its yellowish lateral stripe occupies most of the second, all of the third, and about half of the fourth scale row above the whitish or light green venter. The 19 midbody rows of dorsal scales are keeled; the anal plate is undivided.

Similar snakes   Some ribbon snakes from the South Texas brush country are so heavy-bodied that even experienced herpetologists have mistaken them for Texas garter snakes. The only sure distinction is the position of the garter snake's pale side stripe one dark scale row above the light-hued belly, while the ribbon snake's white side stripe lies two dark scale rows above its pale belly. Among this state's garter snakes, only *T. s. annectens* has pale side stripes that involve the fourth lateral scale row above the belly (in the **eastern (20), checkered (22),** and **blackneck (24—25) garter snakes,** these stripes do not touch the fourth scale row).

Note: The subspecies **red-sided garter snake**, *Thamnophis sirtalis parietalis,* may be present in Northeast Texas. A few specimens have been reported from Grayson, Fannin, Lamar, and Red River counties. These animals may be intergrades with the Texas garter snake, but the red-sided race is distinguished by its lack of a pale lateral stripe on the 4th scale row above its belly line.

Behavior   During the summer months Texas garter snakes are active morning and evening, and their lack of wariness makes them interesting to watch. One individual marked by the author came regularly to a limestone pool among cedar brakes lining the Pedernales River. This 20-inch-long serpent regularly attacked anurans too large for it to swallow and once hung on to a leopard frog for 20 minutes, never managing to engulf more than a single hind leg.

22 Checkered Garter Snake

Thamnophis marcianus marcianus

Nonvenomous   Large checkered garter snakes may nip if handled roughly.

Abundance   Common. In recent years, during its late spring and early summer foraging period *Thamnophis marcianus* was by far the most common terrestrial serpent observed in rural South Texas. By the late-1990s, however, this abundance was a thing of the past. Only a handful of checkered garter snakes could be seen in a night's drive over roads which, ten years earlier, had produced sightings of as many as 80 animals in an evening. Habitat in this part of the state has not changed appreciably, so the checkered garter's decline in this area may be a normal population fluctuation.

Size   Adult *T. m. marcianus* average 15 to 28 inches in length; the record specimen measured 42½ inches.

Habitat   In Central and North Texas the checkered garter snake seems to prefer grassy upland areas near water, where it is widespread but not numerous. In the Tamaulipan thorn brush of the Rio Grande plain, checkered garters are much more common. Here, their activity is closely tied to rainfall: When the soil is moist from precipitation, garter snakes' annelid and anuran prey is abroad on the surface, and the humid air allows olfactory predators like *T. m. marcianus* to follow their scent.

Prey   Captive checkered garter snakes feed voraciously on worms, tadpoles, mice, and frogs. A variety of other small vertebrate, insect, and annelid prey is undoubtedly taken in the wild, while *T. m. marcianus* is also among the handful of serpents that sometimes feed on carrion. See **Eastern Blackneck Garter Snake (24).**

Reproduction   Live-bearing. Birth occurs between late May and October—an Oct. 6 parturition, by a 28-inch-long female rescued from a cat at a La Salle Co. campground is the latest date on record—with 38 newborns averaging 7.8 inches in length. (In a somewhat unusual ophidian developmental process, young checkered garter snakes are partially nourished through their mother's placenta.) Following their birth, the young, which exactly resemble their parents except with more vivid coloring, are extremely plentiful in South Texas' brush country (it is not unusual to find healthy neonates lying full length in mesquite-shaded cow paths), where many of them provide prey for the region's numerous ophiophagas milk and kingsnakes.

Coloring/scale form   The checkered garter snake's white or very light yellow vertebral stripe is flanked, on each side of the pale, gray-green back and sides, with a double row of black squares. (Checkered garter snakes from the Hill Country may have a tendency toward melanism: During 1979, Jozsef Laszlo and Alan Kardon displayed at the San Antonio Zoo two melanistic *T. m. marcianus,* both of which were found in Comal Co.; other all-black specimens have come from Kerr and Medina counties. Albino specimens are also known from the wild and are commonly propagated in captivity.)

The checkered garter snake's most distinctive marking, however, is the yellowish crescent behind the jaw, posteriorly bordered by a large black spot on the side of the neck. Laterally, a light-hued stripe occupies only the third row of scales above the belly on the foreparts, but widens to include the second scale row over the rest of the body; the whitish-yellow ventral scales sometimes have black-tipped edges. Arranged in 21 rows at midbody, the dorsal scales are keeled; the anal plate is undivided.

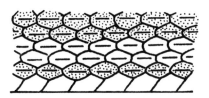

Lateral stripe marking: checkered garter snake

Similar snakes Texas (21) and **blackneck garter snakes (24–25)** lack a prominent yellow crescent behind the jaw and have only 19 midbody rows of dorsal scales. The **western plains garter snake (23)** has a less prominent yellow nuchal crescent, while its anterior lateral stripe occupies both the third and fourth scale rows above its venter. **Ribbon snakes (26–29)** are more slender, with 19 dorsal scale rows, unspotted backs, wire-like tails that make up nearly a third of their body length, and a prominent white spot just in front of the eye. The lined snake **(19)** has a smaller head and a double row of black ventral half-moons.

Behavior Named *T. marcianus* for Capt. Randolph B. Marcy, who in 1852 delivered to the Smithsonian Institution the original type specimen (which he obtained during an exploratory expedition along the Red River), the checkered garter snake ranges from central Kansas to Belize. It is also a longtime Texas resident. The fossilized remains of a serpent almost identical to *T. marcianus* were recovered by J. Alan Holman (1964) from the banks of Hardeman Co.'s Groesbeck Creek, in strata dating from the Wisconsin Glacial Period of 50,000 to 100,000 years ago.

Especially likely to be abroad on humid nights preceded by light rain showers, Marcy's garter snakes follow the typical ophidian pattern of foraging at dawn and dusk in spring and fall, then becoming entirely nocturnal during the hottest months. At this time, they are active later into the summer than most serpents, but only in the cooler hours between midnight and dawn. In the manner or ringneck, ground, and other subcaudally red or banded snakes, occasional specimens exhibit a defensive posture in which the tightly curled yellowish underside of the posterior third of the trunk is everted. First photographed by Donna Marvel beside a Rio Grande irrigation ditch, this behavior is so unusual that among hundreds of *T. m. marcianus* observed over fifteen years, D. Craig McIntyre has observed similar tail-curling only once.

23 Western Plains Garter Snake
Thamnophis radix haydenii

Nonvenomous   This animal will not bite unless handled, when it may snap abruptly in its own defense.

Abundance   Uncommon in Texas. Within most of its predominantly Midwestern territory, *T. r. haydenii* is locally abundant, but records for Texas are sparse.

Size   Adults average 20 to 28 inches; the record length is 40 inches.

Habitat   This subspecies' popular name suggests a grassland range, though its microenvironment is more likely to involve the borders of streams, washes, and gullies that bisect the prairie.

Prey   Amphibians, insects (especially grasshoppers), and, among the young, earthworms are the principal prey of *T. r. haydenii*.

Reproduction   Live-bearing. Litters average 29 offspring.

Coloring/scale form   Dorsally, the western plains garter snake resembles a checkered garter: its white or very light yellow vertebral stripe is flanked with a closely-spaced double row of black squares. Below them, a prominent pale yellow lateral stripe occupies only the third and fourth scale rows above the belly; below it another row of squarish black spots appears. (The off-white to pale greenish ventral scales may also bear a line of dark distal spots.) With a maximum of 21 rows of strongly-keeled scale rows, *T. r. haydenii* has more numerous dorsal scales than any other garter snake but the checkered; its anal plate is undivided.

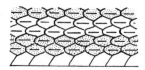

Lateral stripe marking: western plains garter snake

Similar snakes   This is a difficult animal to distinguish from the **checkered garter snake (22)**, whose light yellow, posteriorly black-bordered neck crescent is more prominently defined, and whose light side stripe does not reach the fourth scale row above its belly line. **Ribbon snakes (26–29)** are much more slender, with proportionately longer tails, unspotted backs, unmarked whitish lips and bellies, a prominent white spot just ahead of the eye, and 19 rows of dorsal scales.

Behavior   Seasonally active from March to November, western plains garter snakes retire below ground during the hottest weeks of summer, for they are quite sensitive to high temperatures, becoming overheated at more than 90°F. This species is relatively hardy in cool weather, though, for on sunny autumn days too chilly for most reptiles to be abroad large numbers of *Thamnophis radix haydenii* are sometimes observed crawling onto asphalt roads—where many are slain by traffic—where they pause to absorb warmth from the blacktop.

Eastern Blackneck Garter Snake
Thamnophis cyrtopsis ocellatus

Nonvenomous *Thamnophis cyrtopsis ocellatus* generally defends itself only by discharging feces and musk, but a large individual may nip if molested.

Abundance Common. Because of the eastern blackneck garter's vivid colors and diurnal foraging, it is often noticed in the residential neighborhoods of San Antonio, New Braunfels, San Marcos, and Austin. New residential developments spreading from this urban corridor onto the Edwards Plateau frequently result in new houses being built during the winter over the brumation crevices of *T. c. ocellatus*. When these beautiful little serpents emerge in spring they find themselves literally on the new residents' doorsteps. Surprisingly, this often causes consternation since, in popular mythology, bright orange and black dorsal markings on a snake, however small and innocuous, means danger.

Size Adult *T. c. ocellatus* average 16 to 20 inches in length; the record is 43 inches.

Habitat The eastern blackneck garter snake's primary habitat is moist, wooded ravines and streamside bottomland throughout Texas' central Hill Country; now, well-watered, heavily-foliaged residential neighborhoods approximate this environment and support healthy populations of *T. c. ocellatus*.

Prey In an extensive study of predation in this and two other *Thamnophis* species in Travis Co., M. J. Fourquette (1954) found that the eastern blackneck garter takes mainly tadpole prey during spring and early summer, then adult frogs the rest of the year. (Along the Balcones Fault west of Austin, Fourquette found that its anuran prey was primarily the locally abundant cliff frog, although slimy salamanders, red-spotted toads, and ground skinks were also noted.)

In this area, the eastern blackneck garter snake competes for food mainly with the redstripe ribbon snake, which also favors amphibian prey. The garter snake takes primarily amphibians it finds on land, however, while the predominantly aquatic ribbon snake seeks frogs and salamanders in water. (To a limited extent, the eastern blackneck garter also competes with the checkered garter snake for terrestrial amphibian prey, although much of the checkered garter's diet consists of earthworms and small lizards, neither of which are regularly eaten by the blackneck garter snake; the checkered garter snake's mostly nocturnal foraging presumably also lessens predatory competition between it and the more diurnal eastern blackneck garter.)

Reproduction Live-bearing. The average brood is 9 young, 8 to 10½ inches in length.

Coloring/scale form First described by C.B.R. Kennicott in 1860, the eastern blackneck garter snake takes its name from the Greek *cyrto*, "curved," and *opsis*, "appearance"—a reference to the hemispherical black blotch located just behind its jaw. Flanking this snake's orange vertebral stripe, a row of large black dorsolateral blotches, separated by tiny light-and-dark bars, encroaches downward into the forward portion of the broad yellow side stripe (which occupies the second and third scale rows above the venter), giving it a wavy appearance. Posteriorly, these blotches diverge into a double row of staggered black spots. Arranged in 19 rows at midbody, the dorsal scales are heavily keeled, the anal plate is undivided.

LINED, GARTER, RIBBON SNAKES

73

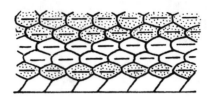

Lateral stripe marking: eastern and western blackneck garter snakes

Similar snakes   No other *Thamnophis* occurring within the range of *T. c. ocellatus* has a single row of very large black blotches on either side of its neck. (Posteriorly, the western blackneck race has black checkerboard dorsolateral patterning.) The **redstripe ribbon snake (27)** is much more slender, has a long, wire-like tail, unmarked white upper labial scales, and a prominent white spot in front of its eye. The pale side stripe of the **Texas garter snake (21),** unlike that of *T. c. ocellatus,* occupies part of the fourth scale row above its belly.

Behavior   Blackneck garter snakes are diurnally active during even the hottest summer months, almost always near some sort of aquatic milieu. Vision is used for capturing prey, but sight is less important to garter snakes than scent in locating prey, for the instinctually-recognized smell of appropriate prey species such as earthworms, anurans, and fish is what elicits predatory attacks.

Despite its gaudy appearance, the blackneck garter's bright vertebral stripe functions as sophisticated camouflage: As *T. c. ocellatus* slides away from danger, its black dorsal spots and orange vertebral pigment flash intermittently through intervening leafy undergrowth, focusing a predator's visual attention on what seems to be a flickering but stationary ribbon of orange.

Western Blackneck Garter Snake
Thamnophis cyrtopsis cyrtopsis

Nonvenomous   Blackneck garter snakes nip only if they are molested or handled roughly.

Abundance   Common. In well-watered and vegetated habitats, this reptile may be abundant: In summer it is often found on roads at night in the vicinity of dry creekbeds and culverts. Sherman Minton's (1959) experience in Brewster Co. is also typical:

> In late July, almost every pool in the little canyon below Boot Spring was occupied by 2 to 6 of these snakes. They were sunning on rocks or swimming in pursuit of *Hyla arenicolor* (canyon treefrog) tadpoles, which were found in the stomachs of all those collected.

Size   Adults average 16 to 28 inches in length; the largest western blackneck garter on record measured 41¾ inches.

Habitat   In West Texas *Thamnophis cyrtopsis* is generally a mountain- and plateau-dweller absent from intervening low-lying valleys.

Prey   See **Eastern Blackneck Garter Snake (24).**

Reproduction   Live-bearing. Broods of 3 to 25 young have been recorded.

Coloring/scale form   On the western blackneck garter snake's forebody, the pale orange vertebral stripe divides a single row of large black dorsolateral squares; this splits, posteriorly, into a double row. The crown is bluish gray, strikingly set off from the big black neck patch that is the source of its common name, and which laterally borders the rear of its skull. The pale side stripe occupies the second and third scale rows above the venter throughout this animal's length, and the chin and belly are white, sometimes with a faint greenish or yellowish-brown cast. There are 19 rows of keeled dorsal scales at midbody and the anal plate is undivided.

Similar snakes   The subspecies **eastern blackneck garter snake (24)** has a single row of much larger, rounded or V-shaped dark anterior dorsolateral blotches, the lower tips of which reach downward into a wide yellow lateral area, giving this pale side stripe a wavy configuration. Posteriorly, the black checkerboard dorsolateral patterning of the western blackneck race is scarcely evident. The **checkered garter snake (22)** is not usually found in the upland locales where the western blackneck garter most often occurs, but is distinguished by the prominent yellow crescent located just behind its jaw, by the anterior restriction of its pale side stripe to the third row of scales above its belly, and by its 21 midbody rows of dorsal scales. **Ribbon snakes (26–29)** are more slender, with proportionately longer tails, unmarked white upper labial scales, and a white, half moon-shaped spot just forward of the eye. Ribbon snakes also lack the garter snakes' black-blotched back.

Behavior   *Thamnophis cyrtopsis* is frequently encountered basking on creekside rocks from which, if disturbed, it flees by swimming rapidly across the surface to the opposite bank; cornered, it may flatten its body against the ground and writhe as menacingly as possible.

LINED, GARTER, RIBBON SNAKES

26 Western Ribbon Snake
Thamnophis proximus proximus

Nonvenomous   See **Redstripe Ribbon Snake (27)**.

Abundance   Common. One of Texas' four races of *T. proximus* is likely to occur near any body of fresh water in the eastern
⁹⁄₁₀ of the state.

Size   Most adults are 20 to 34 inches long, with such slender bodies that
3 female western ribbon snakes between 27 and 34 inches in length—as with all
Thamnophis, females are the larger gender—averaged less than 6 ounces in weight.

Habitat   Throughout ribbon snakes' wide range, which stretches from Wisconsin
to Costa Rica, these creatures most often inhabit creek, lake, and pond margins;
they are also found in arid brush country, but seldom far from water. See **Arid Land
Ribbon Snake (29)**.

Prey   Ribbon snakes' food animals vary with the seasons: 92% of the stomach
contents of one Brazos Co. sample trapped during late spring consisted of tadpoles. At other times of the year frogs and toads—whose digitaloid skin toxins
garter snakes are metabolically equipped to digest—lizards, and small fish may be
the principal prey. Besides mammalian and avian carnivores, ribbon snakes are
themselves preyed upon by big, fast-moving snakes like racers and coachwhips.

Reproduction   Live-bearing. One female *T. p. proximus* captured by Bill and
Donna Marvel near Stanford, Oklahoma, gave birth to 21 young shortly after midnight on Aug. 8, while three Smith Co. litters, recorded by Neil Ford of the University of Texas at Tyler, were deposited July 10, 18, and Aug. 20. The two smaller
females each gave birth to 18 young, the larger one to 23, all of them about the
same size: between 9½ and 10 inches in length, slimmer than a pencil at midbody,
and about ¹⁄₁₀ ounce in weight.

Because juvenile ribbon snakes seldom turn up in field collections, mortality
among first- and second-year individuals is thought to be quite high, especially in
years with very dry and/or cold winters. Donald R. Clark (1974) reports heavy winter die-offs among juvenile western ribbon snakes, presumably because their smaller ratio of bulk to surface area renders them more vulnerable to desiccation during
their critical November-through-February brumation period.

Among Clark's East Texas population, sufficient rainfall before and during denning appeared to be the primary factor determining survival of juvenile *T. p. proximus,* for dry autumn weather limited the abundance of small frogs and resulted
in low fat levels among the young about to enter winter dormancy. Little precipitation later in the year, combined with very cold winter weather then resulted in an
estimated mortality of 74% of this vulnerable age group during its 4½ months' brumation.

Coloring/scale form   The western ribbon snake's unmarked dark gray-brown
dorsum is split by a broad orange vertebral stripe. Like that of all ribbon snakes, its
yellowish lateral stripe occupies the third and fourth scale rows above its yellowish-
green venter. The white upper labial scales are unmarked. (The lips, lateral stripe,
and belly of individuals living north and east of Dallas often have a bluish cast, however.) Two tiny white dashes punctuate the rear of the blackish crown and a rear-
ward-curved white spot occurs just in front of each eye. The strongly keeled dorsal
scales are arranged in 19 rows at midbody and the anal plate is undivided.

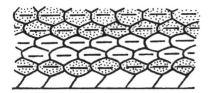

Lateral stripe marking: garter snake
(All garter snakes have the same side-striped spacing.)

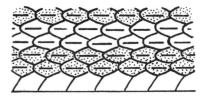

Lateral stripe marking: ribbon snakes

Similar snakes   Texas' four geographically distinct races of *Thamnophis proximus* are the result of Douglas Rossman's 1963 separation (from the western ribbon snake, known since 1823) of the **Gulf Coast ribbon snake (28),** which typically has a brownish- to olive-green back and sides and an olive-tan to dull gold vertebral stripe; the **redstripe ribbon snake (27),** which has a dark gray back, a wine-red vertebral stripe, and gray-green lower sides; and the **arid land ribbon snake (29),** whose back is usually gray-brown, although individuals from the Canadian and Cimarron River drainages sometimes display a darker ground color, with both a distinctive thin black ventrolateral seam and a broad orange vertebral stripe that lightens to gold on the nape. All interbreed freely, producing intermediate forms that vary clinally as the range of each subspecies merges with that of adjoining races. **Garter snakes (20–25)** have stockier bodies with shorter tails, larger heads lacking a white spot in front of the eye, and dark vertical seams between the upper labial scales.

Behavior   First termed *Thamnophis,* Greek for "bush serpent," by Leopold J. F. Fitzinger in 1843, both garter and ribbon snakes are indeed at home in the brushy environs of lake and stream shorelines. Here the ribbon snakes are frequently somewhat arboreal, for in Collin Co. Jim Stout observed nine juveniles basking on the branches of a brush-filled gully. The western ribbon snake, *T. proximus proximus,* was long thought to be but a subspecies of the eastern ribbon snake, *T. sauritus sauritus* (*proximus* means "neighboring") until Rossman (1963b) demonstrated that in the few regions where these animals occur together the two do not recognize each other as potential mates. Because of this reproductive isolation Rossman concluded that western and eastern ribbon snakes are actually the separate species, *T. proximus* and *T. sauritus,* respectively, whose differentiation may have occurred when the range of their common ancestor was split by the cold weather pushed southward by the advance of late Pleistocene glaciers. (This cooler climate presumably left the eastern segment of the ancestral ribbon snake population isolated in Florida, its western counterpart in northern Mexico, for so long that after cold abated and the two groups were again able to extend their ranges northward, they had diverged too far along separate genetic paths to be able to interbreed—although both still maintained similar orientation in habitat and diet.)

27 Redstripe Ribbon Snake
Thamnophis proximus rubrilineatus

Nonvenomous   Like most *Thamnophis*, ribbon snakes, if seized roughly, can nip and hang on tenaciously despite their small heads.

Abundance   Common. See **Western Ribbon Snake (26).**

Habitat   Confined mainly to the Edwards Plateau, this race is endemic to Texas. In the Hill Country's juniper/savannah community, *Thamnophis proximus rubrilineatus* is almost always found in or near water. Here, it is easily observed because of its diurnal activity pattern: When not actively foraging, it basks on rocks, logs, and the raised cypress knees that occur along many waterways in this region. Such individuals typically remain motionless until approached very closely, or even touched, when they streak away across the water's surface to hide beneath overhanging rocks or vegetation on the opposite bank. During late August and September newborn redstripe ribbon snakes can often be found sheltering under creekside limestone flags.

Prey   Ribbon snakes' prey is seasonally variable, but is almost always obtained from aquatic environments. In spring, tadpoles constitute much of the diet; at other times, small fish, salamanders, and adult frogs and toads—whose digitaloid skin toxins ribbon snakes are metabolically equipped to digest—are principal food animals.

On land, ribbon snakes use scent-tracking to locate fossorial food animals such as earthworms, as well as to ferret lizards and small anurans from beneath grass and litter. See **Eastern Blackneck Garter Snake (24).**

Reproduction   Live-bearing. Breeding occurs from April through June. Litters of up to 20 are deposited between July and September.

Coloring/scale form   The narrow vertebral stripe splitting the dark gray back of this subspecies can vary from deep wine red near the tail to bright orange at the nape, although entirely orange-striped specimens not infrequently turn up throughout the range.

Similar Snakes   The 4 geographical races of *Thamnophis proximus* found in Texas interbreed to produce clinal variations intermediate between the redstripe ribbon, the **Gulf Coast ribbon snake (28),** which typically has a brownish- to olive-green back and sides and an olive-tan to dull gold vertebral stripe; the **arid land ribbon snake (29),** whose orange vertebral stripe bisects an olive-brown to gray back and tan lower sides, and the **western ribbon snake (26),** whose dark gray-brown back is split by a broad orange vertebral stripe. **Garter snakes (20—25)** have stockier bodies with shorter tails, larger heads that lack a white spot in front of the eye, and dark vertical seams between their upper labial scales.

Behavior   The ribbon snake's conspicuous vertebral stripe is believed to help it evade predators: Seen through thick vegetation, as it moves away from the viewer this bright spinal stripe appears to remain in place, gradually narrowing as the snake slides deeper into the bushes.

Even knowing full well that such a partially hidden snake is moving away, it is still always a surprise to see its tailtip suddenly slip from view, and predators clearly have the same response. So many manage to catch only the ribbon snake's tailtip—which is easily twisted off—that nearly 20% of the *Thamnophis proximus* in one Kansas study lacked complete tails.

Gulf Coast Ribbon Snake

Thamnophis proximus orarius

Nonvenomous *Thamnophis proximus* does not bite humans unless it is handled roughly.

Abundance Common. See **Western Ribbon Snake (26)**.

Size See **Western Ribbon Snake (26)**.

Habitat *Thamnophis proximus orarius* is almost invariably found near water, inhabiting coastal marshes, moist prairie, and low hammocks above surrounding wetlands (one favored microhabitat is the levees that impound rice field irrigation lakes). In Jefferson Co. these reptiles are found right on the upper Gulf beach, but inland terrain near water is also occupied.

Prey Ribbon snakes typically forage along shorelines, taking insects, crustaceans, and small vertebrates. Nearly as aquatic as the water snakes (*Thamnophis* is believed to be ancestral to the *Nerodia* water snakes), ribbon snakes rely on diving into water for protection. Without this refuge they are evidently quite vulnerable, for I have seen these little snakes heavily preyed upon by cattle egrets in the drying bed of the Nueces River.

Reproduction Live-bearing. Breeding begins early in the year: Gravid *T. p. orarius* have been discovered as early as April, and by July, 88% of females examined in one study were found to be pregnant. Recorded broods for *Thamnophis proximus* have ranged from 5 to 33 (one Duval Co. specimen gave birth to 33 young on Oct. 18–20–a very late parturition date for this animal).

Coloring/scale form Notable for its mint-green upper labial scales, chartreuse venter, and a less contrasting dorsal pattern than upland ribbon snakes, *T. p. orarius* has a brownish-green back whose pale vertebral line is almost the same color as its olive-tan side stripes. (Individuals from Duval and McMullen counties have cream-colored vertebral stripes, however, and are often so large and thick-bodied that they closely resemble the Texas garter snake (**21**). Those from eastern Harris and southern Liberty Co. may have a golden spinal stripe, with a dark back and sides.)

Similar snakes Texas' 4 races of *Thamnophis proximus* intergrade to produce variations between the Gulf Coast ribbon and the **western ribbon snake (26),** which has a darker back and wine-red vertebral stripe; the **redstripe ribbon snake (27),** whose wine-red to bright orange vertebral stripe splits a dark gray back; and the **arid land ribbon snake (29),** whose back is usually gray-brown, with both a thin black ventrolateral seam and a broad orange-to gold vertebral stripe. (Among look-alike garter snakes such as the Texas garter (**21**), the position of the pale side stripe—one dark scale row above the light-hued belly—is the only sure way to distinguish it from the largest ribbon snakes, whose white side stripe lies two dark scale rows above the pale belly.)

Behavior In studying a population of Gulf Coast ribbon snakes on the Sarpy Wildlife Refuge, a cypress-gum swamp northwest of New Orleans, Donald Tinkle (1957) established that in this subtropical climate ribbon snakes are active almost year-round—although their most extensive foraging occurred immediately after summer rains when frogs and toads were abroad. Tinkle found that his marked snakes occupied territories several acres in size although, because they foraged throughout the study area, he encountered them most frequently on earthen ridges extending into the swamp. Here, in cool spring weather, they basked in the sunny upper layers of blackberry vines; in summer they sought the protection of the wooded parts of the ridges.

29 Arid Land Ribbon Snake
Thamnophis proximus diabolicus

Nonvenomous   Ribbon snakes nip if they are molested.

Abundance   Common. See **Western Ribbon Snake (26).**

Size   The longest of Texas' ribbon snakes, *Thamnophis proximus diabolicus* has been recorded to just over 4 feet in length.

Habitat   Ribbon snakes' ability to subsist around even small bodies of water allows this westernmost race of *T. proximus* to occupy much of West Texas. Along river courses crossing the High Plains, the arid land ribbon snake occurs as far upstream on the Pecos River as Artesia, New Mexico, and is absent only from the driest, most westerly parts of the Northern Chihuahuan Desert.

In large measure this is because of man. Since the latter part of the nineteenth century, ranchers have been pumping water from Panhandle aquifers into stock tanks. These artificial ponds offer frogs and toads an aquatic reproductive niche and provide them with flies drawn to the ponds' manure-covered banks. As a result, these anurans' predators, the ribbon snakes previously restricted to the heads of the narrow creeks on the dry shortgrass prairie, have now colonized waterholes everywhere on the High Plains.

Like their relatives the garter snakes, ribbon snakes are able to prey on these anurans because enlarged adrenal glands allow them to partially neutralize toads' toxic epidermal secretions. These secretions contain the digitaloid poisons that cause dogs that have bitten a toad to gag and froth at the mouth, and can slow or even stop the heartbeat of small predators not metabolically equipped to counter their neurologically-suppressive effect.

Prey   See **Western Ribbon Snake (26).**

Reproduction   Live-bearing. See **Gulf Coast Ribbon Snake (28).**

Coloring/scale form   Because the type specimen for *Thamnophis proximus diabolicus* was taken near the Devil's River, this snake owes its subspecies name to the Greek *diabolikos*. Its back is usually gray-brown—though individuals from the Canadian and Cimarron river drainages sometimes display a darker ground color—with a distinctive thin black ventrolateral seam and a broad orange vertebral stripe that lightens to gold on the nape.

Similar snakes   Throughout the Panhandle, *T. p. diabolicus* intergrades with the **western ribbon snake (26)**, which generally has a darker back and a slightly narrower vertebral stripe. Likewise, on the Stockton and western Edwards plateaus the arid land ribbon snake intergrades with the **redstripe ribbon snake (27)**—the latter having a ruddier vertebral stripe than the arid land race—while, as far northwest as Laredo on the Rio Grande plain, the arid land ribbon snake's range overlaps that of the olive-backed, vertebrally greenish tan-striped **Gulf Coast ribbon snake (28).**

Behavior   The arid land ribbon snake's behavior, although slightly adapted to the drier conditions of its range, is similar to that of Texas' three other subspecies of *Thamnophis proximus.*

Diamondback Water Snake
Nerodia rhombifer rhombifer

Nonvenomous   If cornered, large diamondback water snakes can be vigorous biters with an extraordinary ability to excrete large quantities of musk.

Abundance   Abundant. On the coastal plain south of Houston *Nerodia rhombifer rhombifer* is the most common aquatic serpent; it is less numerous in the central and northeastern parts of the state. In Southwest Texas the diamondback water snake inhabits more arid terrain than most of the state's aquatic snakes, and because waterways in this area are prone to seasonal drying, *N. r. rhombifer* is significantly exposed to predation during late summer. At this time newborns are at their most numerous and I have seen great blue herons and egrets plucking juvenile diamondback water snakes from shrinking pools in the Nueces River.

Size   Most adults are 20 to 34 inches; the record is just over 60 inches.

Habitat   *Nerodia rhombifer rhombifer* may be found in or around almost any rural body of water in the eastern two thirds of the state; here, man-made objects left along the banks are a frequent source of shelter. During rainy periods diamondback water snakes may also forage in moist grassland a mile or more from water.

Prey   This animal's food choice varies considerably with locale, but in most situations prey is mainly frogs and rough fish (few healthy game fish, which are too fast for water snakes to capture, are taken). As with other water snakes, carrion seems to be an important part of the diet, which is the reason *N. r. rhombifer* is seen nosing around the dead and dying fish held by fishermens' stringers.

Reproduction   Live-bearing. Twenty-two litters, all deposited between the first of August and mid-October, averaged 37.3 young 8¼ to 10¼ inches in length.

Coloring/scale form   Blackish-brown lines form a diamond-shaped network across the dark olive to grayish-brown back. These lines intersect dark vertical bars along the diamondback water snake's sides; its yellowish venter is randomly marked with small black crescents. The 25 to 31 midbody rows of dorsal scales are strongly keeled; the anal plate is divided.

Similar snakes   Water snakes' heavy bodies and dark coloring most often cause them to be mistaken for the **western cottonmouth (95),** which is distinguished by its slit-pupil eye and sunken heat-sensing pit between eye and nostril. Unlike the rounded heads of water snakes, the cottonmouth's angular head is distinguished by flat, undercut cheeks which abruptly intersect its crown. *Nerodia* water snakes typically swim and dive vigorously, moreover, while the cottonmouth's entire body is buoyantly suspended on the surface.

Behavior   One predatory strategy involves sensitive lateral areas along the trunk; when these spots are touched, *N. rhombifer* snaps sideways in an automatic strike response that, as it swims along pond and river banks, increases its chances of seizing prey trapped between its body and the shore.

AQUATIC SNAKES

81

31 Yellowbelly Water Snake
Nerodia erythrogaster flavigaster

Nonvenomous   In self-defense, yellowbelly water snakes
will flatten their necks and bodies and make false strikes. If
pressed further they will bite—and large *Nerodia* are strong
enough to do so with vigor, typically causing long scratches as they
quickly jerk free—as well as discharge both feces and foul-smelling musk
excreted by cloacal glands located just inside the vent.

Abundance   Common. *Nerodia erythrogaster flavigaster* is one of the two (the
other is the broad-banded water snake) most abundant aquatic serpents in much of
East Texas. Because it has a stout body that becomes even more heavily proportioned with age, yellowbelly water snakes are frequently mistaken for the venomous
cottonmouth, but the vast majority of "moccasins" found around rural and suburban ponds are actually yellowbelly, blotched, or diamondback water snakes.

Size   Adults are usually between 28 and 48 inches in length. The record size is 62
inches—almost certainly a female because males do not reach more than three-quar-
ters the length or girth of the largest females.

Habitat   The yellowbelly water snake inhabits most rural wetland environments
east of the blackland prairie, though it is most numerous in swamps, the current-
less water of oxbow river segments, bayous, and the marshy verges of floodplain
lakes and ponds in East Texas.

These aquatic milieus are rich in both food sources and shelter—murky water is a
good place to hide, but there is nothing in the biology of water snakes to limit them
to a wet environment. For example, if food is available and predators are not present—captives often ignore artificial pools except just before shedding—these animals are able to thrive away from aquatic habitats (juveniles, being less mobile and
more vulnerable to predation, are more likely to keep to the comparative safety of
aquatic milieus).

Prey   Young *N. e. flavigaster* eat small fish, tadpoles, and aquatic insects; adults
feed primarily on fish, frogs, and other amphibians. One instance of predation on
the latter was noted by Bill Marvel:

> At 2 p.m. on March 16 I was standing beside a roadside ditch when a 36-
> inch yellowbelly water snake backed out of the water with a 10-inch lesser
> siren grasped about mid-body. The snake crawled up the embankment, where
> it began "walking" its jaws along the siren's body toward the head. The siren
> attempted to escape by burrowing among the grass roots and by twisting
> movements that forced the snake to turn on its back. The siren also uttered
> several shrill distress cries. Although the snake crawled across my boots during
> this struggle it did not seem to notice my presence. After it had swallowed the
> siren it raised its head, flicked its tongue, then crawled back into the ditch and
> swam away under water. The whole operation took about 45 minutes.

Reproduction   Live-bearing. See **Blotched water snake (32)**.

Coloring scale/form   Latin for "yellow," *flavi*, combined with *gaster*, Greek for
"belly," describes this subspecies as the yellow-bellied race of the eastern redbelly
water snake, *N. e. erythrogaster*. Slightly paler on its lower sides, the yellowbelly
subspecies' unpatterned dark back varies from the gray-backed animals found in
East Texas and Louisiana to specimens intermediate in coloring between this race

and the vertebrally pale-barred, laterally dark-blocked western subspecies, the blotched water snake, *N. e. transversa*. Marked only by the dark vertical sutures of the labial scales, the lips and chin are yellow, as is the venter.

Juvenile *N. e. flavigaster* differ in appearance from adults; their faintly pinkish ground color is conspicuously patterned over the forebody with dark dorsal bands which break up posteriorly into dark saddles alternating with vertical lateral bars. The venter is pale yellow, with dark pigment lining the forward edges of the mid-body ventral scutes. The keeled dorsal scales occur in 23 rows at midbody and the anal plate is usually divided.

Similar snakes   Water snakes' albumin proteins indicate that they are close relatives of the garter and ribbon snakes. (*Nerodia* are thought to be a Pliocene evolutionary departure toward aquatic life on the part of some members of the much older, more terrestrially-adapted garter snake genus *Thamnophis*.)

Yellowbelly water snakes are dark-bodied serpents with heads distinctly wider than their narrow necks (when flattened in threat, their "triangular" shape suggests, to many people, the **western cottonmouth (95)**. But the cottonmouth has a vertically-slit pupil unlike the circular pupil of all water snakes, as well as a sizable dark heat-sensing pit between its eye and nostril; its angular head is distinguished by flat, undercut cheeks that abruptly intersect its crown.

Behavior   For the most part *Nerodia* (the current genus name for North American water snakes previously classified as *Natrix*) have not made a radical physical accommodation to aquatic life. Instead, they have been able to take advantage of the benefits of life in the water by behavioral adaptations. Most important is these snakes' technique for gaining heat in cooler aquatic milieus by basking on logs and floating aquatic vegetation. Frequently seen draped along tree limbs overhanging water, (like most aquatic serpents *N. e. flavigaster* is a good climber) yellowbelly water snakes are also encountered crossing roads in the evening, especially following rainstorms that bring out feeding frogs.

During their breeding season, frogs and toads move away from ponds—which are filled with predatory fish—to deposit their eggs in the ditches and temporary puddles that give their tadpoles a better chance of survival. This, of course, leaves the adult anurans without shelter, and drawn by the easy prey offered by these annual congregations, yellowbelly water snakes often venture far from their home lakes and rivers.

32 Blotched Water Snake
Nerodia erythrogaster transversa

Nonvenomous   See **Yellowbelly Water Snake (31)**.

Abundance   Common. In the central and west central parts of Texas, *N. e. transversa* is the predominant water snake.

Size   Most adults are 2 to 3 feet in length; the record is 58 inches.

Habitat   The chocolate-blotched newborns are often in shallower, more dappled microenvironments—both small streams and the inlets of larger bodies of water—than the more uniformly colored adults. (The most westerly *N. e. transversa*, which occupy rocky streambed channels, retain distinct dorsal patterning throughout their lives.)

Prey   Most reptiles partition habitat; snakes usually partition prey species. The diverse population of sympatric water snake species in the eastern Texas instinctually partitions its food resources, with *Nerodia erythrogaster* taking mostly of fish and frogs.

Reproduction   Live-bearing. Like their relatives the garter snakes, water snakes are characterized by large numbers of offspring. *N. e. transversa* fits this pattern, depositing, after a 3½-month gestation period, litters containing from 11 to over 30 young. These range from 9 to 11½ inches in length and, after their birth in late summer, are often numerous in farm ponds and other shallow bodies of water where their mortality to wetland-foraging predators such as raccoons and herons is extremely high.

Reproduction   Live-bearing. Breeding occurs on land in spring; the 5 to 27 young—7½ to 10½ inches long and almost identical to young yellowbelly water snakes—are born in late summer.

Coloring/scale form   Blotched water snakes are gray-brown above, often with a hint of olive. Over the spine, short, dark-edged pale bars are evident, while dimly-defined dark vertical bars mark the sides. The belly is yellow, with the edges of larger animals' ventral plates lightly tinged with brown. (The young are indistinguishable from juveniles of the subspecies yellowbelly water snake.) The 23 to 27 midbody rows of dorsal scales are heavily keeled; the anal plate is divided.

Similar snakes   Blotched water snakes are stout-bodied, short-tailed serpents that darken with age, heightening their resemblance to the **western cottonmouth (95)**. But the cottonmouth has a vertically-slit pupil unlike the circular pupil of all water snakes. The cottonmouth also has a dark heat-sensing pit between its eye and nostril and an angular head whose flat, undercut cheeks abruptly intersect its crown. Intergrades between the blotched and **yellowbelly water snake (31)** occur in East/Central Texas, but the typical yellowbelly is unmarked above, with light yellow posterior edging on its ventral scales.

Behavior   During temperate weather blotched water snakes are crepuscular or diurnal foragers, but during the hottest months they are active mainly at night. Like other *Nerodia*, they are drawn to water flowing into their ponds, perhaps in anticipation of small fish being swept downstream, although they are as likely to lie for hours in the sterile outflow of a well pump as in the mouth of a natural creek.

33 Broad-banded Water Snake
Nerodia fasciata confluens

Nonvenomous   See **Florida Water Snake (34).**

Abundance   Uncommon in parts of its extensive East Texas range, *N. f. confluens* is often abundant along the upper coast: In the marshes of Chambers and Jefferson counties it is the predominant water snake.

Size   Adult length averages 20 to 30 inches; the record is 45 inches.

Habitat   Broad-banded water snakes occur in and around permanent bodies of slow-moving or current-less water—forest-bordered ponds, lakes, and small streams—as well as in wet prairie and coastal wetlands, sometimes right down to the margins of salt water.

Prey   *Nerodia fasciata confluens* preys primarily on fish, frogs, toads, salamanders, and crayfish taken on both diurnal and nocturnal forays. Swimming parallel to the shore, it is able to seize the frogs that, flushed from bankside resting places, fling themselves into the water directly in its path. At other times, broad-banded water snakes may be seen slowly searching the bottoms of shallow ponds.

Reproduction   Live-bearing. Mating has been reported to occur in April, followed, after 70 to 80 days of gestation, by litters of up to 50 young. Only the largest females deliver this many offspring, however, and most broods are closer in number to the 15 young—all between 8½ and 9 inches in length and about ⅛ ounce in weight—deposited July 20 by a 32½-inch-long Smith Co. female.

Coloring/scale form   Ground color is yellowish-gray, with dark-edged gray-brown to black dorsolateral crossbands. Juveniles are more boldly patterned, while very old individuals may be almost entirely dark brown. A blackish stripe extends from the eye across the gray-brown cheeks through the posterior supralabial scale. The dappled yellow venter is generally marked with squarish brown blotches, but Herpetologist William Lamar reports that some individuals have bright red ventral blotches and even crossbars. The 21 to 25 midbody rows of dorsal scales are keeled; the anal plate is divided.

Similar snakes   The animal now known as the subspecies **Gulf salt marsh snake (35)** was formerly classified as only a color phase of the broad-banded water snake, but the relationship of the banded and striped water snakes is still problematical. Because some populations of *Nerodia fasciata* were longitudinally striped, predominantly salt-marsh-living animals, while other groups were cross-banded snakes living mostly in freshwater environments, during the 1980s, the striped, brackish-habitat populations were separated to form a new, salt-marsh snake species, *Nerodia clarkii*.

Yet, interbreeding has since been reported between banded water snakes and the newly taxonomically separated salt marsh snakes: Where their ranges overlap, individuals exhibiting combinations of the dark dorsolateral bands of the broad-banded water snake and the longitudinal stripes of the Gulf salt marsh snake occur. This calls into question whether these animals are actually a single species that should never have been divided, or two separate species that are still closely related enough to sometimes interbreed—an issue that involves our basic concept of what constitutes a species.

Behavior   See **Florida Water Snake (34).**

34 Florida Water Snake
Nerodia fasciata pictiventris

Nonvenomous   If cornered, *N. f. pictiventris* may discharge an odorous musk from its cloaca, flatten its forebody and strike in defense.

Abundance   A population is established in southeastern Cameron Co.

Size   In Florida, most adult *N. f. pictiventris* measure 22 to 40 inches in length. The record is much larger, however: 62.5 inches.

Habitat   Texas' colony of Florida water snakes owes its existence to the live animal business operated in Brownsville by W. A. "Snake" King, which between 1907 and 1956 imported and sold thousands of wild creatures to zoos, circuses, and snake charmers. To provide food for more notorious reptiles such as king cobras, hundreds of water snakes from the Southeast were imported and held in ramshackle cages, many of which were torn open by the violent hurricane of September 5, 1933. In addition, rather than maintaining these nondescript "food snakes" during slack seasons, King's firm annually released large numbers in the local resacas and parks, from which, it was hoped, they might be recaptured when business improved; that not all were recovered is evident in the appearance here of newborn Florida water snakes a half-century after their predecessors' introduction.

Prey   *Nerodia fasciata pictiventris* takes a variety of aquatic life, including crayfish, salamanders, frogs, and fish.

Reproduction   Following a midwinter breeding season, the Florida population gives birth in late spring to as many as 57 young, 6 to 9½ inches long. This fecundity has contributed to its survival in Texas: By late summer, young *N. f. pictiventris* are often abundant.

Coloring/scale form   The dorsal ground coloring of *N. f. pictiventris* is variable from tan to dark brown, with bright red to brown to black crossbands and dark lateral blotches; some individuals are almost entirely black. (This variant is especially likely to be mistaken for the cottonmouth.) The grayish cheeks are always lighter than the dark crown, however, and are marked behind the eye with a brown stripe that extends posteriorly through its last supralabial scale. If its dorsum is sometimes nondescript, the Florida water snake's venter is its signature: Its painted (*pictum*, in Latin) belly is known for the bold, wavy markings (from red to dark brown to black) that border its yellowish scales. The young are paler, with sharply-defined dark dorsolateral crossbands. There are 23 to 27 rows of keeled dorsal scales at midbody and the anal plate is generally divided.

Similar snakes   The only other *Nerodia* found in Cameron Co. is the **diamondback water snake** (30). Dark lines form a rhomboid pattern on its gray-green to gray-brown back and dark vertical bars line its sides; it lacks pale cheeks crossed by a dark postocular stripe.

Behavior   On cool, sunny days Florida water snakes spend hours basking on partially submerged logs or on overhanging tree limbs, but in the hottest months these reptiles are active mainly at night. During the Rio Grande Valley's short cold spells, Florida water snakes retire to bankside dens or burrow beneath vegetative debris.

Gulf Salt Marsh Snake
Nerodia clarkii clarkii

Nonvenomous   *Nerodia clarkii clarkii* will bite only if molested.

Abundance   Formerly quite numerous on the Gulf Coast; now less common due to commercial development and pollution of Texas' tidal wetlands.

Size   Adults are 15 to 30 inches long; the record is 36 inches.

Habitat   Salt marsh snakes live in both brackish and entirely saline tidal estuaries (*N. c. clarkii* is seldom found in freshwater). Favored microhabitats include the shelter of littoral debris, crayfish and fiddler crab burrows, and matted vegetation in the salt grass-lined margins of tidal mud flats.

Prey   Primarily fish, especially shallows-living species such as killifish and small mullet, which are often taken when they become trapped by the falling tide, as well as crayfish and shrimp.

Reproduction   Live-bearing. Little is known, but the 7- to 8½-inch-long young (which, except for bolder dorsolateral striping, resemble the adults) weigh only ¼ to ⅓ ounce at birth.

Coloring/scale form   On each of the Gulf salt marsh snake's upper sides, a pair of dark brown dorsolateral stripes stands out against a paler, grayish ground color. The venter is reddish-brown, with a central row of cream-colored ovals laterally flanked by a row of pale spots. The keeled dorsal scales occur in either 21 or 23 rows at midbody, there is a double row of subcaudal scales, and the anal plate is divided.

Similar snakes   In Texas, no other aquatic serpent has the Gulf salt marsh's strongly contrasting light and dark dorsolateral striping. The **western cottonmouth (95)** has slit, vertical pupils, a pointed snout above an underslung lower jaw, and sunken facial pits.

   Salt marsh snakes were once classified as subspecies of the freshwater banded water snake, *Nerodia fasciata*. Because salt marsh snakes have morphological differences from *N. fasciata* and rarely enter fresh-water, they are presently recognized as the separate, saline-environment salt marsh snake, *Nerodia clarkii*; but where their ranges overlap, intergrade animals with both the pale cheeks and lateral blotches of the **broad-banded water snake (33)** and the longitudinal gray dorsolateral stripes of *N. clarkii* occur.

Behavior   The fluid conservation difficulties faced by marine reptiles are as severe as those confronting desert-dwellers. Not only is freshwater absent from their environment but seawater—which is saltier than their body fluids—exerts a continual osmotic draw on their electrolyte balance. Scaly reptilian skin is a good barrier against external dehydration, but, because intestinal membranes are salt-permeable, if seawater is ingested, the hydraulic imperative of liquids to equalize discrepancies in mineral content draws the less-salty fluid from blood and body tissues into the stomach, eventually dehydrating any reptile not metabolically equipped, like the sea turtles, to rid itself of the extra salt. Among Texas snakes, only *N. clarkii* has established itself in an entirely saline niche, apparently by drinking rainwater when it is available, and at other times by swallowing nothing but prey animals whose body fluids are as dilute as its own.

AQUATIC SNAKES

36 Mississippi Green Water Snake

Nerodia cyclopion

Nonvenomous   Although Behler and King (1979) report that rather than striking, *Nerodia cyclopion* usually attempts to repel an assailant by regurgitating and voiding feces and a viscous musk from cloacal glands located just inside its vent, three Mississippi green water snakes in my experience snapped as vigorously as any other large water snake—although because of the difficulties posed by their aquatic environment few large water snakes are taken without a bit of a struggle.

The Mississippi green water snake's dark, seemingly unmarked thick body, combined with its inclination to flatten its head and neck if molested, typically causes it to be confused with the venomous cottonmouth.

Abundance   Very uncommon. Far to the east of its limited Texas range, the Mississippi green water snake may be abundant in cypress swamps, but it appears only sporadically in other aquatic habitats. It is very spottily distributed along and just inland from the upper Gulf Coast, as well as within the Sabine River drainage as far north as Marshall.

Size   Most adults are 30 to 38 inches; the record is 51 inches.

Habitat   In Texas, the Mississippi green water snake is much more restricted in both range and habitat than the widespread yellowbelly, blotched, and diamondback water snakes. While Garton, Harris, and Brandon (1970), who gathered most of the extant field data on *N. cyclopion,* found it to be a woodland-swamp-living reptile in Illinois; along the Gulf Coast Mississippi green water snakes often occur in open marshland vegetated only with reeds and cattails. *N. cyclopion* also occupies the brushy verges of rice field irrigation lakes, connecting canals, and bar ditches, as well as larger, partially wooded waterways such as Hull's Bayou near Dickinson. According to Roger Conant (1975), it is occasionally even found in brackish water.

Prey   An examination of 75 Mississippi green water snake stomachs revealed frogs in 10, fish in 4, and a single large salamander in another; the young reportedly feed on insects, tadpoles, and minnows.

Reproduction   Live-bearing. Litter size averages 15 to 25, 6- to 9½-inch-long newborns.

Coloring/scale form   The uniformly dark and pale speckled gray-green dorsum is paler in ground color among younger animals, and newborns are more distinctly spotted and crossbarred than adults. The Mississippi green water snake's definitive characteristic, however, is the row of small subocular scales that separates the lower

Green water snake

Other water snakes

half of its eye from the supralabial scales. The venter is also distinctive: The pale forebelly darkens posteriorly to gray, heavily infused with yellow half moons. The keeled dorsal scales occur in 27 to 29 rows at midbody; the anal plate is divided.

Similar snakes The angular head (sharply pointed snout, underslung chin, and slab-sided cheeks) of the **western cottonmouth (95)** contrasts with water snakes' more oval head. Both the cottonmouth's indented dark facial pit between eye and nostril and its narrow vertical pupil—visible from several feet away—are sure identifying marks. If cornered, water snakes may strike, but they never gape motionless in threat as the cottonmouth sometimes does. Cottonmouths' tails narrow sharply from their thick posterior bodies (the longer tails of water snakes have a more gradual taper), and among newborn cottonmouths the tail tip is grayish yellow; young water snakes' tails are brown.

All of Texas' other **water snakes (30—35, 37, 38)** lack subocular scales.

Behavior Elsewhere in its broad range, the Mississippi green water snake is occasionally seen during the day basking at the water's edge, but in Texas *Nerodia cyclopion* seems to be an almost exclusively nocturnal forager seldom observed either in the water or along the shore except by spotlighting after dark.

AQUATIC SNAKES

37 Brazos Water Snake
Nerodia harteri harteri

Nonvenomous   Brazos water snakes will nip only if seized or molested.

Abundance   Threatened. Protected by the State of Texas.
Nerodia harteri is the only species of snake unique to Texas, and while it is extremely restricted in range, it is not threatened with extinction.

Size   Most adults are 16 to 32 inches; the record is just over 35 inches.

Habitat   Nerodia harteri hides under stones in shallow water or shelters beneath lake- or river-bank rocks. Until the late 1980s it was thought to exist only in rocky portions of the upper Brazos River and its tributary streams—a habitat so limited, with many stretches scheduled to be inundated by reservoir impoundments, that both this reptile and its subspecies, the Concho water snake, *Nerodia harteri paucimaculata*, were thought to be in danger of extermination.

The ecological attention this situation received (in part due to accounts presented in the first edition of this volume) resulted in an intensive investigation by James Dixon, of Texas A&M University et al., of both races of *Nerodia harteri*. When this 5-year-long study appeared in 1992, it showed that, where only a few thousand *Nerodia harteri* of both races had been thought to exist, computer projections indicated that their numbers were probably in the tens of thousands. Although Brazos and Concho water snakes seem to have originally been exclusively riffle-dwellers, both subspecies have adapted to life in the newly-constructed lakes that have replaced much of their original streambed habitat, and Brazos water snakes are now found along rocky shorelines in both Lake Granbury and Possum Kingdom Lake. See **Concho Water Snake (38).**

Prey   The opportunity to seize small fish as they become momentarily vulnerable in rocky riffles has historically been the primary factor determining the Brazos water snake's microhabitat. How it manages, over long periods, away from these shallow rapids remains to be seen.

Reproduction   Live-bearing. The September and early October parturition of 4 females captured while gravid resulted in the birth of 7 to 22 young that measured 7¼ to 9 inches in length.

Coloring/scale form   The type specimen of *N. h. harteri*—taken in 1940 by veteran Palo Pinto Co. reptile fancier Phillip "Snakey" Harter—is defined by its medium brown vertebral stripe flanked by a double row of brown spots (each row has 58 to 65 spots, more than any other indigenous water snake). Ground color is tan, the throat is pale yellow, and the venter carrot-colored with the ends of the ventral scales spotted or darkened. The posterior chin shields are separated by 2 rows of small scales; the keeled dorsal scales occur in 21 to 25 (usually 23) midbody rows, and the anal plate is divided.

Similar snakes   The subspecies **Concho water snake (38)** has a less-pigmented venter and a single row of small scales between its posterior underchin shields.

Behavior   Nerodia harteri is a partly diurnal forager whose exposed habitat requires it to both hide from predators under rocks—where it can remain under water for more than an hour—and to move fast when discovered: No other indigenous serpent swims as rapidly, typically streaking diagonally downstream toward the opposite bank.

8 Concho Water Snake
Nerodia harteri paucimaculata

Nonvenomous   See **Brazos Water Snake (37).**

Abundance   Endangered. Federally protected and protected by the State of Texas. The only snake species unique to Texas, *Nerodia harteri* has always been restricted in range, with the subspecies Concho water snake inhabiting even narrower geographic boundaries than the Brazos race. Recently, these boundaries have been narrowed still further. Since 1968, nearly half the Concho water snake's original streambed-shallows habitat has been inundated by the construction of Coke County's Spence Reservoir; this has left just 69 miles of the Concho water snake's original Concho and Colorado River habitat. Here, some 41 riffle sites in Tom Green, Concho, Coleman, and McCulloch counties were thought to contain almost the entire world population of 330 to 600 Concho water snakes, but because Stacy Dam was scheduled to flood at least 24.8 additional miles of this habitat and severely cut downstream flow during dry weather, Concho water snakes were expected to be confined to less than 22 miles of sparsely riffled streambed—a remnant environment too vulnerable to development (these shallows are the best places to build low-water crossings) to preserve the race from extinction.

Environmental alarms were sounded in both popular and herpetological literature, but a 1992 study by James Dixon, of Texas A&M University et al., indicated that although Brazos and Concho water snakes may have been originally mostly streambed riffle-dwellers, both subspecies have successfully adapted to the newly-constructed lakes that have replaced much of their streambed habitat. Concho water snakes are now found along rocky portions of the banks of Lake Spence, Lake Ivy, and Lake Moonen, and are so far from being in danger of extinction that they are now considered for declassification as threatened animals. See **Brazos Water Snake (37).**

Size   Adult length ranges from 16 to 32 inches.

Habitat   Some 135 miles southwest of the Brazos River headwaters where *N. h. harteri* is found, the same sort of fast-flowing upper Colorado and Concho River riffles are home to Texas' even more range-restricted endemic race of the Harter's water snake, *N. h. paucimaculata.* Still waters in this area are inhabited by the quite different blotched water snake, *Nerodia erythrogaster transversa.*

Prey   See **Brazos Water Snake (37).**

Reproduction   Live-bearing. See **Brazos Water Snake (37).**

Coloring/scale form   Not discovered until 20 years after its Brazos subspecies, the Concho water snake has a paler dorsum and less conspicuous ventral spots—hence its designation *N. h. paucimaculata,* or "fewer-spotted." A single row of small scales separates its posterior underchin shields, its keeled dorsal scales occur in 21 to 25 (usually 23) rows, and the anal plate is divided.

Similar snakes   The subspecies **Brazos water snake (37)** has a double row of small scales between its underchin shields. The **blotched water snake (32)** has vertebral crossbars and dark lateral blocks.

Behavior   See **Brazos Water Snake (37).**

AQUATIC SNAKES

39 Graham's Crayfish Snake
Regina grahamii

Nonvenomous   See **Gulf Crayfish Snake (40)**.

Abundance   Uncommon. Despite its wide Texas range, the Graham's crayfish snake is not generally dispersed, although this species is locally abundant in a few places.

Size   Small and slender, most adult *R. grahamii* measure only 18 to 30 inches in length; the maximum size is 47 inches.

Habitat   On the coastal plain, Graham's crayfish snake inhabits sloughs, rice field irrigation ditches and, where crayfish are abundant, muddy bottomland pastures. The aquifer-fed headwaters of rivers emerging from the Balcones Fault constitute another habitat: *R. grahamii* is common in the headwaters of the San Antonio River.

Prey   The first to report on this animal's diet was John K. Strecker (1926), who wrote that *Regina grahamii* "feeds largely on crayfish and a small species of freshwater prawn." Recent studies have found the stomachs of several Graham's water snakes contained only freshly molted crayfish, but frogs and snails may also be taken.

Reproduction   Live-bearing. Lawrence Curtis and R. J. Hall (1949) first observed courtship, which occurs early in May, at night, in the water. At this time, a group of pheromone-drawn males may entwine themselves around a female, forming a compact mass within which only one copulation evidently occurs. More often, breeding pairs are solitary, floating wrapped together, their tails hanging downward.

Deposited in August and September, recorded litters have ranged from 6 to 39 (26 broods averaged 17.4 young, 7 to 9½ inches in length), and Strecker reported finding 4 or 5 newborns sheltering together under flat rocks at the water's edge. Males may breed as early as their second spring, females not until their third year.

Coloring/scale form   Except for a pale vertebral line, the back and upper sides are dark grayish brown, while a wide, yellowish tan side stripe—edged by a serrated black seam—occupies the first three scale rows above the yellowish venter. The belly's lateral border is delineated by a line of angular black spots; a row of brown midventral dots is better defined toward the tail. The keeled dorsal scales occur in 19 rows at midbody and the anal plate is divided.

Similar snakes   The **Gulf crayfish snake (40)** has a shiny, chocolate-colored back; its pale belly is marked with a double row of rearward-arched dark brown crescents. The **Gulf salt marsh snake (35)** has a gray-striped back and sides, at least 21 rows of dorsal scales, and a dark venter whose midline bears a row of cream-colored ovals.

Behavior   Named for soldier, engineer, and naturalist James Duncan Graham, a member of the 1852–53 Mexican Border Survey that first described much of Texas' herpetofauna, *Regina grahamii* forages at night during the summer months but engages in more crepuscular activity in spring and fall. Because of its reclusive temperament, the Graham's crayfish snake is able to subsist in urban park ponds where less cryptic water snakes would soon be killed. This may make its presence something of a surprise, for on rainy spring nights Graham's crayfish snakes have been found crawling across suburban lawns in Waco—the only time *R. grahamii* is ever seen in this area.

Gulf Crayfish Snake
Regina rigida sinicola

Nonvenomous   Like all crayfish snakes, this shy, cryptic little reptile does not bite human beings even if it is handled.

Abundance   Very uncommon.

Size   Most adults are less than 20 inches; the record is 31⅜ inches.

Habitat   In the southeastern U.S., the Gulf crayfish snake inhabits bottomland forest and flooded stands of cypress. In Texas, *Regina rigida sinicola* lives in more open terrain: the freshwater marshes, lakes, and inundated rice fields of the coastal plain. It also occupies irrigation ditches, wet prairies, and muddy pastures where crayfish are common. Here, it is both aquatic and semi-subterranean, its primary microhabitat being the burrows of the crayfish on which it feeds. *R. r. sinicola* also burrows into the earth beneath rotting stumps, logs, and planks at the water's edge and, presumably because neither this semi-subterranean lifestyle nor predation on slow-moving crayfish calls for agility, crayfish snakes are decidedly stiff-bodied—they feel taut to the touch—an attribute from which their Latin species name, *rigida*, is derived.

Prey   The stomachs of most crayfish snakes have contained only freshly-molted crayfish, but lesser sirens, small fish, frogs, and aquatic insects such as dragonfly nymphs may also be taken.

Reproduction   Live-bearing. Eleven newborns measured between 7 and 8½ inches in length.

Coloring/scale form   The back is shiny chocolate brown, sometimes with dimly darker-striped sides above a yellowish-tan lateral stripe (split by a thin black seam) that occupies the first and second scale rows above the belly line. The labial scales, as well as the unpatterned sides of the throat, are yellowish, and the pale venter is marked with a double row of rearward-arced black crescents that form a single line beneath chin and tail. The keeled dorsal scales are arranged in 19 rows at midbody and the anal plate is divided.

Similar snakes   The yellowish lateral band of the **Graham's crayfish snake (36)** extends 3 scale rows above the belly, where it is separated from the grayish-brown back by a faintly serrated dark horizontal line. The Graham's water snake's belly also bears a single row of small midventral spots. The **Mississippi green water snake (36)** is dark-speckled above, has 27 or more rows of dorsal scales and a single row of little subocular scales that separates its eye from the big scale plates along its upper lip. The **yellowbelly water snake (31)** also lacks a longitudinal color demarcation along its sides; it has 23 or more rows of dorsal scales and an unmarked venter.

Behavior   Crayfish snakes are predominantly nocturnal creatures with a secretive, semi-subterranean lifestyle. *R. r. sinicola* forages mainly between March and early November but even during this time it is almost never observed except during drainage ditch excavation or at night after heavy rain. Its predators can include giant salamanders: One 40-inch-long two-toed amphiuma trapped by Florida Game and Fresh Water Fish Commission biologist Kevin Enge disgorged a large crayfish snake.

AQUATIC SNAKES

41 Western Mud Snake
Farancia abacura reinwardtii

Nonvenomous   This big, docile serpent is generally unwilling to bite, even when first handled in the field.

Abundance   Common. Formerly very abundant along most of the Gulf Coast, especially in Wharton, Matagorda, Brazoria, and Galveston counties, *F. a. reinwardtii* is seen there less often at present. Just inland from the Gulf in Chambers and Jefferson counties, this animal is still evident along Highway 87. Other scattered populations occur throughout inland East Texas, including one in Panola Co. at the north end of Toledo Bend Reservoir. Here, despite mud snakes' secretive, aquatic/burrowing habits, they can be among the most numerous serpents that appear on roads through wetland areas on rainy spring nights.

Size   Adult mud snakes may reach over 6 feet—most measure between 30 and 48 inches—but at hatching the young may be as small as 6¼ inches.

Habitat   Western mud snakes live in and around sluggish, undisturbed bodies of freshwater with swampy margins and profuse aquatic vegetation. Microhabitat includes the underside of logs and debris on hummocks in flooded bottomland forest.

Prey   A prey-specific predator, *F. a. reinwardtii* has a heavily muscled neck, jaws, and body adapted to overpowering the giant salamanders—sirens and amphiumas—that are its principal prey. (Its horny tailtip helps the mud snake overcome this large, vigorous prey, by giving it a point of purchase on the eels' slippery sides.) Captives also accept frogs and fish as food.

Reproduction   Egg-laying. Mud snakes deposit their eggs during July and August, and do so prolifically: One clutch numbered 60. Much larger clutches have been reported, but are probably the result of communal egg-laying. The eggs are parchment-like in texture, and adherent, forming a glued-together mass. They are typically laid in a moist substrate such as a bankside cavity, inside which the female may exhibit parental care by remaining coiled about her clutch throughout its 8- to 12-week incubation period.

At least 5 mud snake nests, one in northern Florida and 4 in Louisiana, have been located *within* the nests of American alligators. The huge amount of vegetative material that alligators amass to warm their eggs with the heat generated by composting plant matter also benefits the eggs of *Farancia abacura*—whose incubation period closely matches the 9-week incubation of alligator eggs. Additional benefits from this commensal nesting are the fact that female alligators actively defend their nests from raccoons and other carnivores, while the elevation of alligator mounds minimizes the mortality of *Farancia abacura* eggs caused by flooding.

The 6¼ to 9-inch-long young—which exhibit the largest difference in size between hatchling and adult of any native serpent—hatch in early autumn. As is reported for the western mud snake's eastern races, these hatchlings may remain in their nest cavity for months, perhaps until the following spring. This could enhance their chances for survival because the aquatic habitat of *Farancia* is at its driest during autumn, when the neonates' amphibian prey is scarce and simultaneously being sought by large numbers of newborn natricine water snakes.

Coloring/scale form   Western mud snakes live in wet soil, but they are anything but muddy in coloration. Their glossy blue-black dorsums are marked with fewer than 52 round-topped, reddish-pink lateral blotches, which extend up their sides from the venter. Among juveniles, these red blotches reach all the way to the lower back. Black rectangles checker the pinkish-red venter; posteriorly this pattern becomes black subcaudal crossbands. The 19 midbody rows of dorsal scales are smooth, except for the vertebral rows directly above the cloaca, where they may be keeled. There is no preocular scale and, like all *Farancia,* the terminal caudal scale is enlarged and stiffened into a point. The anal plate is almost always divided.

Similar snakes   No other indigenous serpent bears the mud snake's distinctive color pattern. The **western cottonmouth (95)** is brownish or blackish gray above, lacks reddish scallops along its lower sides, and has an angular, slab-sided head characterized by sunken facial pits and vertical pupils.

Behavior   Western mud snakes are aquatic, nocturnal burrowers that do not climb. Because their lives are largely spent in a slippery, viscous medium, the pointed tailtip may have developed—besides its role in helping to restrain prey—as a means of gaining traction to press through mud.

  F. a. reinwardtii typically responds to restraint by curling its body tightly around one's hands and wrists, pressing in its tail's hardened, hornlike tip so firmly that it was once believed that this spur could deliver a mortal sting. When mud snakes' habit of lying in a circular coil was factored into the story, the legend arose of the horn-tailed hoop snake that could take its stinger in its mouth, roll down a fleeing man, and tail-sting him to death with venom "powerful enough to kill a tree."

42 Texas Patchnose Snake
Salvadora grahamiae lineata

Nonvenomous   See **Mountain Patchnose Snake (43).**

Abundance   Common. *Salvadora grahamiae lineata* occurs in almost every well-vegetated, rural terrestrial habitat throughout its range.

Size   Adults generally measure between 20 and 34 inches in length; the record is just under 4 feet.

Habitat   Most abundant in the woods and farmland of the state's central Cross Timbers, *S. g. lineata* is often found along woodland/meadow boundaries. Similar habitat is occupied in the oak-juniper savannahs of the Edwards Plateau, while Texas patchnose snakes are present, but less abundant, in the thorn brush woodland of South Texas.

Prey   As captives, Texas patchnoses prefer lizard prey, but smaller snakes, mice, frogs, and buried reptile eggs—reportedly rooted out with the aid of the enlarged rostral scale at the tip of the snout—have also been found in the stomachs of wild individuals.

Reproduction   Egg-laying. Reproduction was first recorded by Roger Conant in 1940: A Palo Pinto Co. female laid 10 adhesive-shelled, yellowish-white eggs 1⅛ inches in length and ⅝ inch in diameter on April 1, a time when most other serpents in Central Texas have just begun courtship. Two other clutches of 5 and 7 eggs were deposited during the first week in May by a pair of Travis Co. females; these hatched 88 days later into young slightly paler than the adults, with whitish sides. The neonates were very active, vibrating their tails in excitement and striking about at random.

Coloring/scale form   As an adult, *S. g. lineata* has a blackish back split by a yellowish vertebral stripe which occupies the vertebral scale row plus half of each adjacent row. Its sides are olive-brown, and a thin brown line (the *lineata* of its Latin name) seams the third row of scales above the whitish belly on the foreparts, the second row on the posterior trunk. An enlarged rostral scale (the source of the patchnose's common name) tips the snout (*grahamiae* refers to James Duncan Graham, a pioneer naturalist and member of the 1852–53 Mexican Border Survey that first systematically cataloged much southwestern herpetofauna). The 17 midbody rows of dorsal scales are smooth, there are 7 or 8 upper labial scales, and the anal plate is divided.

Similar snakes   In northeastern Terrell Co. the Texas patchnose begins to intergrade with its western subspecies, the **mountain patchnose snake (43).** This race has pastel gray sides and a faintly peach-hued vertebral stripe 3 scale rows in width. **Garter (20–25)** and **ribbon (26–29) snakes** have darker, often checkered backs, at least 19 midbody rows of keeled dorsal scales, and an undivided anal plate. They lack a large flat rostral scale and most have a pair of small white dots on the rear of the crown.

Behavior   Despite its enlarged rostral scale, *S. g. lineata* is not a fossorial animal, and rather than diving into a hole when flushed from hiding beneath flat rocks or corrugated siding around old farms, this diurnal, fast-moving serpent typically streaks away into the grass like a racer. Compared to most snakes, the Texas patchnose seems to be active in unusually cool weather because I have seen these animals abroad in Travis Co. during December and February.

3 Mountain Patchnose Snake
Salvadora grahamiae grahamiae

Nonvenomous When first captured, the mountain patch-nose snake typically flails about, and may even give a single panicky nip, but if handled gently it quickly calms down and is unlikely to bite again. Its upper rear teeth are slightly enlarged, a charac-teristic of many colubrids whose saliva is somewhat toxic to their small prey, though it poses no danger to humans.

Abundance Common. Widely distributed throughout its range, in suitable micro-habitat *S. g. grahamiae* is sometimes abundant.

Size Slightly smaller than the closely-related Texas patchnose, the mountain race usually measures between 18 and 30 inches in length. The record is 37½ inches.

Habitat *Salvadora grahamiae grahamiae* occupies a variety of stony and/or brushy habitats throughout the Trans-Pecos. In the succulent desert west of the Devil's River, it may be found in the heart-root cavities under decaying agaves and sotol.

Prey This snake's primary prey is lizards, although smaller serpents, reptile eggs, and mice are also eaten; its armored snout is used to press into the subsurface nooks where these creatures find shelter.

Reproduction Egg-laying. See **Texas Patchnose Snake (42).**

Coloring/scale form The mountain patchnose snake's delicate form and subtle coloring make it one of the most beautiful snakes in Texas. Its broad (2 full scale rows in width), very pale yellow vertebral stripe is flanked by contrasting dark lines that set off its silvery- to pinkish-beige sides. An enlarged rostral scale overlaps its adjacent nasal scales and folds back over the snout, giving the patchnose its distinc-tive squared-off profile as well as its common name. The 17 midbody rows of dor-sal scales are smooth, there are usually 8 upper labials, the posterior chin shields beneath its jaw either touch or are separated by a single small scale, and the anal plate is divided.

Similar snakes The subspecies **Texas patchnose snake (42)** has a narrower verte-bral line bordered by a pair of much wider blackish-brown dorsolateral stripes; its buff lower sides are split by a thin dark seam along the third scale row above its belly. A separate species of patchnose, the **Big Bend patchnose snake (44)** is distin-guished by the line of dark hash marks along the fourth lateral scale row above its peach colored venter, its 9 upper labial scales, and the 2 or 3 small scales that sepa-rate its posterior underchin shields.

Behavior Quick and elusive in brush or near cover, the mountain patchnose must still rely on ambush to obtain most of its even faster-moving prey. This may entail a deliberate process of advancing, in a series of short glides, only while its lizard quar-ry is busy with its own foraging. Once in range, *S. g. grahamiae* seizes lizards larger than its own diameter, hanging on doggedly as its victim drags it back and forth. The patchnose's saliva may eventually exert a paralytic effect on the lizard for, though it may take half an hour, the snake ultimately manages to work its way along the tiring lacertilian's body to its snout. Then, stretching its delicate head and jaws over the larger skull of the lizard, the patchnose squeezes the animal into its throat.

44 Big Bend Patchnose Snake
Salvadora deserticola

Nonvenomous   This slender reptile generally does not bite even when first handled in the field.

Abundance   Predominantly Mexican in range, *Salvadora deserticola* is uncommon within its restricted Texas range.

Size   Twenty to 45 inches in length.

Habitat   The Big Bend patchnose inhabits both low-lying terrain such as shrub desert, tobosa/grama grassland, and catclaw/creosote/blackbrush flats, as well as a variety of broken upland terrain.

Prey   Lizards, snakes, reptile eggs, and small rodents are the primary prey of *Salvadora deserticola*—all but the latter typically being rooted from sand-filled depressions with the aid of the enlarged rostral scale.

Reproduction   Egg-laying. See **Texas Patchnose Snake (42)**.

Coloring/scale form   This attractive serpent has yellowish-gray sides separated from its wide, peach-colored dorsal stripe by a flanking pair of dark brown dorsolateral lines. The sandy-beige sides are marked with a line of dark-hued hash marks along the fourth scale row above its pinkish-orange venter. The enlarged rostral scale, widest immediately above the mouth (where it overlaps the adjacent nasal scales), covers the tip of the snout in a distinctive flat patch from which the common name is derived. Below, the lips and throat are unmarked white—there are 9 upper labial scales, and either 2 or 3 small scales separate the posterior underchin shields. The smooth dorsal scales are arranged in 17 rows at midbody and the anal plate is divided.

Underchin: Texas and mountain patchnose snakes   *Underchin: Big Bend patchnose snake*

Similar snakes   The **mountain patchnose snake (43)** has unstriped sides, 8 upper labial scales, an off-white venter, and posterior underchin shields that either touch or are separated by a single scale.

Behavior   Like many diurnal, desert-living serpents, the Big Bend patchnose is inclined to midday basking in cool weather: Sherman Minton (1959) found it abroad as early as March 6 in Brewster Co. During the heat of July, August, and September, it adopts a predominantly crepuscular activity pattern; but, unlike many arid terrain snakes that retire into sub-surface aestivation at this season, *S. deserticola* remains abroad, although at this time it is more often found in the artificially-moist environments of irrigated areas (diurnal foragers like patchnose snakes transpire more water than nocturnal/fossorial serpents).

Its daylight hunting also makes *S. deserticola* susceptible to avian predators. Minton found the remains of a Big Bend patchnose in the nest of a red-tailed hawk, and the Jan. 1983 issue of *Texas Parks and Wildlife Magazine* contains a photograph of a roadrunner offering one of these slender colubrids to its fledglings.

Rough Green Snake
Opheodrys aestivus

Nonvenomous   The rough green snake does not bite humans.

Abundance   Abundant. *Opheodrys aestivus* is widespread throughout the eastern two thirds of the state and is common in suitable moist woodland habitat.

Size   Adults average 22 to 32 inches; the record is 45⅝ inches.

Habitat   Thickly-foliaged trees and shrubs with closely spaced stems that allow it to move about easily are the rough green snake's preferred environment. This microhabitat occurs at the sunlit edges of woods bordering ponds, meadows, and dirt roads, where this small reptile's abundance makes *O. aestivus* so easy to capture that, in the southeastern U.S., thousands are taken for the pet trade. (Almost all of them soon die.)

Prey   Plucked from leaves and stems, most of the rough green snake's prey is insects. In one Arkansas study, 85% of its diet consisted of caterpillars, spiders, grasshoppers, crickets, and odonates. Caterpillars, in particular, are favored because they constituted more than twice as large a percentage of the total than their local prevalence would suggest.

Reproduction   Egg-laying. Spring and summer rainfall influences rough green snakes' reproduction because the more abundant insect prey available in wet years increases females' body fat and thus egg-laying capacity. Rainfall also enhances survival of the 3 to 12 eggs (which are laid in plant litter between April and July), because their small size and partially water-permeable shells leave them prone to desiccation. The grayish hatchlings are 6 to 8 inches long; they can reach adult size in a year, but do not breed until their second spring.

Coloring/scale form   Often called "grass snake," emerald-bodied *Opheodrys aestivus* is color-adapted, instead, to the verdant hue of tree leaves. (After death, these little snakes turn a dull blue.) The lips, chin, and belly are yellow, and the nostril lies across the juncture of adjacent nasal scales. Arranged in 17 rows at midbody, the dorsal scales are keeled; the anal plate is divided.

Similar snakes   The **smooth green snake (46)** is very rare in Texas, only a few specimens having been found in only a handful of upper Gulf Coast counties; it has 15 rows of smooth dorsal scales. The **eastern yellowbelly racer (56)** is a much more robust, gray-green serpent with smooth scales; each nostril is centered in a single nasal plate.

Behavior   Slow-moving, unwary *Opheodrys aestivus* depends entirely on camouflage for protection: When approached it may freeze, swaying with the wind to match the movement of surrounding foliage. During warm weather, this diurnal forager sleeps at night in a loop draped along a branch, its head resting either on the branch or on a body coil. Here, its luminous venter reflects the beam of a flashlight so clearly that in places where green snakes are numerous they are easily found by scanning vegetation along forest roads. Abroad late into autumn (I have observed active Hays Co. specimens the week before Christmas), *O. aestivus* spends the leafless months below ground.

46 Smooth Green Snake
Liochlorophis vernalis

Nonvenomous   This little reptile is harmless to humans.

Abundance   **Endangered. Protected by the State of Texas.**
Very rare in Texas, *Liochlorophis vernalis* is known in this state
from fewer than 10 specimens, all collected in similar grassland terrain in
Austin, Chambers, Harris, and Matagorda counties. (Arnold Grobman
[1950] of the Florida State Museum, an expert on this species, has even suggested that
these individuals may have been escaped captives rather than a natural population.)

Size   The longest Texas specimen was about 15 inches; the shortest, 10 inches.

Habitat   Conversion of the upper Gulf Coast's moist, native short grass prairie to
residential and commercial development has eliminated almost all of the smooth
green snake's native habitat.

Prey   Prey is probably similar to that taken by the rough green snake, except that it
would consist of non-arboreal, grass-living insects.

Reproduction   Egg-laying. In Missouri, G. T. Hille found 3 newly-hatched young
buried 3½ inches beneath a decomposed wooden fence post. There are reports
from the northern part of the range of communal nesting sites, as well as of an
exceptionally short incubation period of as little as 4 weeks. The young have an
olive- to light brown dorsal hue that persists into adulthood on some specimens;
their litter-mates may have acquired emerald backs within weeks of hatching.

Coloring/scale form   Geographically-separated from the major population of
Liochlorophis vernalis some 500 miles to the north, the small Texas group may, if
other specimens are ever found, eventually be recognized as a separate species
because *L. vernalis* from elsewhere in the range are usually bright green above,
while the very few Gulf Coast specimens retain the olive brown coloring of the
young. (*Liochlorophis vernalis* is the new scientific name of the smooth green
snake until recently known as *Opheodrys vernalis*. Both Texas' green snakes formerly shared the genus *Opheodrys*, but the smooth green snake's smooth scalation
is thought to be such a fundamentally different biologic structure from the keeled
scales of the rough green snake that, on the basis of research conducted by venerable herpetologist Hobart M. Smith, it has been given its own genus and species designation.) Its smooth dorsal scales occur in 15 midbody rows; its venter is off-white,
and its anal plate is divided.

Similar snakes   The **rough green snake (45)** is very common, bright green, and
slightly slimmer; it has 17 rows of keeled dorsal scales.

Behavior   Because of its rarity in Texas, practically nothing is known of the
smooth green snake's life history here: Most Texas specimens have been found
only as displaced, non-foraging creatures flushed from unknown microhabitats on
mesic short-grass prairie by flood waters. Outside of Texas, *L. vernalis* (the Latin
species name means "spring" snake) is abundant in parts of a wide range that
includes much of the Midwest (in Michigan, 148 individuals were found hibernat-
ing together). During warm weather smooth green snakes are active during daylight, foraging through dense grass and, unlike the predominantly arboreal rough
green snake, seldom climbing even into low bushes.

1 **Plains Blind Snake,** *Leptotyphlops dulcis dulcis* (almost identical to New Mexico Blind Snake, *Leptotyphlops dulcis dissectus*—#2 in text— except for scales on crown)

3   **Trans-Pecos Blind Snake,** *Leptotyphlops humilis segregus*

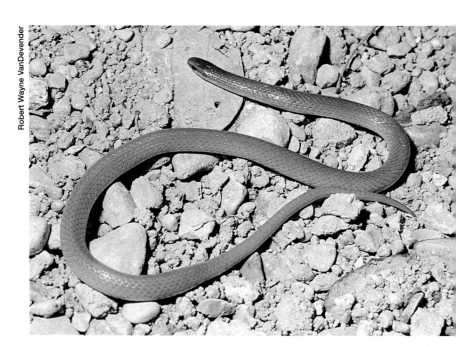

4 Flathead Snake, *Tantilla gracilis*

5 Plains Blackhead Snake, *Tantilla nigriceps*

6 **Southwestern Blackhead Snake,** *Tantilla hobartsmithi*

8 **Blackhood Snake,** *Tantilla rubra cucullata* (The extremely rare Mexican blackhead snake—#7 in text—looks similar to this blackhood snake.)

9   Texas Brown Snake, *Storeria dekayi texana*

10   Marsh Brown Snake, *Storeria dekayi limnetes*

11 Florida Redbelly Snake, *Storeria occipitomaculata obscura*

12 Rough Earth Snake, *Virginia striatula*

13 Western Smooth Earth Snake, *Virginia valeriae elegans*

14 Mississippi Ringneck Snake, *Diadophis punctatus stictogenys*

15   Prairie Ringneck Snake, *Diadophis punctatus arnyi*

16   Regal Ringneck Snake, *Diadophis punctatus regalis*

17a Ground Snake, *Sonora semiannulata*

17b Ground Snake, *Sonora semiannulata*

17c Ground Snake, *Sonora semiannulata*

18 Western Worm Snake, *Carphophis amoenus vermis*

19 Lined Snake, *Tropidoclonion lineatum*

20 Eastern Garter Snake, *Thamnophis sirtalis sirtalis*

21 Texas Garter Snake, *Thamnophis sirtalis annectans*

22 Checkered Garter Snake, *Thamnophis marcianus marcianus*

Donna Marvel

23 Western Plains Garter Snake, *Thamnophis radix haydenii*

24 Eastern Blackneck Garter Snake, *Thamnophis cyrtopsis ocellatus*

25 Western Blackneck Garter Snake, *Thamnophis cyrtopsis cyrtopsis*

Donna Marvel

26 Western Ribbon Snake, *Thamnophis proximus proximus*

Michael J. Bowerman

27 Redstripe Ribbon Snake, *Thamnophis proximus rubrilineatus*

Donna Marvel

28 Gulf Coast Ribbon Snake, *Thamnophis proximus orarius*

D. Craig McIntyre

29 Arid Land Ribbon Snake, *Thamnophis proximus diabolicus*

30 Diamondback Water Snake, *Nerodia rhombifer rhombifer*

31 Yellowbelly Water Snake, *Nerodia erythrogaster flavigaster*

32a Blotched Water Snake, *Nerodia erythrogaster transversa*

32b Blotched Water Snake, *Nerodia erythrogaster transversa* (juvenile)

33 Broad-banded Water Snake, *Nerodia fasciata confluens*

34 Florida Water Snake, *Nerodia fasciata pictiventris*

35 Gulf Salt Marsh Snake, *Nerodia clarkii clarkii*

36 Mississippi Green Water Snake, *Nerodia cyclopion*

Michael J. Bowerman

37 Brazos Water Snake, *Nerodia harteri harteri*

Michael J. Bowerman

38 Concho Water Snake, *Nerodia harteri paucimaculata*

39 Graham's Crayfish Snake, *Regina grahamii*

40 Gulf Crayfish Snake, *Regina rigida sinicola*

41a Western Mud Snake, *Farancia abacura reinwardtii*

41b Western Mud Snake, *Farancia abacura reinwardtii*
(ventral display)

42 Texas Patchnose Snake, *Salvadora grahamiae lineata*

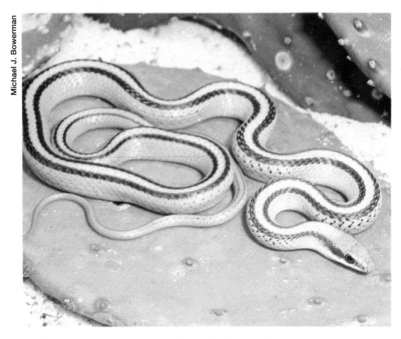

43 Mountain Patchnose Snake, *Salvadora grahamiae grahamiae*

44 Big Bend Patchnose Snake, *Salvadora deserticola*

45 Rough Green Snake, *Opheodrys aestivus*

46 Smooth Green Snake, *Liochlorophis vernalis*

47a Eastern Coachwhip, *Masticophis flagellum flagellum*

47b Eastern Coachwhip, *Masticophis flagellum flagellum*
(juvenile)

48a Western Coachwhip, *Masticophis flagellum testaceus* (inset—red
color phase found in the west and southwest Trans-Pecos)

48b Western Coachwhip, *Masticophis flagellum testaceus* (juvenile)

49 Central Texas Whipsnake, *Masticophis taeniatus girardi*

50 Desert Striped Whipsnake, *Masticophis taeniatus taeniatus*

51a Schott's Whipsnake, *Masticophis schotti*

51b Schott's Whipsnake, *Masticophis schotti* (hatchling)

52 Ruthven's Whipsnake, *Masticophis ruthveni*

53a Southern Black Racer, *Coluber constrictor priapus*

53b Southern Black Racer, *Coluber constrictor priapus* (juvenile)

54 Buttermilk Racer, *Coluber constrictor anthicus*

55 Tan Racer, *Coluber constrictor etheridgei*

56 Eastern Yellowbelly Racer, *Coluber constrictor flaviventris*

57 **Mexican Racer,** *Coluber constrictor oaxaca* (hatchling)

58 **Central American Speckled Racer,**
Drymobius margaritiferus margaritiferus

59 Texas Indigo Snake, *Drymarchon corais erebennus*

60a Eastern Hognose Snake, *Heterodon platirhinos*

60b Eastern Hognose Snake, *Heterodon platirhinos*
(defensive tail coiling and neck swelling)

60c Eastern Hognose Snake, *Heterodon platirhinos*

61 **Dusty Hognose Snake,** *Heterodon nasicus gloydi* (hatchling)

62 **Plains Hognose Snake,** *Heterodon nasicus nasicus*

63 Mexican Hognose Snake, *Heterodon nasicus kennerlyi*

64 Western Hooknose Snake, *Gyalopion canum*

65 Mexican Hooknose Snake, *Ficimia streckeri*

66 Louisiana Pine Snake, *Pituophis ruthveni*

67 Bullsnake, *Pituophis catenifer sayi*

68 Sonoran Gopher Snake, *Pituophis catenifer affinis*

69 Texas Glossy Snake, *Arizona elegans arenicola*

70 Kansas Glossy Snake, *Arizona elegans elegans*

71   Painted Desert Glossy Snake, *Arizona elegans philipi*

72a Texas Rat Snake, *Elaphe obsoleta lindheimerii*

72b Texas Rat Snake, *Elaphe obsoleta lindheimerii* (juvenile)

73a Baird's Rat Snake, *Elaphe bairdi*

73b Baird's Rat Snake, *Elaphe bairdi* (juvenile)

74a Great Plains Rat Snake, *Elaphe gutatta emoryi*
(East and North Texas dark, large-blotched type)

141

74b Great Plains Rat Snake, *Elaphe gutatta emoryi*
(South and far West Texas paler, smaller-blotched type)

75a Trans-Pecos Rat Snake, *Bogetophis subocularis*

75b Trans-Pecos Rat Snake, *Bogertophis subocularis*

75c Trans-Pecos Rat Snake, *Bogertophis subocularis*
(pale or "blonde" color phase)

143

Michael J. Bowerman

75d Trans-Pecos Rat Snake, *Bogertophis subocularis*
(hatchling)

Michael J. Bowerman

76 Prairie Kingsnake, *Lampropeltis calligaster calligaster*

77 Speckled Kingsnake, *Lampropeltis getula holbrooki*

78 Desert Kingsnake, *Lampropeltis getula splendida*

79 Louisiana Milk Snake, *Lampropeltis triangulum amaura*

80 Mexican Milk Snake, *Lampropeltis triangulum annulata*

81a New Mexico Milk Snake, *Lampropeltis triangulum celaenops*

81b New Mexico Milk Snake, *Lampropeltis triangulum celaenops*

Michael J. Bowerman

82 Central Plains Milk Snake, *Lampropeltis triangulum gentilis*
(juvenile)

D. Craig McIntyre

83a Gray-banded Kingsnake, *Lampropeltis alterna*
(light-hued, Blair color phase with orange saddles;
central Val Verde County)

83b Gray-banded Kingsnake, *Lampropeltis alterna*
(light-hued, Blair color phase without orange saddles;
central Val Verde County)

83c Gray-banded Kingsnake, *Lampropeltis alterna*
(dark-hued Blair color phase; southern Val Verde County)

Michael J. Bowerman

83d Gray-banded Kingsnake, *Lampropeltis alterna*
(darker-hued Blair color phase; central Val Verde County)

D. Craig McIntyre

83e Gray-banded Kingsnake,
Lampropeltis alterna
(hatchling; light-hued
alterna color phase;
central Val Verde County)

D. Craig McIntyre

83f Gray-banded Kingsnake,
Lampropeltis alterna
(light-hued alterna color
phase; western Brewster
County)

83g Gray-banded Kingsnake, *Lampropeltis alterna* (medium-hued alterna color phase; Jeff Davis County)

83h Gray-banded Kingsnake, *Lampropeltis alterna* (dark-hued color phase, intermediate between Blair and alterna; northern Brewster County)

83i Gray-banded Kingsnake, *Lampropeltis alterna* (light-hued Blair color phase; western Terrell County)

84 Northern Scarlet Snake, *Cemophora coccinea copei*

85 Texas Scarlet Snake, *Cemophora coccinea lineri*

86   Texas Longnose Snake, *Rhinocheilus lecontei tessellatus*

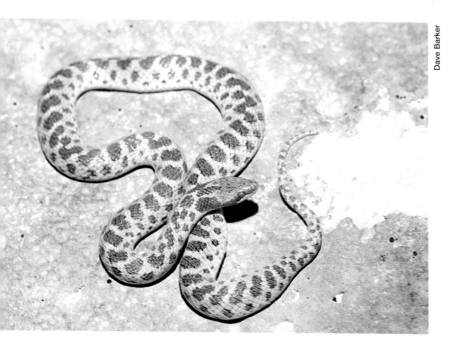

87a Texas Night Snake, *Hypsiglena torquata jani*

87b Texas Night Snake, *Hypsiglena torquata jani*
(far West Texas pale phase)

88 Black-striped Snake, *Coniophanes imperialis imperialis*

89 Northern Cat-eyed Snake, *Leptodeira septentrionalis septentrionalis*

90a Texas Lyre Snake, *Trimorphodon biscutatus vilkinsonii*

90b Texas Lyre Snake, *Trimorphodon biscutatus vilkinsonii* (hatchling)

91 Texas Coral Snake, *Micrurus fulvius tener*

92 Southern Copperhead, *Agkistrodon contortrix contortrix*

93 Broad-banded Copperhead, *Agkistrodon contortrix laticinctus*

94 Trans-Pecos Copperhead, *Agkistrodon contortrix pictigaster*

95a Western Cottonmouth, *Agkistrodon piscivorus leucostoma*

95b Western Cottonmouth, *Agkistrodon piscivorus leucostoma*
(juvenile)

96 Western Pigmy Rattlesnake, *Sistrurus miliarius streckeri*

97 Western Massasauga, *Sistrurus catenatus tergeminus*

98 Desert Massasauga, *Sistrurus catenatus edwardsii*

99 Timber Rattlesnake, *Crotalus horridus*

100 Western Diamondback Rattlesnake, *Crotalus atrox*

101 Northern Blacktail Rattlesnake, *Crotalus molossus molossus*

102 Prairie Rattlesnake, *Crotalus viridis viridis*

Michael J. Bowerman

103 Mojave Rattlesnake, *Crotalus scutulatus scutulatus*

Michael J. Bowerman

104a Mottled Rock Rattlesnake, *Crotalus lepidus lepidus*

104b Mottled Rock Rattlesnake, *Crotalus lepidus lepidus*

105 Banded Rock Rattlesnake, *Crotalus lepidus klauberi*

47 Eastern Coachwhip
Masticophis flagellum flagellum

Nonvenomous   If cornered, this long, wiry serpent vibrates its tail and doesn't hesitate to strike and bite—often several times in succession. Rather than hanging on to an aggressor, coachwhips typically grab and quickly pull away, their sharp teeth leaving shallow scratches.

Abundance   Common. *Masticophis flagellum* is one of the most numerous large terrestrial serpents in its range.

Size   The record eastern coachwhip measured 102 inches in length, but an individual this size would be very unusual: most adult *M. f. flagellum* are between 50 and 72 inches long.

Habitat   Coachwhips occur in virtually every rural environment, but seem to be particularly abundant around abandoned farms where its rodent, lizard, and smaller snake prey is plentiful.

Prey   Coachwhips' prey can include almost any smaller vertebrate, although Texas spiny and tree lizards probably compose much of the diet. Other snakes, mammals, birds, frogs, and baby turtles have also been observed as food animals. Insects are probably the primary prey of juveniles.

Serpentine greyhounds adapted for sight-hunting, coachwhips have specialized bodies; for example, selectively lengthening the segmentation spacing of the three major epaxial muscles helps speed and agility but limits the coachwhip's constrictive ability. (Whipsnakes employ only a primitive form of constriction, pressing a prey animal against the ground with a body coil rather than suffocating it as would a constricting serpent—then disabling their prey with bites from their strong jaws.)

Despite its adaptations for speed and sight-hunting, the coachwhip's primary feeding response is determined by vomerolfaction. Hatchlings with no prior exposure to their natural prey react instinctively to the scents of potential food species, snapping most vigorously at cotton swabs rolled over the skin of lizards and snakes abundant within their range. (If a highly visually-oriented, pursuit-hunting species such as *Masticophis flagellum* is primarily responsive to chemical cues from prey, it seems likely that this sort of reliance on vomeronasal cues as attack triggers is universal, or nearly so, among snakes.)

Reproduction   Egg-laying. Little is known about courtship and nesting among free-ranging *M. f. flagellum*. The 10- to 15-inch-long hatchlings, which emerge in July and August, have dimly-defined brown anterior dorsal crossbars on their tan backs and whitish, anteriorly spotted venters—patterning so different from the adults that in spite of the large eyes, pronounced supraocular scales, slender bodies, and crosshatched tails they share with their parents, the young are frequently assumed to belong to another species.

Coloring/scale form   Adult *M. f. flagellum* exhibit unique two-toned coloring: the unmarked dark forebody fades posteriorly to lighter shades of brown and tan, and even the entirely black individuals sometimes found between Liberty and Texarkana have reddish-tinted tails. The eastern coachwhip's ventral color matches that of its dorsum, while on the posterior trunk, the scales' dark borders create a crosshatched, braided whip-like pattern from which this animal's common name is derived. See **Western Coachwhip (48)**.

Coachwhips' heads are also distinctive: elongate yet wider than the wiry neck, with big eyes (shielded above by projecting parietal scale plates) bordered along their forward edges by a pair of small preocular scales. The smooth dorsal scales are arranged in 17 rows at midbody (13 just ahead of the vent), and the anal plate is divided.

Similar snakes   Where the ranges of the eastern and **western coachwhips (48)** overlap, intergrades are common. To the west of this zone, the western race is distinguished by its lighter-hued, beige to brownish dorsolateral color, often barred with wide light or dark crossbands. Its venter resembles that of the juvenile eastern coachwhip: creamy, with a double row of dark dots beneath the neck. The **southern black racer (53)** lacks the eastern coachwhip's dark-anterior, lighter-posterior coloring, as well as its crosshatched tail; racers also have 15 rows of dorsal scales just ahead of the vent.

Behavior   Like other whipsnakes, *M. f. flagellum* is exceptionally alert, perhaps even curious. To get a better look at an intruder, an adult surprised in the field may, like a slim-necked cobra, raise its head and forebody well off the ground; I have noticed myself being observed by coachwhips that had fled a short way, then paused to look back at me over tall grass—their direct gaze a startling contrast to the absence of long-distance vision in most snakes.

Because *M. flagellum* can both traverse open ground more swiftly than any other North American serpent—and, when pursued, streak up into low trees—coachwhips are able to evade predators well enough to forage in comparatively unsheltered environments. Nevertheless, diurnal movement across open terrain leaves them vulnerable to predation by hawks (Jim and Herman Stout observed a red-shouldered hawk laboring in flight across a Collin Co. pasture with a three-foot-long eastern coachwhip struggling in its talons), and remains of these snakes are commonly found in the nests of large raptors. (The nervous energy that fuels this vigorous lifestyle generates a constant need to move about, and as a result coachwhips are miserable in confinement—though they are such tough, resilient animals that individuals have lived for nearly 17 years in captivity.)

Western Coachwhip
Masticophis flagellum testaceus

Nonvenomous   Western coachwhips are agile biters that may strike past a human assailant's hands at his face or body. See **Eastern Coachwhip (47)**.

Abundance   Among the most common large, nonvenomous serpent in terrestrial rural environments throughout its range.

Size   The young are 12 to 14 inches at hatching, while most adults measure between 4 and 5½ feet in length. The record is 6 feet 8 inches.

Habitat   *Masticophis flagellum testaceus* occupies almost every terrestrial, non-urban habitat in western Texas.

Prey   See **Eastern Coachwhip (47)**.

Reproduction   Egg-laying. See **Eastern Coachwhip (47)**.

Coloring/scale form   Often reflecting the general hue of their terrain, coachwhip populations become progressively paler-hued as one moves westward, although the head and neck are usually slightly darker than the trunk. In Central Texas many individuals have broad light and dark dorsolateral crossbands, while on the limestone Edwards Plateau unmarked silvery-tan coachwhips predominate. Some specimens—the "red racers" of West Texas storytellers—are brick red, or even vermillion pink above. The venter is gray, anteriorly marked by a double row of black spots. Juveniles are tan, dimly crossbarred with brown on the anterior trunk.

This reptile's most distinctive characteristic, however, is the light-dark cross-hatch patterning of its tail. Because each dorsal caudal scale is two-toned—the forward portion is paler than its trailing edge—the coachwhip's posterior body has the look of a braided buggy whip, though its scales are actually quite smooth. They are arranged in 17 rows at midbody (13 rows just in front of the vent), a unique pair of lorilabial scales—the lower one very small—borders the anterior edge of the eye, and the anal plate is divided.

Similar snakes   The **eastern coachwhip (47)** has uniformly dark foreparts and a lighter-colored posterior trunk and tail which, on otherwise all-black East Texas individuals, has a reddish hue. Other **whipsnakes (49–52)** are even slenderer serpents with thin white lateral stripes, reddish undertails, and 15 midbody rows of dorsal scales.

Behavior   A true hot-weather animal, the western coachwhip is often seen sliding across broiling pavement and Trans-Pecos rock fields even when the temperature is above 100°F. No other serpent except the closely related whipsnakes—whose lean configuration, like that of the coachwhip, is resistant to heat and desiccation—is active at this time, and while neither the coachwhip nor its whipsnake kin can go for long without shade under such conditions, being able to hunt at all during the heat of the day when their lizard prey is most active is a major predatory advantage. This diurnal foraging renders *M. flagellum* vulnerable to predation by carnivorous birds: Red-tailed hawks are commonly seen perched on power line poles feeding on western coachwhips, and juveniles are preyed upon by roadrunners. Vehicles also cause many coachwhip deaths, and in South Texas, caracaras specialize in traffic-killed serpents, many of them coachwhips, for *M. f. testaceus* is typically unwary of even heavily-traveled highways.

49 Central Texas Whipsnake
Masticophis taeniatus girardi

Nonvenomous   See **Desert Striped Whipsnake (50).**

Abundance   Common. Despite its geographically-descriptive name, the Central Texas whipsnake seems to be seen more often in the Trans-Pecos portion of its range.

Size   Despite its considerable length—adult size is 28 to 72 inches—*Masticophis taeniatus girardi* is so slender that even the largest individuals have heads no bigger than a man's thumb: One healthy 3½-foot-long specimen weighed but 5.6 ounces.

Habitat   In Central Texas, oak-juniper evergreen woodland is the favored habitat. In the Trans-Pecos, *M. t. girardi* is found in a wider range of environments: dry watercourses, montane canyons and rocky slopes up to 6,000 feet in elevation, and evergreen mountain forest.

Prey   Food animals include lizards, snakes, and small rodents. Newly-caught Central Texas whipsnakes are typically voracious, immediately taking several mice in succession. After settling into confinement their metabolisms slow, and captives eat only a mouse every two weeks and remain healthy.

Reproduction   Egg-laying. See **Desert Striped Whipsnake (50).**

Coloring/scale form   Named in honor of Charles Frederich Girard, a colleague of S. F. Baird, Secretary of the Smithsonian Institution with whom Girard first described some 24 of Texas' ophidian species and subspecies, *M. t. girardi* varies in its dorsal coloring. Individuals from Central Texas are grayish-black above, with whitish scales on the nape and a row of tiny white flecks on both the lowest dorsal scale row above the belly line and the outer tips of the gray- and white-mottled ventral plates—which, posterior to the vent, shade to pink. West Texas individuals may fit this description, have brownish dorsolateral crossbands, or be uniformly mahogany above, with charcoal anterior bellies. Hatchlings have entirely charcoal-hued backs and sides except for a broad, solid white lateral stripe, which in adults consists of separate elongate patches on the third and fourth scale rows above the belly. There are 15 midbody rows of smooth dorsal scales and the anal plate is divided.

Similar snakes   Throughout the northern Trans-Pecos, intergrades occur with the subspecies **desert striped whipsnake (50),** which is distinguished by its gray-brown to rusty dorsolateral coloring and its pair of white lateral stripes (the uppermost of which is longitudinally split by a blackish streak; the lower white stripe touches the outer edge of the venter). Along the southeastern edge of the Edwards Plateau, the **Schott's whipsnake (51)** is distinguished by its bluish-shading-to-olive dorsolateral coloring, its pair of unbroken white lateral stripes, and the orange flecks often found on its neck and anterior sides.

Behavior   Although few serpents in the wild live much beyond the prime of life, even among animals as high-strung as whipsnakes a few survive to old age. In Big Bend, D. Craig McIntyre came upon a 6-foot-long Central Texas whipsnake that showed signs of age ordinarily seen only in captive snakes at the end of long lives in confinement. Drinking deeply from a stock tank, this individual was quite lethargic despite the warm weather, and made no attempt to escape when approached.

Desert Striped Whipsnake
Masticophis taeniatus taeniatus

Nonvenomous   Nervous, fragile animals, whipsnakes invariably flee rapidly from danger, but if cornered or seized may defend themselves with several rapid, entirely superficial nips.

Abundance   Desert striped whipsnakes are locally common in West Texas uplands such as the Guadalupe Mountains.

Size   See **Central Texas Whipsnake (49).**

Habitat   *Masticophis taeniatus* inhabits both rocky succulent desert and evergreen mountain woodland at elevations up to 7,000 feet. Because the rocky faces of highway road-cuts constitute prime habitat for its lizard prey, the desert striped whipsnake is often seen in these man-made canyons where, despite the speed and agility whipsnakes display in more open terrain, they are easily captured as they attempt to ascend the cuts' vertical faces.

Prey   *Masticophis taeniatus* feeds primarily on lizards and snakes—small western diamondback rattlers have been reported as prey—as well as rodents, nestling birds, and insects. Whipsnakes are not good constrictors, however, typically pinning sizeable prey animals to the ground while disabling them by biting their heads. See **Eastern Coachwhip (47).**

Reproduction   Egg-laying. Like other whipsnakes, *M. t. taeniatus* lays clutches of 3 to 12 relatively large, slightly rough-surfaced eggs. The 12-to 15-inch-long hatchlings—no thicker than a pencil and colored like their parents except that their pale nuchal marking is more pronounced—emerge in late summer or early autumn.

Coloring/scale form   The desert striped whipsnake is descriptively named: below its gray- to rusty-brown dorsal ground color three prominent lateral stripes line its sides. The uppermost is off-white, 2 scale rows in width, and longitudinally split by a blackish streak; below this stripe is a dark lateral stripe, and below it a lower white stripe touches the outer edge of the belly. Ventral coloring is solid charcoal to mottled gray and white below the forebody, shading to coral beneath the tail. The dorsal scales are smooth, arranged in 15 rows at midbody, and the anal plate is divided.

Similar snakes   As with other whipsnakes, the desert striped subspecies intergrades with any race of *M. taeniatus* whose range abuts its own; throughout the northern Trans-Pecos this merging involves the **Central Texas whipsnake (49),** which in typical form is distinguished by its black back, white neck patch, and the strip of elongate white dashes—sometimes compared to highway traffic lane indicators—along its anterior sides.

Behavior   Whipsnakes are among the most radically-shaped of serpents, and while their speed and agility is apparent, what is less evident is that their gracile configuration is equally adapted to resisting heat and desiccation (high heat tolerance is vital for this diurnal, desert-living hunter for it allows *M. taeniatus* to forage during the middle of the day when its lizard prey is abroad). Another advantage of the whipsnake's thin body is that it allows these narrow-bodied reptiles to almost disappear by freezing partially upright, which makes their slim profiles as inconspicuous as plant stems.

51 Schott's Whipsnake
Masticophis schotti

Nonvenomous   See **Ruthven's Whipsnake (52)**.

Abundance   Somewhat uncommon. *Masticophis shotti* is seasonally active in Duval, Brooks, Jim Wells, Webb, Kleberg, and Kenedy counties, but it is not numerous there.

Size   Most adult Schott's whipsnakes are 40 to 56 inches long—the record is 66 inches—but even the largest adults are not much thicker than a fountain pen and weigh only a few ounces.

Habitat   *Masticophis schotti* inhabits the coastal plain south of the Balcones Fault whose typical vegetation is mesquite/live oak savannah and the northern edge of the Tamaulipan thorn woodland, or "brush country," as it is locally known.

Prey   Lizards are this reptile's principal prey, but rodents are also taken—captives typically eat mice immediately—as well as other snakes; cannibalism is reported. In the wild, the young probably feed largely on insects or very small lizards.

Reproduction   Egg-laying. Three Texas clutches reported by Howard Gloyd were laid in May and June and consisted of 3, 10, and 12 eggs. None hatched, but reproductive success was achieved during 1996 when a gravid Webb Co. female cared for by Kenny Wray of the University of Texas at Arlington laid 9 nearly two inch-long, rough-surfaced eggs on May 1. Four were infertile, but 72 days later the remaining egg hatched into a 12¾ inch-long offspring whose brick-red cephalic wash and salmon-hued venter were quite different from the coloring of its parent (its photograph, the first ever taken of a juvenile *Masticophis schotti*, is included here).

Coloring/scale form   Formerly known as *Masticophis taeniatus schotti*, Schott's whipsnake has now been re-defined by James Dixon, et al., of Texas A&M University, as the separate species, *Masticophis schotti*. Its bluish- to greenish-gray back and sides contrast sharply with the pair of white lateral stripes and the reddish scales scattered along its whitish lower neck. The venter is cream-colored beneath the chin, stippled with bluish gray at mid-body, and deep yellow to salmon below the tail. The dorsal scales are smooth and arranged in 15 rows at midbody; the anal plate is divided.

Similar snakes   The adjacently-ranging **Central Texas whipsnake (49)**, which inhabits the southeastern Edwards Plateau, is gray-black, with a prominent white nuchal patch and a series of white dashes—sometimes likened to highway lane dividing stripes—along its anterior sides; it lacks the Schott's pair of continuous white dorsolateral lines. To the south, the **Ruthven's whipsnake (52)** is greener, lacks distinct white lateral stripes, has gray or dark orange spots on its white or pale yellow throat, and a bright red undertail.

Behavior   Fast-moving small animals instantly attract this diurnal reptile's attention and are pursued using a stop-and-go tactic in which the whipsnake pauses while its quarry, usually a lizard, is in flight, then darts forward a few inches when the lizard's attention is diverted by its own foraging. Once grasped by the jaws, prey too large to be immediately engulfed is pressed against the ground by a loop of the trunk, then bitten repeatedly in the head to subdue it.

52 Ruthven's Whipsnake
Masticophis ruthveni

Nonvenomous   *Masticophis ruthveni* is nervous and quick to flee danger, but if cornered it does not hesitate to nip in its own defense, after which it may quickly retract its head and neck, raking its teeth across its adversary's skin leaving shallow scratches.

Abundance   Formerly common. Ruthven's whipsnake is now commonly found only near uncut patches of mesquite savannah and thorn woodland that remain in this region; it is often seen as a roadkill in the area Cameron Co. Airport and the Laguna Atascosa National Wildlife Refuge.

Size   Most adults are 40 to 56 inches long; the record is 66⅛ inches.

Habitat   This semi-tropical whipsnake is an inhabitant of the Tamaulipan thorn woodland, a massive thorn thicket reaching from Mexico into southern Texas. Named for Mexico's northeasternmost state, this tangle of catclaw acacia, paloverde, tamarisk, cenizo, and ocotillo was once among the richest biotic communities in the state, comparable to East Texas' Big Thicket in species diversity. But its lush vegetation grew on fertile, level land, and the 1950s agricultural boom leveled most of its native vegetation, decimating the tropical birds, mammals, and reptiles that originally ranged only as far north as the Rio Grande floodplain.

Prey   See **Schott's Whipsnake (51).**

Reproduction   Egg-laying. See **Schott's Whipsnake (51).**

Coloring/scale form   The dorsum is an unmarked olive-green, with lighter-hued blue-green lower sides faintly marked behind the jaw with rusty orange spots. (The leading edge of some of the anterior vertebral scales is cream-colored, shading to olive or reddish gray toward the tail.) The pale yellow forebelly changes to blue-gray, lightly mottled with salmon on the middle third of the trunk; the venter is pink around the vent, and deep red beneath the tail. Juveniles have a black-edged pale side stripe on the adjacent portions of the third and fourth scale rows above the belly but lack the light anterior vertebral scale margins of adults, as well as most of their dark ventral stippling. The smooth dorsal scales occur in 15 rows at mid-body; the anal plate is divided.

Similar snakes   The Schott's whipsnake (62) has much more conspicuous white lateral stripes, a paler forebelly, and a pale pink undertail.

Behavior   In a 1928 monograph, Arthur I. Ortenberger (who, five years previously had named this serpent after his former teacher, Alexander Grant Ruthven, president of the University of Michigan) concluded that essentially nothing was known of the habits of what was then called *Masticophis taeniatus ruthveni* (recent studies by James Dixon et al., of Texas A&M University, have defined this animal as the separate species, *Masticophis ruthveni*).

Like other whipsnakes, *M. ruthveni* is a seemingly curious animal that, with abrupt darting movements investigates any unusual activity within its territory; because most of its U.S. habitat has been lost to agricultural and residential development during the last thirty years, however, further information regarding its natural history will probably come from northern coastal Mexico. See **Schott's Whipsnake (51).**

53 Southern Black Racer
Coluber constrictor priapus

Nonvenomous   See **Eastern Yellowbelly Racer (56).**

Abundance   The southern black racer occurs only as far west as the northeastern tip of Texas.

Size   Most adults measure 20 to 56 inches; 72 inches is the record.

Habitat   *Coluber constrictor* is a habitat generalist that thrives in a variety of rural and even suburban areas. The southern black racer's preferred environment in Texas, however, seems to be deciduous forest-meadowland interface—a vegetative transition zone characterized by the low-level shrubbery that racers favor.

Prey   Racers are wide-spectrum predators, taking whatever smaller creatures are most available. This includes small animals from insects and their larvae to vertebrates such as frogs, toads, lizards, snakes, birds and their eggs, and rodents. In captivity, unlike many other serpents, racers' high metabolism requires them to eat every few days when warm and active. See **Eastern Yellowbelly Racer (56).**

Reproduction   Egg-laying. Seven to 18 rough-textured oval eggs, about 1 by 1⅝ inch-long, are laid in humid subsurface cavities—a few of which are communally used year after year. The 9-to 11-inch-long hatchlings emerge in July and August and, because they are otherwise defenseless, may feign death when handled. Very different in coloring from the adults, young racers are conspicuously patterned with chestnut-brown vertebral saddles and small grayish lateral spots, and do not turn uniformly dark above until they reach about 22 inches in length.

Coloring/scale form   The southern black racer's dorsum is grayish black, with some white generally visible on the chin and throat. The belly ranges from yellowish gray to as dark a charcoal as the back. This subspecies' slender body and elongate head follow the same configuration as those of other racers, but the eye is notable for its dark, orange-red iris. The 17 midbody rows of dorsal scales (15 anterior to the vent) are smooth and glossy and the anal plate is divided.

Similar snakes   The equally dark, but larger and longer-tailed **eastern coachwhip (47)** has a slightly lighter-hued posterior body with a faintly rusty wash on its tail otherwise marked by dark-edged cross-hatching; it also has a dark forebelly and 13 rows of dorsal scales just ahead of the vent.

Behavior   During the spring and summer of 1981 one study found that several *C. c. priapus* maintained fairly well-defined home territories around the rocky outcroppings of several grassy, oak-studded hillsides in Grayson Co. In Florida, southern black racers have been observed more than 10 feet up in trees, where they sought refuge after having eluded a pursuer on the ground. Both in the East and in Texas I have found *Coluber constrictor* to be less wary when hidden in thick branches where, rather than flee, it is inclined to freeze, sometimes until actually touched.

4 Buttermilk Racer
Coluber constrictor anthicus

Nonvenomous   Like other racers, *Coluber constrictor anthicus* will nip in self-defense (even in distress, however, these animals often bluff by striking open-mouthed rather than biting down, and seldom inflict more than shallow scratches).

Abundance   Common. During one week in mid-May, 9 specimens were found on the grounds of a Lake Houston golf course.

Size   Most adults are 30 to 60 inches long; the record is 70 inches.

Habitat   The buttermilk racer favors overgrown fields, meadows, and partially open areas at the edge of woodland, where it often shelters in brier patches and brushy undergrowth. This habitat preference has benefitted *C. c. anthicus* for, as East Texas' old growth forests have been progressively cut for timber, less and less acreage has been allowed to regenerate its forest cover. Now fragmented into a patchwork of fields, residential subdivisions, and golf courses, much of this region has become ideal habitat for the buttermilk racer.

Prey   In the single study of this subspecies' diet, mice were found in the stomachs of 25 adults, lizards were found in 8, frogs in 7, rats in 5, and 3 had eaten birds.

Reproduction   Egg-laying. During the breeding season in April and May, male racers become quite aggressive, with several sometimes courting a single female. Deposited during June, July, and early August in a variety of sites—within the tunnels of small burrowing mammals, beneath rotting boards or sheets of iron siding, in loose soil along the margins of plowed fields—the rough-surfaced eggs measure up to 1⅝ inches in length. (Of 3 *C. c. anthicus* clutches deposited at the Houston Zoo in late May, 2 consisted of 18, the third of 27; the eggs hatched 46 days later into 10-to 11-inch-long young.)

Coloring/scale form   Dorsal ground color is dark bluish or greenish gray on the foreparts, lighter and browner to the rear (especially in Angelina, Polk, Tyler, and northern Jasper and Newton counties, where the buttermilk racer intergrades with its paler subspecies, the tan racer; here, the brownish hue of *C. c. etheridgei* prevails).

   Across its dark ground color the buttermilk racer's back and sides are spattered with off-white scales, densely-packed on some specimens, scattered and few in number on others. Individuals genetically-influenced by the tan racer may exhibit only a long, white-spotted dark patch on the nape. The lips, chin, and lower sides of the neck are pale yellow, while the belly is gray, often with a few little yellow spots. (Among juveniles, the cream ground color is blotched with brown vertebral saddles and small lateral spots.) The dorsal scales are smooth and arranged, like those of all racers, in 17 rows at midbody (15 rows just forward of the vent). The anal plate is divided.

Similar snakes   The **tan racer** (55) is entirely light gray or brown above, with only a few white dorsolateral scales. Young buttermilk racers' dark vertebral saddles, big, yellow-irised eyes, and 17 anterior rows of dorsal scales set them off from adults of the similar-sized burrowing serpents found in the same leaf-litter microenvironment.

Behavior   See **Eastern Yellowbelly Racer (56).**

55 Tan Racer
Coluber constrictor etheridgei

Nonvenomous   See **Eastern Yellowbelly Racer (56)**.

Abundance   *Coluber constrictor etheridgei* is not uncommon within its very limited range.

Size   This subspecies has been recorded to nearly 6 feet in length. Most adults are 3 to 5 feet long, however, while hatchlings measure 8 to 12 inches.

Habitat   *Coluber constrictor etheridgei* is an inhabitant of oak/sweetgum/longleaf pine woodland. Dense second growth stands of previously-lumbered forest is also good habitat, but as East Texas' cut-over stands of pine and oak have become fields, subdivisions, and golf courses, much of the tan racer's always-limited territory has now been usurped by the more open- or brushy-terrain-living buttermilk racer, *C. c. etheridgei*.

Prey   See **Eastern Yellowbelly Racer (56)**.

Reproduction   Egg-laying. The only extant data for this subspecies is that on May 28, a female from east of Woodville in Tyler Co. deposited 30 eggs, a very high number for a racer—whose clutches generally number fewer than 20 eggs—each a little more than an inch in length.

Coloring/scale form   Although the specimen pictured here is grayish, the tan racer's dorsolateral coloring is more often light brown (at first glance it resembles a western coachwhip with a scattering of pale dorsal scales), sometimes with a white-spotted patch of dark bluish or greenish gray on its nape. The venter is unmarked light gray, with some yellowish spots. The dorsal scales are smooth, with a maximum of 17 dorsal rows at midbody (15 just anterior to the vent), and the anal plate is divided.

Similar snakes   East Texas' more widespread **buttermilk racer (54)** has a much darker, gray-blue or gray-green back and much more profuse off-white dorsolateral scales. (Intergrades between the two—with dark forebodies and brownish tails—are common.) Hatchling racers are distinguished from other small terrestrial serpents with brown dorsolateral patterning by their dark vertebral saddles, proportionately large heads and big yellow eyes, and their singular combination of a divided anal plate and 17 rows of smooth dorsal scales at midbody, 15 just ahead of the vent.

Behavior   As with other racers, *C. c. etheridgei* is most easily found in early spring while it is still lethargic (these serpents are almost impossible to capture later in the year when they are warm and active), hiding beneath woodland ground cover or human detritus. It is far more active from May to July, while another seasonal foraging peak occurs in October; based on individuals seen crossing pine woods logging roads, its hunting is generally divided into morning and afternoon periods, especially when the temperature at those times is between 70° and 85°F. See **Eastern Yellowbelly Racer (56)**.

Eastern Yellowbelly Racer
Coluber constrictor flaviventris

Nonvenomous   If cornered, *C. c. flaviventris* may vibrate its tail and if seized is likely to bite with agility. Compared to even a tiny mammal, however, racers are unable to exert much pressure with their jaws and little pricks or scratches are all that result.

Abundance   The most widely distributed member of its genus in Texas, because of its slightly bluish-olive back *C. c. flaviventris* is known, in many rural areas, as "blue racer."

Size   Although reported to reach nearly 6 feet in length, adult eastern yellowbelly racers are generally between 30 and 54 inches long.

Habitat   Weed-grown fields are also traversed on hunting forays (in open terrain, racers may coil under bushes or clumps of bunchgrass), but *C. c. flaviventris* is most often found along woodland-meadow interface. Derelict buildings whose fallen boards and siding also constitute a favored microhabitat.

Although the eastern yellowbelly racer is usually thought of as living in mesic environments, *C. c. flaviventris* also turns up in completely arid desert terrain. One individual I found in a moist area near Marathon was thought to be part of a relict population that had survived in this mesic refuge from the wetter West Texas of Pleistocene times, but another specimen was discovered in the spring of 1997 on a waterless plateau north of Sanderson.

Various theories have linked the genetic affinity of these West Texas racers with either the Mexican racer, *C. c. oaxaca,* or even the far western, Great Basin racer, *C. c. mormon,* but because both these specimens were phenotypically pure eastern yellowbelly racers, their presence in the Northern Chihuahuan Desert merely broadens our view of the broad range of environments in which *C. c. flaviventris* can survive.

Prey   Despite the name *C. constrictor,* racers are not true constrictors. Small prey such as insects is simply snapped up, but when feeding on larger vertebrates—birds, frogs, lizards, snakes, and rodents are recorded—rather than suffocating their prey by constriction, racers overpower these creatures by pinning them against the ground with a coil of their muscular bodies, then disabling the animal by biting its head. Racers are also noteworthy for the deep channels that line the sides of the snout in front of the eyes. These grooves give the large eyes an overlapping field of view directly ahead, thus providing the binocular vision and depth perception so important to a pursuit-oriented diurnal predator of fast-moving prey.

Coluber constrictor flaviventris will eat any small creature it can capture, including rodents, birds (I once found a small eastern yellowbelly racer in a chicken coop housing half-feathered chicks far too large for it to swallow), lizards, frogs, and other snakes. Large insects are also important prey, and during the periodic emergence of cicadas, when in a single acre tens of thousands may crawl out of the earth, eastern yellowbelly racers feed on them almost exclusively.

Reproduction   Egg-laying. With the approach of their early summer parturition, female racers move to denser vegetation than they frequent at other times, subsequently hiding their eggs beneath litter or burying them under a layer of sandy soil. See **Buttermilk Racer (54).**

Coloring/scale form   The eastern yellowbelly racer is a lovely, muted blue-gray-green above, with a bright yellow venter. The young are dorsolaterally brown-blotched, but during their second year, at 16 to 18 inches, in an ontogenetic pattern change they begin to lose their juvenile coloring, beginning on the tail. Seventeen rows of smooth dorsal scales line the middle of the trunk (15 just ahead of the vent), there are usually 7 upper labials, and the anal plate is divided.

Similar snakes   Over much of Southwest Texas the eastern yellowbelly racer may intergrade with the **Mexican racer (57)**, a more southerly and westerly subspecies with a darker back and lighter sides, a greenish-yellow venter, and 8 upper labial scales. See **Buttermilk Racer (54)**.

Behavior   Even in areas of sub-optimal habitat, eastern yellowbelly racers probably occupy ranges of no more than 25 acres; only a few have been known to travel as far as ¾ mile. Yet, by engaging in the vigorous predatory activity that characterizes their genus—racers' nervous temperament makes them restless captives that seldom do well in confinement—*Coluber constrictor* has adaptively chosen a high-risk, predatory exposure-filled lifestyle. Not only are these snakes more likely to be attacked than cryptic serpents, their high energy expenditures may not be offset by the additional prey-calories their active search for prey has evolved to acquire.

Racers' ecological strategy is so different from that of most other snakes, in fact, that in the Carolinas the activity profile of *Coluber constrictor* has recently been charted by Michael Plummer and Justin Congdon (1994). Using radio-telemetry, these researchers determined that thickets were racers' preferred habitat because dense shrubbery allows them to climb to escape danger. On average, racers were active on three out of four days during summer, with their inactive periods (during which most hid in rodent burrows) being devoted to shedding. Home ranges* usually covered several square acres, but big racers had no larger ranges than small ones. Adult males, and females seeking egg-laying sites, traveled farther than other racers, however, and in autumn all activity areas decreased significantly.

Plummer and Congdon also found that, despite the name racer, *Coluber constrictor* is incapable of moving really fast. Its maximum speed is no more than 12 mph, and even at a much slower pace exhaustion is reached in only about 30 minutes. Although well short of the endurance of birds and mammals, this is great stamina for a reptile, which can only be achieved because of racers' sophisticated physiology. For example, within 30 seconds of seizing a mouse a racer's heart rate shoots up to 3 times its resting level, while its arterial blood pressure increases nearly fourfold. This rush of circulating blood lets *C. constrictor* respond nearly as rapidly, from a resting state, as a bird or mammal; as field experience has repeatedly confirmed, a reptile need not be a warm-blooded dinosaur to make use of a quick-reacting neuromuscular system, nor to sustain that system with considerable cardiovascular stamina.

This advanced physiology is also a factor in a subtle quality one notices when handling racers. Unlike most snakes, racers have an almost mammalian presence: They clearly take note of what is going on around them. A newly captured individual may seem to have settled down in one's hands but, in a way not seen among most other snakes, it continues to pay attention to its circumstances and, if an opportunity for escape arises, it is instantly ready to take advantage of it.

---

*An animal's home range is usually defined as its entire area of activity, which contains all its essential needs for food, water, and cover. An animal's territory, in contrast, is the defended part of its home range; although home ranges of different individuals may overlap, territories generally do not. The cruising radius is the usual scope of an animal's daily movement within its home range.

57 Mexican Racer
Coluber constrictor oaxaca

Nonvenomous *Coluber constrictor oaxaca* will nip if molested.

Abundance Uncommon even in undisturbed parts of its South Texas range.

Size Slightly smaller than other Texas racers, most adult *C. c. oaxaca* measure between 20 and 40 inches in length.

Habitat Both Tamaulipan thorn woodland and grassy pastures constitute this subspecies' principal habitat. Here, Mexican racers may be found coiled in clumps of cactus or hidden under boards and debris around unworked farms and stock tanks, but it has also been found in suburban vacant lots and even city parks. (As an intergrade with the eastern yellowbelly racer, the Mexican racer occurs throughout the Trans-Pecos.)

Prey See **Eastern Yellowbelly Racer (56)**.

Reproduction Egg-laying. Deriving reproductive data for an uncommon animal like *C. c. oaxaca* can become an exercise in forensic science, as happened with one freshly traffic-killed, 3-foot-long McMullen Co. female discovered on June 25 by D. Craig McIntyre. This specimen's skin and eye coverings were milky which, when the animal was found to be gravid, meant that the snake was beginning her egg-laying shed. Based on the gestation period of the Mexican racer's subspecies, the eastern yellowbelly racer, this animal's stage of pregnancy would indicate a mid-May copulation date. Using the usual 15 days or so from the beginning of racers' pre-laying shed to egg deposition, would give an expected laying date about July 10. Based on captive *Coluber constrictor* incubation times, this would mean that this Mexican racer's hatchlings would have emerged in early to mid-September. An attempt was made to salvage and incubate the 13 fully formed and shelled eggs, but because they were still in the oviduct—where serpents' eggs are supplied with oxygen by their mother's respiration—by the time these eggs were removed all the embryos had suffocated.

Coloring/scale form Adult coloring of *Coluber constrictor oaxaca* consists of an olive-gray back, darker along the spine (some individuals appear to have a dusky vertebral stripe), with distinctly paler gray-green sides. Some specimens also have dark blue or black skin visible between the scales—colors that may also appear on the forward edges of the scales themselves. The lips, chin, and belly are yellowish green, with a few individuals having yellowish-pink throats. There are 17 mid-body rows of smooth dorsal scales (15 anterior to the vent), usually 8 upper labial scales, and the anal plate is divided.

Similar snakes Unlike the young of other Texas racers, which have rounded brown saddles along the spine, juvenile *C. c. oaxaca* are marked with narrower, jagged-edged dark bands across the forward part of the back; brown flecks are scattered over their buff ground-colored sides, and both the crown and the posterior back are grayish brown. Among adults, the **eastern yellowbelly racer (56)** is more uniformly olive-brown above and has 7 upper labial scales.

Behavior In Southwest Texas, *Coluber constrictor* is most active from mid-April to early July, with another seasonal peak of activity occurring in October. See **Eastern Yellowbelly Racer (56)**.

58 Central American Speckled Racer
Drymobius margaritiferus margaritiferus

Nonvenomous   Its speed and shyness ensure that this animal seldom encounters human beings. If cornered, however, it can strike with such agility that avoiding a nip is difficult.

Abundance   **Endangered. Protected by the State of Texas.** *Drymobius margaritiferus margaritiferus* is the only member of its genus to reach the United States. Here, the northern limit of its range lies at the southern tip of the Rio Grande Valley in Cameron and eastern Hidalgo counties, where it is now among the rarest reptiles in Texas.

Size   Adults are 30 to 40 inches; maximum recorded length is 50 inches.

Habitat   From the Rio Grande to the Yucatan Peninsula the speckled racer occupies dense thickets near freshwater where its amphibian prey is plentiful. Little of this habitat is left in Texas, however, and the speckled racer's continued existence in the U.S. is in doubt. Yet *D. m. margaritiferus* can sometimes still be found in the Audubon Society's 60-acre Palm Grove Sanctuary, as well as within the handful of Texas Palm groves that remain in Cameron Co.—especially those that retain their natural layered floor of decaying fronds. Riparian woodland near Brownsville and brushy Hidalgo Co. creekbeds have also been noted as habitat. See **Ruthven's Whipsnake (52).**

Prey   Central American speckled racers are diurnal predators that most often feed on anurans (in Mexico I have found *Drymobius* by following the cries of a frog held in a speckled racer's jaws).

Reproduction   Egg-laying. Clutches of 2 to 8 nonadhesive, smooth-shelled eggs, approximately 1⅝ inches in length and ⅝ inch in diameter, are laid between April and August; emerging after an incubation of 8 weeks, Central American speckled racer hatchlings are only about 6 inches long. Compared to the adults, they are even more vividly colored, with each dark scale being centered with a bright, yellowish-white spot, often overlain with dark vertebral blotches or crossbands.

Coloring/scale form   This sleek reptile's vividly patterned back (each dark dorsal scale bears a pale yellow dart-shaped spot, a bluish margin near its base, and a black perimeter) is evocative of oriental lacquer work. Hans Schlegle, who named this snake in 1837, described the patina of glossy white dots on its back by combining the Latin *margarita,* or "pearl," with *ferre,* which means "to carry." (*Drymobius* is Greek, and means "of the forest.") The sides are yellowish-green, the neck washed with turquoise, and a black stripe runs from the eye to the posterior lemon-yellow labial scales—the sutures of which are edged with black. Both juveniles and adults have greenish-yellow venters whose scales are bordered, beneath the tail, with black on their trailing edges. Arranged in 17 rows at midbody, the dorsal scales are weakly keeled along the spine and have apical pits. The anal plate is divided.

Similar snakes   No other snake in Texas resembles this animal.

Behavior   In Southern Mexico, Guatemala, and Belize, *Drymobius margaritiferus* is abundant in thickly-vegetated riparian milieus, where it constantly searches damp places for prey. In these countries speckled racers are also seen in both open savannah and woodland, as well as in overgrown fields and even village backyards.

59 Texas Indigo Snake
Drymarchon corais erebennus

Nonvenomous   This beautiful reptile is, with its eastern subspecies, perhaps the most impressive of all North American serpents. When encountered in the field, individuals may hiss, flatten their necks, and vibrate their tails in agitation but—almost amazingly in view of the great size and power of adult indigos—most allow themselves to be handled without aggression; only rarely, when very warm and active, does one bite vigorously enough to inflict deep cuts.

Abundance   **Threatened. Protected by the State of Texas.** Despite being both federally protected and receiving legal protection from the state, the Texas indigo snake is slowly declining in the U.S. Collecting for the pet trade formerly impacted the eastern indigo snake population, and to a lesser extent the Texas race, but the most harmful factor in this animal's current decline is loss of habitat and roadway casualties.

As an essentially tropical animal living at the northern limit of its biological capacity, the indigo is vulnerable to the widespread conversion of its native terrain to agriculture, and *D. c. erebennus* is now largely restricted to uncleared portions of South Texas' mesquite savannah and Tamaulipan thorn woodland. Another small population has radiated westward along the riparian corridor of the Rio Grande and occupies desert terrain as far west as the eastern Trans-Pecos. Here, Damon Salceies recently recorded a large adult in Sanderson Canyon. D. Craig McIntyre's report of a vehicle-killed 2-foot-long adolescent on the Juno road confirms the existence of this Val Verde Co. group and, moreover, indicates that it is breeding successfully.

Fragmentation of the home ranges of Texas indigo snakes by human incursion is also a problem. The warm-weather range of adults has been found to include several hundred acres (adult males use much more territory). This means that only in the South Texas brush country and eastern Trans-Pecos is there enough non-human-occupied space to allow a viable population of these animals—a breeding population's territorial needs are estimated at more than 2,500 pristine acres. Elsewhere, indigo snakes' great size and diurnal foraging make it difficult for them to escape detection, and they are usually quickly exterminated near populated areas by landowners, dogs, and automobiles.

Size   *Drymarchon corais* is the largest nonvenomous snake in North America; individuals of the Texas race over 8½ feet in length are recorded. Adult males average 5 to 7 feet in length, however, and 4 to 6 pounds in weight; females are about a foot shorter and 1½ pounds lighter.

Habitat   Although it occurs in environments ranging from grassy prairie to coastal sandhills to limestone-floored desert, *D. c. erebennus* is most plentiful in the thorn brush woodland and mesquite savannah of the coastal plain south of Beeville. Here, tree-filled riparian corridors constitute its favored terrain, while its microhabitat includes mammal burrows, especially those of armadillos. These subterranean retreats are essential not only as protection from the brush country's host of large mammalian predators but also because to shed its skin *D. c. erebennus* requires a somewhat moist milieu—which in arid terrain it can find only in humid underground tunnels.

Prey   One of the few snakes large and active enough to be easily observed in its foraging, the Texas indigo moves rapidly through burrows and across the bare ground between patches of thorn thicket. On these forays it can sometimes actually be heard sniffing at the entrance of burrows, searching for any vertebrate big enough to attract its attention and small enough to be swallowed. Not a true constrictor, *Drymarchon corais* typically pins its prey to the ground with a body coil, seizes it with its jaws and, if it is not too large, thrashes it back and forth before immobilizing it by biting its head.

The indigo's jaws are so powerful that this tactic is effective in subduing even large pitvipers, whose venom seems to have no effect on the indigo. Nevertheless, a rattlesnake seized at midbody by a big indigo will strike its assailant many times before being overpowered and swallowed. The Texas indigo snake's preferred prey, however, is rodents (new captives immediately take rats), frogs, and nonvenomous snakes, and a great many of these prey animals are taken.* *D. c. erebennus* has such an active metabolism that warm and active adults feed at least once every week, the young every 3 to 5 days.

Reproduction   Egg-laying. Breeding occurs in late fall, when the territoriality of adult males waxes to the extent that they may inflict 6 inch-long razor-like fang cuts on each other's foreparts; copulation is almost as aggressive. From these autumnal pairings female indigo snakes retain sperm until early spring fertilization (sometimes sperm are retained much longer: one female *Drymarchon* deposited fertile eggs after 4 years of isolation). Following 70 to over 100 days of incubation the 4 to 11 pebbly-surfaced eggs (as much as 3 inches in length and 1½ inches in diameter) hatch into dorsally-blotched young, 18 to 26 inches long. Sexual maturity is not reached until 3 years of age.

Coloring/scale form   The adult Texas indigo snake's muscular trunk is covered with big, predominantly smooth black dorsal scales so glossy they seem almost iridescent. Black facial striping is evident on most individuals' slightly brownish foreparts. The venter evidences a singular combination of cloudy orange and blue-gray, with some areas showing more orange, some more gray. There are 17 midbody rows (14 on the posterior trunk) of predominantly smooth dorsal scales, although partial keels may occur on some of the vertebral scales of adult males. The anal plate is undivided.

Similar snakes   No other terrestrial serpent in South Texas has an entirely black back and sides.

Behavior   The Texas indigo snake is seasonally territorial: although in spring and summer males roam for miles, in winter indigo snakes emerge during warm spells, but both sexes keep to small ranges near their residence dens where the same individuals, marked by clipping a subcaudal scale, have been recovered year after year. On their home terrain these animals seem to be familiar with every stick and bush, for if pursued they may make false runs in two or three different directions before doubling back toward their dens.

Indigo snakes' dramatic appearance has created a demand for captives but, besides being illegal to capture, *Drymarchon* are much too restless to make satisfactory cage animals. Unable to settle into the lethargy that confinement requires many rub their snouts raw trying to pry out of their enclosures, while others are so given to voiding musk and feces that handling them is an ordeal. Unlike arboreal snakes like the boas, which are comfortable draped over one's limbs, the terrestrial indigo is ill at ease off the ground and generally makes such efforts to be free of human contact that it is clear it should have been left in the wild.

---

*The high incidence of frogs and other snakes in the diet of wild indigos makes them prone to the herpetofaunal-specific parasitic worms they acquire from these prey species, and most wild caught individuals are heavily parasitized.

60 Eastern Hognose Snake
Heterodon platirhinos

Nonvenomous   The eastern hognose snake has a pair of unique lance-shaped rear teeth (its genus name, *Heterodon*, means different-toothed) but they are located too far back in its mouth to be used in defense, and *H. platirhinos* is entirely harmless to humans.

Abundance   Eastern hognose snakes may be locally abundant in areas that favor its anuran prey—moist, sandy soil and heavy ground cover in which both toads and hognose snakes burrow for shelter.

Size   Most adults are 20 to 33 inches; the record is 45½ inches.

Habitat   *Heterodon platirhinos* inhabits a variety of sandy-substrate terrestrial environments, especially mixed hardwood and upland pine forest and forest/grassland boundaries.

Prey   This scent-hunting amphibian-predator locates the toads, which constitute the bulk of its prey, beneath leaf litter and even a layer of soil by smell, then roots it out with its upturned, plowshare-like rostral scale. *Heterodon platirhinos* is such a predatory specialist on toads—which few other animals are able to eat due to their toxic skin secretions—because it has several highly specialized predatory adaptations that allow it to feed on toads.

These include enlarged rear teeth hinged to the maxillary bone at the rear of its upper jaw. After its flexible lower jaw has partially engulfed a toad and maneuvered the amphibian as far back into the mouth as possible, the hognose swings its long upper teeth forward to puncture the amphibian's swollen body (toads bloat their bodies with air to balloon themselves too large to fit down a snake's throat). This introduces its stringy, opalescent salivary toxins, which soon leave the toad too limp to continue its struggle.

The hognose's other primary adaptation to feeding on toads involves dealing with the amphibian's own toxins. These heart-rate-suppressing digitaloid compounds are excreted by the toad's epidermal glands and (though garter and ribbon snakes manage to feed sparingly on small toads) prevent these anurans from being the principal food of any predator but hognose snakes. To neutralize the toads' bufotoxins, however, *H. platirhinos* has evolved enlarged adrenal glands, some ¼ by 2 in. long in adults, which are 10 times heavier in relation to body weight than those of other North American colubrids.

Frogs are also a principal food of *H. platirhinos,* and lizards may occasionally be taken; in captivity hatchling hognoses will accept crickets. This reptile will also scavenge carrion (I have seen an eastern hognose trying to eat a road-killed leopard frog), but because this species is disinclined to take the domestic mice that most captive snakes are fed, eastern hognose snakes were seldom maintained in confinement until it was discovered that many individuals could be enticed to feed on mice by rubbing the rodents with a live toad to impart its scent.

Reproduction   Egg-laying. Mating occurs March through May, followed by deposition of 4 to 61 (average 22) 1¼ by ¾ inch eggs, more rounded in shape than those of most serpents. Hatchlings measure 6½ to 9½ inches in length and, in an unusual developmental pattern, typically experience their first shed while emerging from the egg.

Coloring/scale form *Heterodon platirhinos* varies enormously in dorsolateral coloring: Individuals can have a khaki-green, yellowish- or reddish-brown ground color, intricately patterned with almost any combination of darker spots and splotches. Some are even black, but in Texas most eastern hognose snakes are yellowish in ground color blotched with darker brown. (As *H. platirhinos* ages, many individuals undergo an ontogenetic color change in which the juvenile patterning darkens until older adults are almost entirely dusky.) There is almost always a big dark splotch just behind the jaw, however, which extends well back onto the neck; an exception is individuals from the Brazos River valley west as far as Lee Co., which are sometimes a military-issue gray-green, entirely without markings.

Because of the eastern hognose's variability, *H. platirhinos* is best identified by its configuration—stocky trunk, short head scarcely distinct from its wide neck, and upturned, pointed snout flanked by sharp-edged labial ridges. A prominent bulge over the little dark eyes is emphasized by a brown band that masks the forecrown; among all color morphs, the underside of the tail is much lighter than the (occasionally orange-blotched) gray venter. The prefrontal scales touch, the heavily keeled dorsal scales occur in 23 to 25 midbody rows, and the anal plate is divided.

Similar snakes The **dusty (61)**, **plains (62)**, and **Mexican (63)** races of the **western hognose snake** have a sandy ground color uniformly patterned with brown dorsolateral spots; their bellies and undertails are heavily blotched with black. **Southern (92)** and **broad-banded (93) copperheads'** dorsolateral bands completely cross the back and sides; the slender neck is much narrower than the copperhead's flat-sided head, whose cheeks are marked by a dark pit between the nostril and the big pale, vertically-pupilled eye.

Behavior The strongly keeled dorsolateral scales of *H. platirhinos* give it the traction to root through the earth with its muscular trunk, using its wedge-like snout like a small plow to force loosened soil to the sides. In the open, this animal's deliberate pace makes it an easy target for predators, and in defense the eastern hognose has developed an elaborate death-feigning ruse. This entails spreading its long ribs to flatten its body (one common name is "spreading adder"), hissing, and making feinting pseudo-strikes that resemble those of a pitviper.

Except that the strikes are carried out with the mouth closed. In fact, unless one has recently handled a toad, even prodding its snout with a finger won't prompt *H. platirhinos* to bite.

If its antagonist persists, the hognose may conceal its head under its tightly spiraled tail. To make itself unappealing as a meal, it may then writhe convulsively, regurgitate, defecate, discharge musk from its cloaca, and turn belly-up, its tongue hanging loosely from its slackened jaw. If placed right side up some hognoses will even flop back over into their death-pose, righting themselves only after the danger has passed.

61 Dusty Hognose Snake
Heterodon nasicus gloydi

Mildly venomous *Heterodon* means "different-" or "multiple-toothed," in reference to this genus' combination of conventional anterior teeth and large, hinged rear ones. Although mildly toxic to its small mammal, lizard, and amphibian prey, the seromucous parotid gland secretions in western hognose's saliva pose no danger to humans because the tips of its long rear teeth lie so far back in the throat that they cannot be used for defense.

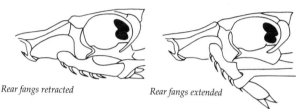

Rear fangs retracted   *Rear fangs extended*

Abundance   Uncommon. *Heterodon nasicus gloydi* occurs in widely separated populations scattered throughout its broad Texas range.

Size   Most adults are 17 to 25 inches; the record is nearly 3 feet.

Habitat   *Heterodon nasicus gloydi* occupies a geographically widespread assortment of most often sandy-soiled grassland microhabitats. As well as shortgrass prairie, these include grassy areas in rocky semi-desert and pasture and pine or hardwood forest interface. On the upper coastal islands dusty hognoses live both on salt grass prairie and in residential areas.

Prey   A generalized feeder, mainly on small mammals, the dusty hognose snake is also reported to prey on amphibians, lizards, and smaller snakes—all subdued by its parotid salivary secretions—as well as on reptile eggs and the young of ground-nesting birds. Carrion is also occasionally eaten, and in captivity reluctant feeders will sometimes take live fish.

Reproduction   Egg-laying. Evidence indicates that breeding may occur only in alternate years. Deposited between early June and August, the 4 to 23 eggs hatch after 52 to 64 days into young 6 to 7½ inches in length, which reach sexual maturity at 18 to 24 months.

Coloring/scale form   In 1952 R. A. Edgren divided the western hognose population into the 3 subspecies recognized today. In all three, the buff ground-colored back is blotched with big dorsal spots while smaller brown patches occur on the lower sides. The **dusty hognose snake (61)**, however, has fewer than 32 medium-sized brown dorsal blotches between snout and vent in males, fewer than 37 in females (males can be identified by their thicker-based tails). This race also has 9 or more small azygous scales separating the prefrontal plates of its forecrown. The **plains hognose snake (62)** has more than 35 slightly smaller dorsal blotches over the same area in males, more than 40 in females, and the same number of azygous cephalic scales. The **Mexican hognose snake (63)** is marked like the dusty, but with no more than 6 azygous scales between its prefrontal plates.

The predominantly black venter has scattered yellowish-white blotches, the 23 midbody rows of dorsal scales are heavily keeled, and the anal plate is divided.

Similar snakes   See **Plains Hognose Snake (62).**

Behavior   See **Plains Hognose Snake (62).**

BROWN-BLOTCHED TERRESTRIAL SNAKES

183

62 Plains Hognose Snake

Heterodon nasicus nasicus

Mildly venomous *Heterodon nasicus nasicus* does not bite humans, but its defensive repertoire includes both imitation strikes made with its mouth so firmly clamped shut that an assailant is only bumped by the snout, and a less dramatic version of the eastern hognose's death-feigning. See **Eastern Hognose Snake (60)**.

Abundance Uncommon.

Size Adults are generally 15 to 25 inches long; the largest Texas specimen, a male from Hale County, measured 35¼ inches.

Habitat Preferred macrohabitat is the short- and mixed-grass prairie of both the Panhandle's Low and High Plains, mainly where canyons or large draws provide at least seasonal water, where there is a gravelly or sandy soil that allows extensive burrowing, and where leaf litter or other ground cover is available as shelter for its small vertebrate prey.

Prey See **Dusty Hognose Snake (61)**.

Reproduction Egg-laying. Reproduction is similar to that of the dusty hognose, but the shorter foraging season of this race's more northerly range makes it more difficult for females to build the fat reserves necessary for successful pregnancy. Because many females examined in midsummer are not gravid, much of the population may breed only in alternate years.

This makes contact between males and the only periodically fecund females unusually important, and because hognose snakes winter in scattered, solitary niches, males have less access to females than do communally-denning serpents. Therefore, during the first weeks after springtime emergence males wander widely in search of mates. Another brief period of copulation occurs in the fall, with spermatozoa from the autumn pairings remaining viable in the female's cloaca throughout the winter.

Coloring/scale form The plains hognose snake's sandy ground-colored back and sides are marked with more than 35 dorsal blotches in males, more than 40 in females. See **Dusty Hognose Snake (61)**. The species' characteristic hognose brown-banded mask across the forehead and eyes is present, as is the typical large brown nuchal blotch, which extends from the rear of the crown well back onto the sides of the neck. Sections of the mostly coal-black ventral pigment are edged with white, yellow, or pale orange, the 23 midbody rows of dorsal scales are heavily keeled, and the anal plate is divided.

Similar snakes The **eastern hognose snake (60)**, despite its variable dorsal pattern, never has a pale tan ground color broken only by small brown vertebral and lateral splotches, and its undertail is always much lighter in hue than its unmarked gray venter. The **western hooknose snake (64)** is a much smaller, crossbanded reptile with 17 rows of smooth dorsal scales.

Behavior Field studies of *H. n. nasicus* in central Kansas show it to be active mostly morning and evening, sheltering at night and during cold weather by burrowing into sandy soil; on the surface it is often found in leaf litter. Its behavioral imperative against biting a large adversary is so strong in the dusty hognose that, rather than close its jaws it will gag on a finger poked into its open mouth.

Mexican Hognose Snake
Heterodon nasicus kennerlyi

Mildly venomous   See **Dusty Hognose Snake (61).**

Abundance   *Heterodon nasicus kennerlyi* occupies two widely separated parts of Texas—the Trans-Pecos and the lower Rio Grande plain. Rare in the Trans-Pecos, this desert-adapted hognose is uncommon but widespread in the mesquite savannah and Tamaulipan thorn brush woodland of South Texas. Here, most records show it to be abroad mainly during damp weather in May and June, then again in September; at these times, over the course of a few days several individuals may turn up in places where no others had been seen for months.

Size   See **Plains Hognose Snake (62).**

Habitat   In South Texas, Mexican hognose snakes live in thorn woodland, most often near arroyos or watercourses where their anuran and small rodent prey is likely to be found, or in grassland. The latter includes both mesquite/prickly pear pastureland and the drier milieu of grass-covered coastal sand dunes. In the Trans-Pecos, *H. n. kennerlyi* occurs sporadically in the rocky desert along the Rio Grande east of Big Bend, but is more likely to be seen in Presidio Co. grasslands. (A common factor is the presence in both areas of gravelly, sandy soil in which hognose snakes can dig to escape harsh weather as well as predators.) *Heterodon nasicus* living north of Interstate 10 and the Marathon basin may constitute an intergrade population between the Mexican and more northerly Dusty hognose races, for they resemble the Mexican race but have very little orange on their venters.

Prey   See **Dusty Hognose Snake (61).**

Reproduction   See **Dusty Hognose Snake (61).**

Coloring/scale form   Coloring is similar to other western hognose species, although a few individuals with almost unmarked dorsums have recently been found in Val Verde Co. See **Plains Hognose Snake (62).**

Similar snakes   Exhibiting almost the same dorsal coloring, size, and body shape as the Mexican hognose is the **desert massasauga (98)**; at night, in the beam of a flashlight, only by looking for the viper's rattle is it possible to tell at a glance which animal is at hand. (This is an interesting case of parallel habitat-selection, for despite being neither related nor sharing the same prey or life history, this small pitviper shares both of the Mexican hognose snake's widely separated ranges.) The **Mexican hooknose snake (65)** is a smaller serpent with 17 rows of dorsal scales and a shallow depression rather than a raised keel behind its tiny upturned snout.

Behavior   Largely fossorial for most of the year, *H. n. kennerlyi* is seldom seen even by ranch hands who spend every daylight hour in South Texas' brush country. Thus, it is always a treat to come across a Mexican hognose on one of its sporadic forays, which generally occur just before dark or at dawn. Because this slow-moving little reptile is vulnerable on the surface to a host of predators—hawks and owls, bobcats, coyotes and foxes, raccoons, and bands of snake-eating javelinas—it is possible that the Mexican hognose is so adapted to the relative safety of fossorial life that it need not employ the defensive death-feigning of other hognose snakes: several individuals I found did not engage in this behavior even when first handled in the field.

BROWN-BLOTCHED TERRESTRIAL SNAKES

64 Western Hooknose Snake
Gyalopion canum

Nonvenomous   This little snake never bites humans.

Abundance   Fairly common. For nearly a century this species was thought to be extremely rare; now, due to increased reporting of observations, *Gyalopion canum* is known to occur widely over the Trans-Pecos and Stockton Plateau.

Size   Most western hooknose snakes are between 6½ and 11 inches in length; the record is a 17¼-inch-long Andrews Co. specimen found by Damon Salceies.

Habitat   *Gyalopion canum* is primarily an inhabitant of grassland, most often shortgrass prairie above 2,500 feet in elevation: It is often found, after the late summer rains have started, in high meadows of the Davis Mts. Western hooknose snakes also occur, although less frequently, both at lower elevations on the north-central plains and in the oak-juniper savannah of the western Edwards Plateau.

Prey   *Gyalopion canum* feeds on spiders, centipedes, and scorpions.

Reproduction   Egg-laying. All that is known about this species' reproduction is that in early July one captive female laid a single, proportionately large 1⅛-inch-long egg.

Coloring/scale form   The dark-speckled buff dorsolateral ground color is crossed with black-edged brown or reddish brown, zigzag-edged vertebral bars that taper to points just above the off-white venter. The most distinctive characteristic of this stub-tailed little reptile, however, is the minuscule upturned hook formed by the hyper-developed rostral scale that tips its snout; posteriorly, this scale splits the internasal scales and reaches back only as far as the juncture of the prefrontal scales. The western hooknose snake's bulbous forehead is crossed with a black-bordered brown band that masks the eyes and extends past the rear of its jaw; above this band a complex pattern of rusty to dark brown bands and splotches (which varies from individual to individual) usually includes an irregularly-shaped longitudinal brown patch across the rear of the skull and nape. Except for being pocked with tiny apical pits, the dorsal scales are smooth and arranged in 17 rows at midbody; the anal plate is divided.

Similar snakes   The **Mexican hooknose snake (65)** is more olive-gray, has an unpatterned (or at least less strongly banded) crown, and narrower, sometimes poorly defined dorsolateral crossbands. There are usually no internasal scales and the upturned rostral scale extends rearward between the prefrontal scales all the way to the frontal scale. The sympatrically-ranging **dusty (61)** and **Mexican (63) hognose snakes** are more robust reptiles with 23 rows of keeled dorsal scales, proportionately larger upturned rostral scales characterized by a raised keel along their edges.

Behavior   Found at the surface mainly under rocks, this slow-gaited burrower emerges only after dark or, following late summer rains, at dusk. Besides hiding, its primary protective strategy is to engage in a series of sudden gyrations, perhaps discomfiting to some predators, that includes extending and retracting the cloaca with a distinct popping sound.

Mexican Hooknose Snake
Ficimia streckeri

Nonvenomous   This animal does not bite human beings.

Abundance   Common. Particularly during May and June *Ficimia streckeri* is often seen at night on the back roads of Webb, Brooks, Jim Hogg, Duval, Zapata, and Starr counties.

Size   Almost all Mexican hooknose snakes in South Texas are between 5½ and 9 inches in length, but the record is a comparatively huge 19 inches.

Habitat   Widely distributed throughout the Tamaulipan thorn brush of the Rio Grande plain, *Ficimia streckeri* is most likely to be found in the vicinity of stock ponds and irrigation canals.

Prey   Spiders are this reptile's preferred prey, but centipedes and other small invertebrates may also be taken. This little snake has a hooked, upturned rostral scale which, along with its slightly bulbous forehead, closely resembles the cephalic configuration of unrelated western hooknose snake. (The similarly-upturned snout of the much larger hognose snakes is used for digging for shelter and rooting out hidden prey, but it is not clear whether the hooknose snakes' similar-appearing adaptation is directed toward uncovering food animals—spiders are seldom fossorial—or whether the Mexican hooknose snake's miniature snout-plow is primarily used as an aid to burrowing.)

Reproduction   Egg-laying. No reproductive behavior is recorded.

Coloring/scale form   Ground color is olive- to grayish-brown with 50 or more thin dark vertebral crossbars narrowly spaced from the nape, where there is a single wider crossband, to tailtip. The upturned rostral scale has a surprisingly sharp point; there are usually no internasal scales because the enlarged rostral occupies this area, separates the prefrontals, and reaches all the way back to the frontal scale. (Posteriorly, the forehead exhibits the bulging brow characteristic of serpents which have evolved a hyper-developed rostral scale.) Except for a large brown spot below the eye, the lips, throat, and lower sides are pale buff; the venter is off-white. Arranged in 17 rows at midbody, the dorsal scales are smooth, pocked with tiny apical pits. The anal plate is divided.

Similar snakes   The **western hooknose snake (64)** has both internasal scales and a rostral that does not extend rearward as far as its frontal scale. Its black-edged dorsal crossbands are wider, while its brown-blotched crown is followed by an irregular longitudinal blotch along the nape. The **Mexican hognose snake (63)** has 23 rows of keeled dorsal scales and a larger rostral backed by a perpendicular ridge.

Behavior   *Ficimia streckeri*, whose name honors herpetologist John K. Strecker, is a slow-moving creature whose principal means of self-defense is its exceptional burrowing ability. When picked up, this animal vigorously noses downward through one's fingers—an attribute that allows it to disappear into soft earth within moments. The Mexican hooknose's other defensive tactics include slowly weaving its elevated head and forebody in an approximation of the defensive posture of the vipers, while a threatened individual may suddenly flip its entire body back and forth, making a sharp little popping sound by extending its cloaca through its vent.

66 Louisiana Pine Snake
Pituophis ruthveni

Nonvenomous   Pine snakes do not bite unless they are attacked, but they are great bluffers. Before the sawmills moved into East Texas during the 1920s, *Pituophis ruthveni* was quite common, attracting written comment on its large size and the dramatic defensive stance in which it rears its forebody off the ground and hisses loudly enough to be heard for several yards. See **Bullsnake (67)**.

Abundance   Endangered. Protected by the State of Texas. An inhabitant of loose, sandy soils, the Louisiana pine snake is thought to be a remnant member of a widespread, desert-evolved Pleistocene fauna now adapted to a sandy-soiled forest habitat. In historical times the Louisiana pine snake's range was moderately large, and included the Big Thicket lowlands north of Harris Co. as well as most of west/central Louisiana. Now, only small populations of Louisiana pine snakes are scattered within this area: Neil Ford of the University of Texas at Tyler found one extremely localized group in Wood Co.

Until the last two years, *Pituophis ruthveni* was known only from historical records and some 17 individuals preserved in museum collections, but in a federally-funded study undertaken by Craig Rudolph of the Southern Forest Experimental Station in Nacogdoches, drift fence trapping in the area's National Forests has located more than a dozen additional specimens. From them, Rudolph is beginning to unravel the population dynamics of this very rare reptile.

Size   Most adult Louisiana pine snakes are between 3 and 5 feet in length; the record is just under 6 ft.

Habitat   Despite their name, pine snakes do not live in trees. Instead, they are terrestrial, burrowing residents of East Texas' longleaf pine/hardwood forest community, which comprises their primary habitat.

This environment is so unsuitable for the Louisiana pine snake's primary prey species, the pocket gopher, that *P. ruthveni* has disappeared from most of its former range. Yet the Louisiana pine snake may not be quite as rare as its infrequent sightings suggest, because its secretive subterranean life—rodent prey is captured in subsurface burrows, where pine snakes remain sequestered after feeding—lets it avoid contact with humans. A recent telemetry tracking study done in Louisiana found that over the course of an entire year one adult *P. ruthveni,* resident in the burrows of a pocket gopher colony, moved about underground within an area of only a few square yards and was *never* detected on the surface.

Prey   Pocket gophers are pine snakes' primary—and usually habitat-determining—prey. This is because, whether pines or hardwoods, old growth timber is so shady that its underlying ground cover is mostly herbaceous—the essential forage of pocket gophers, which need the nutrients of either crops or ground-living herbs to maintain large populations.

Predation on these rodents, which have formidable defenses against predators, is accomplished by two singular hunting techniques. Unlike generalized ophidian predators such as the rat snakes, *Pituophis ruthveni* typically unhesitatingly dives down gopher burrows. It has to move fast because gophers are rapid diggers and can in a moment throw up a barricade of dirt plugging their burrow behind them; a creeping rat snake encounters only a dead-end tunnel.

The pine snake is better adapted to overcome this defense. Aided by their conical skulls and muscular necks, Louisiana pine snakes observed in a glass-walled subterranean chamber twisted their heads sideways to scoop dirt out of their path. When their gopher quarry was overtaken, and there was no room to wrap around and constrict it in its tunnel, Rudolph observed *P. ruthveni* force past the gopher, pinning it against the side of its burrow with a body coil and suffocating it without exposing the pine snake's head to the rodent's big orange incisors.

Other food animals include rodents and young cottontails, as well as ground-nesting birds and their eggs, but the stomachs of three specimens found as road-kills in Louisiana contained only amphibian remains. The few road-kills examined in Texas have contained no prey, however, except for two that had fed on turtle eggs. These animals were probably empty of prey because *P. ruthveni* would be unlikely to occur on the surface—where it would be vulnerable to a drift fence trap—except when hungry and moving from one feeding area to another, or during the males' search for a female's pheromone trail.

Reproduction Nothing is recorded; probably similar to other *Pituophis*.

Coloring/scale form Fewer than 40 irregularly shaped chocolate dorsal saddles mark the posterior three quarters of the backs of most *Pituophis ruthveni*, though a pair maintained at the Lufkin Zoo vary markedly in coloring. The male, taken from the western edge of the range in the Angelina National Forest, has a grayish-tan crown, a dark masking line through its eyes and across its forehead, a light brown ground color, and a black crossbarred tail; the female, from Newton County on the Louisiana border, is an almost uniformly brown serpent whose dark dorsal mottling obscures her vertebral saddles and extends to both crown and tail. The venter is creamy, with brown or black spots along its sides. The central rows of the 28 or more midbody rows of dorsal scales are more heavily keeled than the lateral rows, there are 4 prefrontal scales, and the rostral scale is enlarged and pointed. The anal plate is undivided.

Similar snakes Called pine snakes in the East, bullsnakes in the Midwest, and gopher snakes in the West, members of the genus *Pituophis* share similar configuration. Among this genus, however, relationships are cloudy. The Louisiana pine snake's East Texas woodland habitat is ecologically distinct as well as geographically separate from the eastern Cross Timbers boundary of the bullsnake's territory, which is well to the west of the pine snake's forest home. Moreover, both significant morphological differences (primarily the smaller head and less heavily-scaled snout of *Pituophis ruthveni*) and the dissimilar lifestyles of these two populations are sufficiently distinct to justify their separation into different species.

Similarly, according to Steven Reichling (1995), a comparable gap exists between the Louisiana pine snake and the eastern *Pituophis melanoleucus* subspecies of the southeastern U.S. This, Reichling maintains, indicates long-standing differences in their respective evolutionary histories sufficient to warrant classification of the Louisiana pine snake as *Pituophis ruthveni*—a species separate from both the western *Pituophis catenifer* and the eastern *Pituophis melanoleucus*, but inconclusive relationships such as those among *Pituophis* are always subject to re-interpretation.

Behavior Most published records of *P. ruthveni* have been of road-killed animals run over (often during rainy weather) at dusk or dawn. This indicates a probable crepuscular foraging pattern characteristic of serpents that prey on the small mammals most active at these times.

67 Bullsnake

Pituophis catenifer sayi

Nonvenomous   Bullsnakes vary in defense behavior, either because of individual differences in temperament or in response to circumstances such as temperature. For example, some wild adults allow themselves to be picked up, while others rear the head and forebody, curve, hiss, and attempt to bite. None will strike unless molested, however.

Abundance   Very common. Along with the western diamondback rattlesnake, the bullsnake is the most abundant large reptile in western Texas.

Size   Most adults range from 4 to 6 feet in length, but bullsnakes can grow much larger; along with the **Texas indigo snake (59)**, *P.c. sayi* is the state's longest snake. The largest specimen ever taken is the 8-foot, 6½-inch-long Wichita Co. giant captured by Dr. Robert Kuntz of the Southwest Research Center in San Antonio.

Habitat   One of the most widely distributed snakes in Texas, *P. c. sayi* occupies every sort of dry, open-country terrain in the central two thirds of the state: Bullsnake/gopher snake intergrades are equally at home at lower elevations and at up to 7,000 feet elevation in the Guadalupe Mountains.

Prey   *Pituophis catenifer sayi* feeds primarily on burrowing rodents, especially pocket gophers and ground squirrels. The bullsnake's muscular neck, heavy skull, and upturned rostral scale enable it to root through even gravelly soil in pursuit of these animals. In defense, gophers may push up a defensive plug of soil to seal their tunnels behind them, and are sometimes successful: I have seen a bullsnake turn away from a burrow just back-filled by a frantically-digging gopher. (This reluctance to dig may have been because, as a regular resident of a large gopher colony that well-fed bullsnake may not have needed to press every predatory opportunity.)

Still, in an area heavily populated by rodents even a single *P. c. sayi* exerts a major predatory impact, and an undisturbed group of *P. c. sayi* can lower rodent numbers enough to mitigate the need for poisoning around crop fields where mice and cotton rats, as well as gophers, proliferate. Other prey, such as young rabbits and ground-nesting birds, is also usually warm-blooded; juveniles are reported to eat lizards as well as insects.

Reproduction   Egg-laying. Courtship involves springtime olfactory tracking along a pheromonal scent trace laid down by the female. Up to 24 eggs (the record number deposited by a robust, 6½ lb female maintained by *Pituophis* enthusiast Jim Constabile) are deposited in loose soil during June and July. The leathery, adhesive-shelled eggs (which measure from 2 to more than 3½ inches long) form a single large cluster, from which the 12½- to 19-inch-long young emerge. Along with indigo snakes and diamondback rattlesnakes, bullsnake hatchlings are the largest North American snake neonates, and in early autumn are abundant throughout western Texas.

Coloring/scale form   Of native serpents, only *Pituophis catenifer* has a khaki-hued, brown-freckled crown much paler than its brown-block patterned back; on its tail dark crossbands stand out against a mustard ground color. A slightly elevated transverse ridge—from which its common name is derived—crosses its forehead like the boss of a bull's horn; along it a darker band angles back through the eye and across the cheek. Cephalic scalation is also unique: 4 small prefrontal scales back the long narrow rostral plate. Arranged in 29 to 37 rows (usually 33 at midbody), the dorsal scales have apical pits and are most strongly keeled along the spine. The laterally speckled venter is off-white, the anal plate undivided.

Similar snakes   The **Sonoran gopher snake (68)** is a slightly paler, more reddish brown-blotched, subspecies whose rostral scale is a bit broader than that of the bullsnake (the bullsnake's rostral scale is narrower than it is wide). The Sonoran race predominates to the west and northwest of Texas, entering the state only in El Paso and Hudspeth counties, although it intergrades with the bullsnake throughout the Trans-Pecos. Troy Hibbitts, of the University of Texas at Arlington, reports finding that both sorts of rostral scales occur with about equal frequency throughout the Trans-Pecos; nevertheless, everyone, including herpetologists, had long regarded these animals as bullsnakes.

The **Louisiana pine snake (66)** is darker and less distinctly patterned, with fewer than 40 non-rectangular vertebral blotches. (Both the bullsnake and its more westerly Sonoran race are more "bull-headed" than their fossorial eastern relatives, because it takes a heavy skull and neck to make headway in their calcareous hardpan environment.) Adult **Texas rat snakes (72)** have dark brown heads, 27 rows of dorsal scales, 2 prefrontal scales and a divided anal plate. **Texas (69)** and **Kansas (70) glossy snakes** have a pale longitudinal line along the nape, a white venter and 2 prefrontal scales.

Behavior   Diurnal as well as nocturnal, bullsnakes may be abroad at any hour. In western desert terrain, where ground cover is sparse enough to observe its movements from a distance, I have followed individuals for more than a quarter mile as they foraged across the desert. Because *P. c. sayi* often creeps along using only energy-efficient rectilinear locomotion, it is vulnerable to human activity and many are run over crossing roads. Generally terrestrial, bullsnakes may scale trees when pursued if no shelter is available on the ground.

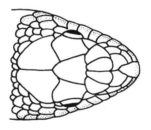

Prefrontal scales: bull, pine, and gopher snakes

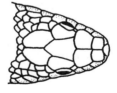

Prefrontal scales: glossy snakes

68 Sonoran Gopher Snake
Pituophis catenifer affinis

Nonvenomous   See **Bullsnake (67).**

Abundance   Common throughout the western United States, *Pituophis catenifer affinis* appears in Trans-Pecos Texas primarily as an intergrade with the bullsnake, for pure *P. c. affinis* range only into the western tip of the state.

Size   Adults are generally 3½ to 5 feet long; the record is 92 inches.

Habitat   The Texas habitat of this subspecies includes short grass prairie, shrub and succulent desert, and barren mountain slopes.

Prey   Primarily small burrowing mammals, especially pocket gophers and ground squirrels. In gopher and ground squirrel colonies *P. c. affinis* simply takes up residence in the burrows. Young rabbits and the eggs and nestlings of ground-living birds are also reportedly taken, and young gopher snakes may eat lizards.

Reproduction   Egg-laying. Bogert and Roth (1966) report dominance rivalry among male Sonoran gopher snakes in which the contestant most successful in the pair's preliminary head-rearing skirmishes then attempts to maintain its superiority by swaying above the forebody of its adversary for as much as an hour, from time to time dropping its anterior trunk onto the snake below. See **Bullsnake (67).**

Coloring/scale form   Throughout the eastern and southern part of Trans-Pecos Texas the Sonoran gopher snake intergrades with the **bullsnake (67).** (The gopher snake is lighter and sometimes more reddish in overall coloring, with some individuals having an almost pinkish-tan cast; there are also slightly more numerous rusty-brown rectangles spaced along the spine between similar-sized golden brown blocks and the gopher snake's rostral scale is broader than the rostral of the bullsnake.) The throat is white, shading to pale yellow at midbody; scattered dark spots tip the outer edges of the posterior ventral scales. Like other *Pituophis,* four prefrontal scales border the rear of the rostral; the 29 or more midbody rows of dorsal scales are heavily keeled along the spine, and the anal plate is undivided.

Similar snakes   *Pituophis* taxonomy—and thus the degree of relatedness among this genus' numerous species and subspecies—has been an area of controversy for decades. Following the early division of E. D. Cope and O. G. Stull, *Pituophis* expert Bart Bruno believes that *P. c. affinis* and *P. c. sayi* exhibit a close relationship that separates them from the pine snake group to the east and the Rocky Mt. and Pacific Coast-ranging gopher snakes to the west. Of 15 Guadalupe Mountains *Pituophis catenifer,* 8 had higher, slightly narrower, bullsnake-type rostral scales, 5 were intermediate between the bullsnake and gopher snake, and 2 had the broader, lower rostral scale typical of the Sonoran gopher snake. For other similar snakes see Bullsnake (67).

Behavior   Large size, diurnal foraging, and slow gait make adult *Pituophis* ill suited for either flight or concealment, leaving dramatic posturing as this reptile's principal defensive strategy. By raising its forebody, puffing its neck, and rapidly vibrating its tail a large individual can present nearly as intimidating a facade as a big rattlesnake, especially when it slides forward a few feet toward its attacker. Contributing to this bluff is the fin of throat cartilage that protects the trachea from swallowed prey animals. When *P. catenifer* exhales sharply, this flap reverberates in a glottal reverberation startlingly suggestive of a rattlesnake's warning tail buzz.

9 Texas Glossy Snake
Arizona elegans arenicola

Nonvenomous   Large individuals may bite if molested.

Abundance   Uncommon in the northeastern part of its range—a long peninsula of sandy-soiled terrain stretching northwest from the Rio Grande plain across the north central Cross Timbers—A. e. arenicola is one of the more abundant serpents encountered on warm spring and early summer nights south of Falfurrias and Hebbronville.

Size   Adults are most often 20 to 30 inches in length, and rarely grow longer than 3 feet. Recorded to 54⅝ inches.

Habitat   *Arizona* means "dry land," and *arenicola* means "sand-loving." Both names aptly describe the siliceous habitat of glossy snakes. In the northeastern part of the range this is usually sandy pasture used for growing bermuda grass hay, where the author has found Texas glossy snakes in Lee and Milam counties.

Much farther from its South Texas population center, A. e. arenicola was first recorded east of the Trinity River by James Dixon of Texas A&M University, who defined this subspecies in 1960. South of San Antonio this reptile is more numerous, but it is abundant only from Duval Co. to the Mexican border. Occasionally found in cropland, it is more often resident here in the Tamaulipan thorn woodland of the coastal plain.

Prey   Based on the behavior of recent captives, *Arizona elegans* feeds mainly on lacertillian prey (whiptails, racerunners, and spiny lizards are numerous in the Texas glossy's range), scented out after dark while they sleep. Small mammals are probably also sometimes taken, although few newly-caught specimens accept mice as prey.

Reproduction   Egg-laying. Little is recorded, but in September and early October up to 2 dozen young, 9½ to 11 inches in length, emerge from buried clutches of 2¾ inch-long eggs.

Coloring/scale form   The Texas glossy snake's dorsolateral ground color is off-white, marked by 41 to 60 (average 50) large brown vertebral blotches with very thin dark borders. Its definitive marking, however, unique to glossy snakes, is the pale longitudinal line that runs along its spine just behind the crown; a brown band masks the eyes and crosses the cheeks. The smooth dorsal scales, which reflect the nacreous patina suggested by the glossy's name, occur in 29 to 35 (average 32) rows at midbody, there are 2 prefrontal scales, the venter is uniformly white, and the anal plate is undivided. See illustration at **Bullsnake (67)**.

Similar snakes   See **Kansas Glossy Snake (70)**.

Behavior   All three of Texas' glossy snake races are thought to have once been members of an ancient, xeric-adapted fauna that occupied a dry corridor joining the desert Southwest to the Florida peninsula. After this arid-land community was fragmented by the cooler, wetter climate that prevailed along the Gulf Coast during the late Pleistocene, A. e. arenicola survived in relict populations living on sandy, desert-like soil well into the eastern part of Texas. Here, as in the southern part of its range, A. e. arenicola is almost never seen above ground except well after dark.

BROWN-BLOTCHED TERRESTRIAL SNAKES

70 Kansas Glossy Snake
Arizona elegans elegans

Nonvenomous   See **Texas Glossy Snake (69)**.

Abundance   Northwest of a line through Del Rio, San Saba, and Gainesville, the Texas glossy snake, *A. e. arenicola,* is replaced by its western plains and Chihuahuan Desert subspecies, *Arizona elegans elegans* (*elegans* refers to this animal's presumably elegant dorsolateral patterning). The Kansas race is distinguished from the Texas glossy snake by its slightly more numerous (41 to 69, average 55) vertebral blotches and its lower number of dorsal scale rows (29 to 31 at midbody, average 30).

Size   Though perhaps a bit larger on the average (adults range from 20 to 47 inches in length), the Kansas glossy snake is similar to the Texas glossy in its behavior, scalation, and reproductive cycle, as well as in its predominantly sandy-soil habitat.

Prey   Similar to Texas glossy snake—mostly lizards (side-blotched and earless lizards are numerous in this reptile's range). Kangaroo and pocket mice have been found in the same burrows as Kansas glossy snakes, however, and captives are reportedly often willing to accept mice as food.

Habitat   Although widespread, *A. e. elegans* seems to be either very spottily distributed or only sporadically abroad on the surface. Perhaps both are the case for, like other races of glossy snake, its abundance seems to vary radically from place to place within its range. For example, Jameson and Flury's (1949) exhaustive West Texas fieldwork failed to yield a single Kansas glossy snake, yet *A. e. elegans* was more numerous than any other snake collected by McKinney and Ballinger (1966) in the lower Panhandle. In a different locale, Frederick Gehlbach of Baylor University found this race of glossy snake to be not uncommon in the shrub desert around the Guadalupe Mountains, while Abilene Zoo director Jack Joy reports that large *Arizona elegans elegans* with a faintly pinkish ground color and olive-brown dorsal blotches are found regularly in Tom Green Co. Elsewhere in its broad Texas range the Kansas glossy snake is seldom reported.

Similar snakes   The Kansas glossy snake is paler, with slightly less distinct dorsolateral patterning than its subspecies, the **Texas glossy snake (69)**. It also has statistically more numerous dorsal blotches (41 to 69, average 55) and fewer dorsal scale rows (29 to 31, average 30). The **bullsnake (67)** has a pale, speckled head, keeled dorsal scales, 4 prefrontal scales and an enlarged rostral scale, and lacks the glossy snake's whitish vertebral line along the nape.

The **prairie kingsnake (76)** also lacks the glossy snake's light vertebral line just behind the head, while its venter is pigmented with dark brown squares. The **Texas night snake (87)** has a prominent chocolate-colored blotch of either side of its neck, an irregularly-shaped dark vertebral bar just posterior to its crown, and a divided anal plate.

1 Painted Desert Glossy Snake

Arizona elegans philipi

El Paso Co. and a bit of western Hudspeth Co. harbor animals found nowhere else in Texas, primarily because of this area's long stretch of sand dunes. This Sahara-like milieu harbors a biotic community that includes such xeric, sand-adapted animals as the Apache pocket mouse and the most westerly of Texas' glossy snakes, *Arizona elegans philipi*. The Painted Desert glossy snake, whose subspecies name honors Philip M. Klauber, son of L. M. Klauber, the world-famous authority on rattlesnakes, is similar to the state's two more easterly glossy snake subspecies in most physical respects, and in places other than the West Texas dunes its favored habitat is the same: mostly creosote- and blackbrush-covered sandy or gravelly slopes, sagebrush flats, and grassland. Throughout the rest of the western Trans-Pecos, this race intergrades with its sub-species the **Kansas Glossy Snake (70)**.

The Painted Desert glossy snake's activity cycle is one of exclusively nocturnal foraging on the surface and subterranean retreat during dawn, daylight, and dusk. Its reproductive behavior, size, and preferred prey parallel those of Texas and Kansas glossy snakes (*A. e. arenicola* and *A. e. elegans,* respectively); but *A. e. philipi* differs from those more eastern glossy snake races by having a higher number of body blotches (average 64.2), a slightly longer tail (about 15% of its total length), and a slightly lower average (27) number of dorsal scale rows.

Like most arid-land reptiles, whose dorsolateral camouflage coloring must mirror the glaucous hue of the prevailing desert substrate, the Painted Desert glossy snake is paler than its eastern relatives, with its golden brown dorsal blotches often compressed over the spine into a waisted, hourglass shape. The white vertebral stripe along the neck typical of all glossy snakes is present, but the Painted Desert glossy snake lacks the well-defined dark mask of its more easterly subspecies; a faint umber line running from its eye to the corner of its jaw suggests this marking, however.

72 Texas Rat Snake
Elaphe obsoleta lindheimerii

Nonvenomous   Texas rat snakes are vigorous in their own defense and if threatened, may make several bluffing, open-mouthed strikes. Pressed further, *E. o. lindheimerii* will bite—though the pressure of its jaws is so light that only scratches usually result—defecate, and emit foul-smelling musk from its cloacal glands.

Abundance   Very common. The Texas rat snake is the long, dark brown-mottled snake that most often appears in suburban areas throughout the eastern half of the state. It is the one most likely to be found high in trees, hidden in barn rafters or attics, or in abandoned automobiles or machinery. After the grayish young hatch in late summer, they often appear around suburban houses and, like the adults, bite when picked up.

Size   Adult *E. o. lindheimerii* are long and slender, averaging 42 to 72 inches—a length which in East Texas has earned the Texas rat snake the nickname "piney woods python"; the record is just over 7 feet.

Habitat   Abundant in both deciduous woods and pastureland, this reptile (named for pioneer Texas naturalist Frederick Jacob Lindheimer) also occurs in almost every terrestrial and aquatic-margin environment from East Texas pine forest to coastal prairie marsh.

Prey   Adult *E. o. lindheimerii* feed almost entirely on warm-blooded prey, and are a major predator on birds and their nestlings. (A flock of screaming blue jays and other passerines screaming retaliation at a Texas rat snake coiled high in the branches is a common woodland sight.) Also called "chicken snake" for its attraction to henhouses, *E. o. lindheimerii* is equally likely to be seen by suburban residents who set out caged birds on their patios. Small mammals are also primary prey, with larger ones being overpowered by constriction.

Reproduction   Egg-laying. Hatchling Texas rat snakes are 12 to 14 inches long, with lead-gray crowns striped by a pair of solid chocolate lines that form a forward-facing spearpoint. Another chocolate band masks the eyes and extends rearward to the posterior upper labials.

Coloring/scale form   Texas rat snakes' dark brown, rectangular vertebral blotches are separated by yellowish brown transverse areas about 4 scale rows in width; reddish skin may be evident on the sides of the neck. Older adults are much darker in color. The pale venter is blotched with dark squares partially obscured by a grayish overwash, while the underside of the tail tip is usually solid gray. Of the 27 midbody rows of dorsal scales, those along the spine are most strongly keeled; the anal plate is divided.

Similar snakes   In the northeastern tip of the state, the Texas rat snake intergrades with *E. obsoleta*, the **black rat snake**. Adult **Baird's rat snakes (73)** are faintly striped above and lack dorsal blotches. Juvenile **great plains rat snakes (74)** have a black-edged brown V on their pale crowns and a pale subcaudal centerline. The **prairie kingsnake (76)** has smooth scales and an undivided anal plate.

Behavior   The Texas rat snake's wiry musculature and sharp-edged belly scales—which it can dig like spikes into tree bark—make it an agile climber, but it also frequently patrols creek banks from the water.

Baird's Rat Snake
Elaphe bairdi

Nonvenomous   Although some Baird's rat snakes are entirely non-aggressive, even when first picked up in the field, other individuals may hiss and nip if cornered.

Abundance   Very uncommon. *Elaphe bairdi* is spottily dispersed throughout the central Hill Country (backroads in the vicinity of Leakey, Vanderpool, and Barksdale are the sites of numerous nocturnal sightings, especially after summer rainfall). This snake is found less often in the Trans-Pecos.

Size   Most adults are between 24 and 40 inches long; one enormous specimen measured 62 inches.

Habitat   *Elaphe bairdi* is principally an inhabitant of the Cretaceous limestone canyons of the Edwards Plateau, as well as of both montane forest and low-lying desert in the Trans-Pecos. Although this range includes some of the most arid terrain in Texas, most of this area is composed of unsuitable habitat, with the result that Baird's rat snakes are found most often in mesic canyon communities; one small male taken just before shedding was unable to rid itself of its old skin until it had soaked in a pan of water for several days.

Prey   Like other rat snakes, *Elaphe bairdi* is a generalized predator, constricting prey that includes birds and their eggs, lizards, rodents and other small mammals. Lizards may be taken by the young.

Reproduction   Egg-laying. Mating during May and early June results in the midsummer deposition of usually fewer than 10, 1¾ by 1 inch, smooth-shelled eggs (which adhere to form a single cluster). These hatch in 70 to 85 days into 11-to 13-inch-long cross-banded gray offspring, which experience an ontogenetic color and pattern change as they mature: During their second year their prominent cross-dorsal lines merge into the faint longitudinal stripes of the adult.

Coloring/scale form   Beneath a translucent sheen, the Baird's rat snake's forebody is washed with a golden tint—the result of myriad tiny orangish crescents, one of which rims the forward margin of each dorsal scale. (A rare, yellowish-tan color phase dimly marked with gray stripes occurs to the west of Big Bend.) The lips and chin are light gray-brown to pale yellow, colors that continue beneath the forebelly, then darken to pale salmon, scalloped with gray, under the tail. The weakly keeled dorsal scales are arranged in 27 rows at midbody and the anal plate is divided.

Similar snakes   The adult **Texas rat snake (72)** has a dark brown head and neck, as well as rectangular chocolate blotches along its trunk.

Behavior   Like the Baird's sparrow and sandpiper, this animal's name honors zoologist Spencer Fullerton Baird, secretary of the Smithsonian Institution throughout the second third of the nineteenth century. A great rival of U.S. Boundary Commissioner William Hemsley Emory (for whom the Great Plains rat snake, *E. g. emoryi,* is named in spite of the fact that Baird first described it), Baird encouraged much of the burst of zoological activity that accompanied the opening of the West. Often in partnership with Charles Frederich Girard, he first described some 24 of Texas' ophidian species and subspecies, including the western diamondback rattlesnake, the Texas rat snake, the black-striped snake, the desert kingsnake, Schott's whipsnake, and the Texas coral snake.

74 Great Plains Rat Snake
Elaphe guttata emoryi

Nonvenomous   Although a large individual may nip if picked up roughly, most Great Plains rat snakes are docile and easily handled.

Abundance   Common. *Elaphe guttata emoryi* is widely distributed and may be found in nearly every terrestrial macrohabitat within the state. It seems to be most numerous, however, on the southern coastal plain.

Size   Most adults are 2½ to 3½ feet; the record is 60¼ inches.

Habitat   Great Plains rat snakes occupy terrain that varies from upland prairie to coastal tidewater marsh to East Texas bottomland forest. In the western part of the state this animal is found in both the arid Northern Chihuahuan Desert and rocky montane forest.

Elaphe guttata emoryi is also more of a chthonic creature than is generally recognized, for it is a common inhabitant not only of creviced canyon walls, but of deep, inaccessible caves: Webb (1970) reports one individual found 60 feet below the surface. Subterranean caverns offer food in the warmer months; like Texas' other rat snakes, *E. g. emoryi* is a regular predator on Mexican free-tailed bat nursery colonies. In winter, caves, rock quarries, and abandoned building foundations offer temperate shelter. Here, Great Plains rat snakes have been found brumating in company with both Texas rat snakes and copperheads; the cellar of one derelict farmhouse in Woods Co. Oklahoma housed 6 wintering Great Plains rat snakes and 27 eastern yellowbelly racers.

Prey   *Elaphe guttata emoryi* eats mostly warm-blooded animals that it kills by constriction. Rodents, as well as birds and their young are primary prey. (South of Marathon I found a Great Plains rat snake wedging its way up the furrowed bark of a cottonwood in whose lower branches a pair of vermillion flycatchers were frantically defending their nest.) Frogs and lizards are also sometimes preyed upon, but smaller snakes are not ordinarily taken.

Reproduction   Egg-laying. The record-sized clutch is probably that of a Murchison Co. female maintained by Gus Renfro that deposited 25 fertile eggs during the first week in July. The first description of reproduction—of a more typical clutch of 15—was published, however, by John E. Werler (1951):

> On June 14 . . . a 44¾-inch-long female from near Brownsville laid 5 smooth, adhesive eggs. Ten more were deposited the following day, averaging 1.8 inches in length, 1.1 inches in width. Slits first appeared in 2 of the eggs on Aug. 7, and these snakes emerged from their shells on August 8. Two additional snakes escaped from their shells on August 9, another on August 10, and the last two on August 12.

The young ranged in length from 14.6 to 15.6 inches. Another set of smaller, 11-inch-long hatchlings I maintained had grown to about 29 inches in length after 14 months; at 9 years of age one of these animals measured 44 inches in length and weighed just under 3 pounds.

Coloring/scale form   Dorsal patterning involves some geographic variation. As the background substrate, against which snakes' dorsal camouflage determines their survival, lightens as one moves westward, many *E. guttata* exhibit gradually lightening ground color. In southwest Texas most *E. guttata* are paler and grayer, with smaller and more numerous dorsal blotches, than easterly specimens. (One recorded by D. Craig McIntyre at Presidio, on the western edge of the species' range, had nearly 80 dorsal blotches so abbreviated they resembled thin crossbars.)

Ventral and subcaudal scale counts are also a bit higher in Southwest Texas and work by Hobart M. Smith et. al (1994) proposes that this southwestern population be classified as a new subspecies, *E. g. meahllmorum.*

Individuals from Central and North Texas tend to have larger, darker brown vertebral blotches on a medium brown ground color, while a few Great Plains rat snakes from East Texas have reddish backs and necks like the corn snake, an eastern race that lives on russet-hued oak leaves and pine needles.

The Great Plains rat snake's most distinctive marking, however, is the diamond-shaped brown band, whose apex lies between the eyes, that patterns its crown; juvenile Great Plains rat snakes have a dark-edged brown mask. The venter is blotched with brown—more heavily in eastern specimens—while the distinctive underside of the tail has a pair of dark distal stripes bordering a pale central line. Among all *Elaphe guttata,* the 27 to 29 midbody rows of dorsal scales are weakly keeled along the spine; the anal plate is divided.

Similar snakes   The **prairie kingsnake (76)** has smooth dorsal scales and an undivided anal plate. Adult **Texas rat snakes (72)** have uniformly dark brown heads and necks and uniformly gray undertails; juveniles have a lead-gray crown and a solid chocolate eye mask. **Glossy snakes (68—70)** have a pale line along the nape, a white venter, and an undivided anal plate.

Behavior   This abundant but secretive reptile is named for William Hemsley Emory, the long-whiskered United States Boundary Commissioner who, in authorizing the initial mapping of the Texas-Mexican border, subsequently saw his name attached to several plant (Emory oak) and animal species first described by members of his survey expeditions, as well as to the highest peak in Big Bend.

Predominantly nocturnal during its March to October activity period, *E. g. emoryi* emerges from hiding only well after dark. When rainstorms drive most terrestrial snakes to shelter, Great Plains rat snakes are typically the first serpents to emerge again onto the wet nighttime pavement; in West Texas very large individuals are sometimes flushed from their subsurface haunts by flash flooding. See **Bullsnake (67).**

75 Trans-Pecos Rat Snake
Bogertophis subocularis

Nonvenomous   Trans-Pecos rat snakes almost never defend themselves against human beings.

Abundance   Uncommon, but not rare. *Bogertophis subocularis* is one of those cryptic, mostly subterranean Chihuahuan Desert serpents that are widespread yet seldom seen except on warm, humid nights during the breeding season in May and June. For the most part "Subocs"—as these snakes are termed by the enthusiasts who seek them out here—appear only on backroads in Val Verde, Terrell, Presidio, Brewster, and Jeff Davis counties, although one was found crossing US Highway 90 between WalMart and Luby's in Del Rio.

Size   Only adult *B. subocularis* measuring 30 to 48 inches in length are normally seen in the wild—though I found one 12¾-inch-long neonate with a fresh umbilical scar in Big Bend in late September. Specimens have been recorded to 5½ feet.

Habitat   The Trans-Pecos rat snake's macrohabitat is barren flats and succulent desert slopes of ocotillo, lechuguilla, and sotol cactus in the northern Chihuahuan Desert; microhabitat includes rocky outcroppings and road-cuts. A less xeric environment in which this species also occurs is the oak-juniper woodland (sometimes at altitudes above 5,000 feet) of West Texas' "mountain islands."

Prey   Despite the lacertillian food preferences of some wild-caught individuals, *B. subocularis* is probably a generalized feeder on smaller vertebrates with the exception of other snakes. I have seen one of these animals coiled on a caveside ledge just below a mass of flightless young Mexican free-tailed bats, on which it was undoubtedly feeding.

Reproduction   Egg-laying. First accomplished by Jonathan Campbell at the Fort Worth Zoo during the 1960s, captive propagation has since become widespread. Twenty-five pairings among *B. subocularis* maintained by D. Craig McIntyre reveal that only during a brief annual fertility cycle will the female accept a mate, for nearly all these copulations took place between June 18 and 30.

Deposited during July, August, and September, the proportionately large eggs range from 3 to 11 per clutch, and require a comparatively long incubation of up to 88 days. (Some *B. subocularis* clutches have taken more than 100 days to hatch, but because serpent embryos begin developing as soon as the egg is formed, longer incubation in the nest cavity may only mean that the mother has not retained her eggs internally for as long as females whose eggs hatch after shorter incubation.)

This species' long incubation and late-season breeding pattern—one road-killed Davis Mts. female was still gravid with unlaid eggs in late August, and the eggs of captives often hatch as late as Thanksgiving—means that the higher elevations of this animal's range have become quite cold by the time its young are ready to emerge. Rather than face this hostile time of year newborns may remain below ground until the following spring, perhaps rarely emerging at all during their first year. (Very small individuals have been found in June, and it has even been postulated that springtime deposition of eggs fertilized the previous autumn may rarely occur.)

Delicate little creatures 11½ to 13 inches in length, hatchling *B. subocularis* are paler than the adults but share the same dorsal pattern. Sexual maturity is reached in 2 to 3 years, and fertility can last for at least an additional 13 seasons as some of McIntyre's females have produced fertile eggs at more than 16 years of age. One individual captured as an adult in 1971 has since laid more than 60 eggs and holds the species' longevity record of 26 years.

Coloring/scale form   Against a soft, mustard-brown dorsolateral ground color two parallel black lines are joined by 27 to 41 intervening crossbars that form a series of H-shaped patterns along the spine. On the tail these crossbars become small saddles. (A few *B. subocularis* from southern Brewster and southern Presidio counties, have a paler, yellowish ground color with faint vertebral patterning. Individuals from north of El Paso are reportedly also sometimes lighter-hued, but grayish.)

Because Trans-Pecos rat snakes are highly regarded by reptile fanciers—besides its unique coloring, this nocturnal reptile's big dark eyes make it appealing to humans—breeders have exaggerated these naturally occurring color morphs into almost pastel-hued *B. subocularis* with separate, rounded dorsal blotches.

The Trans-Pecos rat snake is unique among North American serpents in possessing 40 pairs of chromosomes instead of the usual allotment of 36 or 38, while its scalation is also unusual. A row of small subocular scutes (possessed by no other North American snake, and from which the species' Latin name, *subocularis*, is derived) separates the scales of its upper lip from the eye. The venter is a silky off-white on the throat that darkens to olive-buff by midbody; some individuals show dim undertail striping. Only the 7 vertebral rows of dorsal scales, which occur in 31 to 35 rows at midbody, are keeled. The anal plate is divided.

Similar snakes   Formerly classified with other North American rat snakes in the genus *Elaphe,* in 1988 the Trans-Pecos rat snake was shown by H. G. Dowling and R. Price to be genetically distinct enough to warrant its taxonomic placement in the separate genus, *Bogertophis,* along with another desert-living colubrid, the Baja California rat snake, *Bogertophis rosaliae.* No other Texas serpent shares either the Trans-Pecos rat snake's unique mustard-brown dorsolateral ground color or its distinctive dark vertebral pattern.

Behavior   Like many xeric-adapted reptiles *B. subocularis* responds to the harsh climate of its Chihuahuan Desert range by restricting its movements on the surface to temperate summer nights. During the day, as well as for winter brumation, it withdraws into mammal burrows or descends into the desert's subsurface labyrinth of creviced limestone. Living mostly in this sheltered milieu, the Trans-Pecos rat snake may have never needed to evolve fight-or-flight behavior for, illuminated by headlights, *B. subocularis* typically makes no attempt to escape when approached on foot, lying quietly instead as if in a trance.

Another result of long periods spent underground is vulnerability to parasites which need darkness and humidity. One is a tick, *Aponomma elephensis,* first identified by W. G. and P. B. Degenhardt, that is found on no other living creature. A large number of these arachnids may congregate near the tip of the Trans-Pecos rat snake's tail, reportedly siphoning away enough blood to cause the terminal inch or two to mortify and drop off. This must be a rare occurrence, however, for of dozens of wild-caught *B. subocularis* I have yet to see one with a stub tail.

76 Prairie Kingsnake
Lampropeltis calligaster calligaster

Nonvenomous   This mild-tempered reptile may vibrate its tail in fear, but even when picked up in the wild it seldom nips humans.

Abundance   Uncommon. Prairie kingsnakes are widely distributed across the eastern half of Texas, but their burrowing lifestyle is so secretive that they are only rarely seen.

Size   Adults average 2 to 3 feet; the record is 58⅛ inches.

Habitat   As its common name implies, the prairie kingsnake is predominantly an inhabitant of grassland. This includes the dry, tallgrass prairie of Central and North Central Texas, moist salt-grass savannah along the upper Gulf Coast, and the grassy dunes of coastal barrier islands from Lavaca Bay to Sabine Pass, where piles of driftwood on the leeward side of the island are good microhabitat. Less often occupied are rocky hillsides and riparian woodland, but even in forested areas the prairie kingsnake is entirely terrestrial.

Prey   Like other kingsnakes, *L. c. calligaster* is a powerful constrictor, but one more oriented toward warm-blooded prey than other kingsnakes: Food animals include mice, rats, gophers, moles, and birds. Frogs and toads, lizards, and other snakes are also reported as prey.

Reproduction   Egg-laying. No natural nests are recorded but hatchling *L. c. calligaster* evidently live deeply fossorial lives: No wild newborns have ever been observed. In captivity, clutches of 6 to 17 smooth-shelled eggs are deposited during late June and July, hatching into relatively small, 6- to 8-inch-long young that feed readily on anoles, ground skinks, and small snakes; one specimen has been maintained at the Oklahoma City Zoo for over 13 years.

Coloring/scale form   The prairie kingsnake's yellow-brown dorsal ground color is marked with 50 or more irregular brown dorsal saddles; its sides are marked with jagged brown spots. A ground-colored vertebral strip stretches forward from the anterior back to a spearpoint-shaped marking on its crown, while a dark lateral stripe masks the eyes.

  Lampropeltis calligaster calligaster also exhibits ontogenetic color variation, darkening with age and sometimes developing, from its dorsal blotches, four dimly defined dusky stripes or even, among very old prairie kingsnakes, a solid umber back. The yellowish to cloudy gray venter–*calligaster* means "beautiful belly"–is checked with large, squarish rusty-brown blotches. The smooth dorsal scales occur in 25 to 27 midbody rows; the anal plate is undivided.

Similar snakes   The **Great Plains rat snake (74)** has weakly keeled vertebral scales, a pale buff rather than olive-brown ground color, a dark-edged undertail tip and a divided anal plate. **Texas (69)** and **Kansas (70) glossy snakes** have a pale longitudinal line along the nape, at least 29 rows of dorsal scales, and an unmarked white venter.

Behavior   Prairie kingsnakes are secretive reptiles that seldom emerge from beneath rocks, clumps of grass, or the depths of small-mammal burrows except for limited surface foraging, which typically occurs at dusk in spring and fall, but only well after dark during the hottest months. These animals are also occasionally encountered crossing roads on still, humid spring and summer nights, and because most such individuals are males, many are probably engaged in the search for a reproductively receptive female's pheromone scent trail.

77 Speckled Kingsnake

Lampropeltis getula holbrooki

Nonvenomous   If molested, the speckled kingsnake may swell its neck, then both bite and chew with determination. If treated gently, however, this reptile quickly becomes accustomed to handling, although if one's hands should smell of prey, it may try an exploratory nip.

Abundance   Fairly common. During wet spring weather, in good East Texas bottomland as well as along the upper coast *L. g. holbrooki* may be abundant.

Size   Recorded to 74 inches in length, adult speckled kingsnakes are robust, cylindrically-bodied reptiles whose muscular necks are nearly as large in diameter as their heads. Most adults are 18 to 36 inches long; hatchlings are 6 to 9 inches in length and about the thickness of a pencil.

Habitat   *Lampropeltis getula holbrooki* occupies a variety of terrestrial and semi-aquatic environments, among them pine and deciduous woodland (where rotting logs and stumps are a favored microhabitat), grassy pastures, estuarine coastal marshes, including saline tidal flats, and succulent-covered barrier beach dunes—where speckled kings are found sheltering beneath piles of driftwood. Intergrade individuals exhibiting the genetic influence of the subspecies desert kingsnake inhabit both the Crosstimbers and non-agriculturalized microhabitats within the Blackland Prairie.

Prey   Speckled kingsnakes are scent-oriented hunters that prey on a variety of smaller vertebrates. Other snakes, including members of their own species, as well as venomous pitvipers are also devoured. Although pitvipers are formidable adversaries that may strike and envenomate them repeatedly, kingsnakes are largely immune to Crotalid venom and overcome these vipers by immobilizing them with powerful constriction. Then the kingsnake's robust neck and jaw muscles let it quickly work its way forward to engulf the head of the serpent about to be swallowed. Small mammals, birds, fish, and frogs are also taken; a favorite food is turtle eggs.

Reproduction   Egg-laying. See **Desert Kingsnake (78)**.

Coloring/scale form   Each shiny black or dark brown dorsal scale bears a yellowish-white spot. Juveniles are more profusely light-freckled than adults because their scales are smaller, and many of their light-colored spots are clumped together in pale lines that cross the back, leaving dark intervening areas. The venter is predominantly yellow, checked or blotched with black, the dorsal scales are smooth and arranged in 21 to 23 rows at midbody, and the anal plate is undivided.

Similar snakes   In a band ranging in width from fifty miles at the Gulf Coast to nearly 300 miles along the Red River, the speckled kingsnake occupies an overlapping range with its western subspecies, the **desert kingsnake (78),** which is distinguished by its predominantly black venter and crown, its 23 to 25 dorsal scale rows, and its mostly black or dark brown dorsolateral scales.

Behavior   *Lampropeltis getula holbrooki* is almost always encountered on the ground where, as a slow-moving serpent, its principal defense against large predators is to retreat into burrows or beneath sheltering debris. It can also climb, although slowly, and swim well, as it often does in both flooded bottomland and tidal flat milieus.

LARGE KINGSNAKES

78 Desert Kingsnake
Lampropeltis getula splendida

Nonvenomous Confronted with a large predator, the desert kingsnake may still put on a valiant defensive display, drawing its neck into an S-shaped curve, vibrating its tailtip and striking openmouthed.

Abundance Uncommon. *Lampropeltis getula splendida* is widespread but not numerous except in the thorn brush country of South Texas and, as an intergrade, in the central Blackland Prairie. Desert kingsnakes also range throughout extensive montane areas west of the Pecos River, but they are not common there or in the Chihuahuan Desert. In this part of the state large individuals may remain below ground most of the time, however. In Andrews Co., after torrential rains had flooded many snakes from their subsurface haunts, Damon Salceies found a gravid female *L. g. splendida* almost five feet long. See **Bullsnake (67)**.

Size Most adults average 22 to 38 inches; the record is 60 inches.

Habitat The desert kingsnake may occur in any rural habitat in the western half of the state but, despite its common name, it is most likely to be found in mesic parts of its range, especially near water tanks or within riparian corridors. Prairie grasslands are also good desert kingsnake habitat, and road-killed specimens are often seen in the vicinity of the Marfa lights viewing area.

Prey *Lampropeltis getula splendida* feeds on other snakes, lizards, and small mammals, as well as on clutches of reptile eggs detected beneath the surface by smell. In part because of their resistance to pitviper venom, desert kingsnakes are able to prey on the young diamondback rattlesnakes that are common within their range, and at even the scent of *L. getula* adult western diamondbacks edge hastily backward, shielding their heads with defensive loops of their bodies.

Reproduction Egg-laying. Courtship and copulation among *L. g. splendida* occurs between March and June. Clutches of 5 to 12 adhesive-surfaced eggs are deposited in late June or July, sometimes buried as deeply as a foot to prevent drying through their moisture-permeable shells. After about 60 days of incubation the 8½- to 10-inch-long hatchlings emerge, weighing about ⅓ ounce and as shiny as porcelain figurines. Brightly yellow-speckled in vertebral cross-lines, they also exhibit a lateral row of big, dark brown spots which, as they mature are gradually fragmented by encroaching yellow flecks.

Coloring/scale form The desert kingsnake's glossy dorsum is black or very dark brown, finely speckled with off-white or yellow. These pale flecks form dimly-defined narrow vertebral crossbands, between which the intervening rectangular areas are black. Pale yellow scales may predominate along the lower sides. The venter of both adult and young is mostly black, with white or pale yellow blotches marking the outer ends of the ventral plates. The smooth dorsal scales are arranged in 23 to 25 rows at midbody and the anal plate is undivided.

Similar snakes Throughout Central Texas intergrades with the **speckled kingsnake (77)** prevail, and while individuals with characteristics of both subspecies occur, the speckled kingsnake is distinguished by its predominantly yellow- or white-spotted body and head, its mainly yellow, black-blotched venter, and its 21 to 23 rows of dorsal scales.

Behavior See Speckled Kingsnake (77).

Louisiana Milk Snake
Lampropeltis triangulum amaura

Nonvenomous   Louisiana milk snakes seldom bite even if picked up. Like other members of the kingsnake family, occasional individuals may nip tenaciously, but most *L. t. amaura* are so small that their nips are inconsequential.

Abundance   Very uncommon. Louisiana milk snakes are widespread, but rarely encountered because of their retiring, semi-subterranean lifestyle. Because of their bright colors, *L. triangulum* are avidly sought by reptile enthusiasts, and for years every subspecies was protected from capture in Texas. Collectors' impact on the natural population is now thought to have been minimal, however, and despite major inroads into the Louisiana race's habitat by timbering and land clearing, *L. triangulum* is no longer protected as a threatened animal.

Size   Recorded to 31 inches in length, most adult *L. t. amaura* are much smaller, averaging only 16 to 24 inches and no thicker than one's forefinger.

Habitat   The Louisiana milk snake's two primary habitats are A. the upper coastal plain, where it is often found beneath driftwood, planks, and littoral debris marking the spring tide line of the Gulf barrier islands, and B. East Texas' riparian bottomland. Here, Louisiana milk snakes are cryptic, fossorial inhabitants of forest floor debris, except when the ground is inundated, usually by late winter rainfall. At this time, milk snakes are sometimes found wedged into the narrow space beneath the loosening bark of dead longleaf and loblolly pines. (Because the soil is frequently saturated for months on end in these riverbottom areas, milk snakes' winter brumation also occurs deep within such elevated dead trunks and stumps.)

Prey   Much of the diet of *L. t. amaura* consists of the small serpents that, along with its secondary prey of skinks and spiny lizards, share its forest-floor microhabitat of leaf litter and humus. Mice and small rodents are also taken by the larger adults.

Reproduction   Egg-laying. See **Central Plains Milk Snake (82).**

Coloring/scale form   The typical Louisiana milk snake is characterized by a black snout, which is often so mottled with white that the animal seems to have been nosing into flour; the posterior portion of its head is entirely black, followed by a pale collar. Broad red bands, ranging in number from 13 to 21 (average 16.2), are spaced along its trunk, pinched in at the belly line by narrower black borders. Between these black rings are light-hued bands whose color varies from pale yellow among the population living in the southern, coastal section of the range (therefore subject to gene flow from the deep yellow-banded Mexican milk snake) to white in Northeast Texas. In both areas, the belly is predominantly pale along a central strip where the red and black pigment that encroaches onto the outer portion of the ventral scales seldom intrudes.

As this color variation suggests, Texas' four races of milk snakes are difficult to define with precision because their ranges overlap so intricately. Not only are there broad zones of intergradation where the territories of adjacently-ranging subspecies meet, but Bern Tryon of the Knoxville Zoo has written that *throughout* the ranges of all Texas' milksnakes, individuals typical of neighboring races can be found. For example, D. Craig McIntyre found a perfectly typical Louisiana milk snake in LaSalle County, deep within the range of the Mexican milk snake.

Arranged in 21 midbody rows, the dorsal scales are smooth; the anal plate is undivided.

Similar snakes   Milk snakes' red and pale yellow or white dorsal hues never touch as they do on the **Texas coral snake (91)**. Unlike *L. triangulum,* the coral snake has wide black body bands (as broad as its red ones) and a divided anal plate.

The red dorsolateral bands of the **Mexican milk snake (80)** seldom narrow at the belly line and are generally darker along the spine; it has a black-blotched midventral area and a black snout. The **Central Plains milk snake (82)** has more profuse white flecks on its head and snout, and a higher number—20 to 32 (average 25.6)—of narrower, more orangish dorsolateral rings. The **Texas longnose snake (88)** has roughly rectangular red and black vertebral saddles above black-speckled yellowish lower sides. It has 23 rows of dorsal scales, its unmarked venter is white, its elongate snout is tan, and under its tail is a single row of subcaudal scales unlike the double row of the milk and other nonvenomous snakes. The **northern scarlet snake (84)** has a pointed red snout, an unmarked white belly, 19 midbody rows of dorsal scales, and red dorsolateral saddles that do not reach the venter.

Behavior   *Lampropeltis triangulum amaura* is a cool-weather reptile, suffering less inhibition of movement from lowered temperatures than most other snakes. (In chilly conditions that render neighboring serpents so slow-moving that photographing them is relatively easy, Louisiana milk snakes still present a fast-wriggling challenge.) This trait enables *L. t. amaura* to forage later into the fall—and begin breeding earlier in the spring—than most southern woodland serpents.

It also adapts these animals to hunt effectively during the cooler hours of darkness, to which their coloring is also suited because milk snakes' dramatically contrasting dorsal hues may function in the same way as does the coral snakes' bold pattern, as camouflage. Although milk snakes' bright colors instantly draw attention in daylight, those bright dorsolateral hues act as camouflage at night—the only time that milk snakes forage on the surface—when red looks gray to even color-visioned snake predators such as owls, while the mammalian carnivores that feed on small terrestrial serpents are largely color-blind. Moreover, by approximating dark shadows, the milk snake's black crossbands break up the visual continuity of its serpentine shape while its intervening pale dorsolateral rings further fragment its profile against the light-dappled patchwork of the nighttime forest floor. That its contrasting body bands are effective in either hiding from (or perhaps deterring) larger carnivores is confirmed by the fact that coral snakes and milk snakes have a significantly lower incidence of tail loss and other predator-caused injury than do non-banded serpents.

Mexican Milk Snake
Lampropeltis triangulum annulata

Nonvenomous   Mexican milk snakes grow large enough to bite in self-defense, but do so only if seized roughly.

Abundance   Uncommon. *Lampropeltis triangulum annulata* is widespread throughout both the "brush country" of South Texas and the irrigated farmland that has replaced much of it.

Size   The largest of Texas' milksnakes, adult *L. t. annulata* average 20 to 32 inches in length. The record is a truly huge—for a milk snake—54 inches.

Habitat   Mexican milk snakes are most often observed in the Tamaulipan thorn woodland of the lower coastal plain. See **Schott's Whipsnake (51)**. Another very different habitat is the coastal barrier islands, where these animals are found under high-tide driftwood.

Prey   Like most *Lampropeltis*, milk snakes are powerful constrictors of other serpents, from rattlers to smaller members of their own species. Other food animals are lizards and small mammals, both of which are usually accepted by recent captives.

Reproduction   Egg-laying. See **Central Plains Milk Snake (82)**.

Coloring/scale form   Fourteen to 20 (average 17.6) broad, dark red dorsolateral bands, often peppered along the spine with black, cover the upper trunk (the lower edges of these reddish bands extend onto the otherwise pale belly scales, where they are cut off by blotchy strips of black pigment that occupy the midventral area). Black body bands border each side of the red bands, and are about as wide as the intervening yellow bands; a few light anterior labial spots sometimes mark the otherwise black head. Arranged in 21 rows at midbody, the smooth dorsal scales are small and glossy; the anal plate is undivided.

Similar snakes   Milk snakes' red and yellow (or white) body bands touch only black bands, never each other; the **Texas coral snake (91)** has adjacent red and yellow bands as well as much broader black dorsal bands (as wide as its red bands), which also encircle its belly. Its anal plate is divided.

   Where their ranges intersect, the **Mexican** and **Louisiana milk snake (79)** races show intermingled characteristics, while throughout both animals' ranges individuals typical of neighboring races can be found. To the west, *L. t. annulata* merges with the **New Mexico milk snake (81),** which is distinguished by its greater average number of red dorsal bands (22.1), black dorsolateral rings much thinner than its comparatively broad white (rather than yellow) pale body bands, and its lighter-hued midventral area. The **Texas longnose snake (86)** is distinguished by rectangular red and black vertebral saddles, cream-colored scales scattered along its sides, an extended brown or pinkish snout, and 23 rows of dorsal scales. Its venter is whitish, and bears a single row of ventral scales beneath its tail.

Behavior   As vividly tri-colored reptiles, milk snakes are anything but milky in appearance, their name apparently having stemmed from early attempts to explain their presence in dairy barns. Milk snakes were probably drawn there in search of nestling mice, but because all *Lampropeltis* are so slow-moving it was thought that these little snakes could only subsist by twining up the legs of milk cows after dark to suck milk from their udders.

RED- AND BLACK-BANDED SNAKES

81 New Mexico Milk Snake
Lampropeltis triangulum celaenops

Nonvenomous   See **Louisiana Milk Snake (79)**.

Abundance   Very rare. Throughout its wide range, this animal is almost never seen; most of the few recorded specimens were encountered at night during May and June, moving rapidly across Trans-Pecos ranch roads.

Size   Most adults are between 14 and 22 inches in length; the largest of 7 Texas specimens measured 25¼ inches.

Habitat   According to ecologist Robert Wayne Van Devender, in Texas, better-watered portions of the northern Chihuahuan Desert's evergreen montane woodlands constitute the best habitat for *L. t. celaenops*. Other environments where New Mexico milk snakes have been found include riparian corridors in the Davis Mountains and stony, low-lying desert terrain. In the latter biome, during June 1997, Joe Forks found one *L. t. celaenops* on a rocky plateau 9 miles north of Sanderson and another in the even harsher desert environment of Big Bend's Black Gap; these were the first specimens he had seen in 21 years' field and road collecting in the Trans-Pecos. Another New Mexico milk snake was recently found in a grassland milieu along Highway 176 in Andrews Co.

Prey   The New Mexico milk snake feeds primarily on smaller snakes, lizards located by scent in the crevices where they retreat for the night, and burrow-dwelling rodents.

Reproduction   Egg-laying. See **Central Plains Milk Snake (82)**.

Coloring/scale form   The New Mexico milk snake's 17 to 25 (average 22.1) black-bordered carmine dorsolateral bands are separated by narrower white bands, within which scattered brown flecks give a grizzled appearance. The black body bands are often slightly wider over the posterior spine, the midbelly is largely without black pigment, and the black snout is flecked with white. Arranged in 21 rows at midbody, the smooth dorsal scales have an enamel-like surface to which the genus' Latin name, *Lampropeltis*, or "shining shield" refers. The anal plate is undivided.

Similar snakes   In the eastern part of its range *L. t. celaenops* shares the territory of the **Texas coral snake (91)**, whose red and sulfur body bands touch (milk snakes' red bands are bordered by black bands).

Because their ranges overlap, Texas' four milk snake races are difficult to distinguish, but in general, the **Central Plains milk snake (82)** has narrower, more numerous (20 to 32, average 25.6), orangeish dorsolateral bands, while along its ventral midline splotchy black pigment separates the lower edges of these bands. The **Mexican milk snake (80)** also has a black-pigmented midbelly, deep yellow body bands, and fewer, wider red bands (average 17.6). The **Texas longnose snake (86)** often has rectangular red and black vertebral saddles, 23 rows of dorsal scales and a white belly with a single row of undertail scales.

Behavior   In addition to winter dormancy most western milk snakes undergo a similar subsurface retirement to escape the heat and aridity of July, August, and September. Even during spring and fall, these animals apparently spend the daylight hours deep in subterranean crevices, where the humidity is higher and the temperature more constant than on the surface; they are most likely to be seen abroad on still, spring or early summer nights of high humidity or light rain, and are more frequently observed in years with higher than average precipitation.

2 Central Plains Milk Snake

Lampropeltis triangulum gentilis

Nonvenomous See **Louisiana Milk Snake (79).**

Abundance Rare. Although widely distributed, this animal is seldom found above ground.

Size Most adults are 16 to 24 inches long; the record is just over 3 feet.

Habitat Little is recorded of the life history of *L. t. gentilis* in the wild. It inhabits a wide sweep of basin and rangeland where its specific habitat preferences are largely unknown. It has been found, however, on brushy hillsides in rolling, short- or tallgrass prairie, especially where the soil was slightly moist, broken with large rocks, and loose enough for burrowing.

Prey Nothing is recorded of prey taken in the wild, but the young probably feed mainly on lizards, skinks, and miniature serpents such as blind snakes, and young garter snakes, *Tantilla*, as well as on earthworms and insects. In captivity, like other milk snakes, adults readily constrict and feed on other snakes as well as small rodents.

Reproduction Egg-laying. The reproduction of captives indicates that after spring-time breeding and gestation, milk snakes deposit clutches of up to ten ¼- by ⅝-inch-long, adhesive-shelled eggs. After 65 to 80 days' incubation these hatch into 7½- to 11-inch-long young whose coloration is exactly the same as that of their parents.

Coloring/scale form Both dorsal patterning and coloration in this milk snake subspecies are variable. Northern individuals have less vividly-colored dorsolateral bands than those from the southwestern Panhandle and North Central Texas, which intergrade with more brightly colored southern races of *Lampropeltis.* Among northern *L. t. gentilis,* the reddish-orange dorsolateral bands are duller in hue, narrower, and more numerous (20 to 40, average 25.6) than those of other milk snakes, and are darkened by black scales over the posterior spine. These russet bands are bordered by narrow black rings that may almost entirely encircle them low on the sides and belly (only intermittently do the yellowish-gray dorsolateral rings cross the venter). The snout and forehead are mottled with white, the 21 mid-body rows of dorsal scales are smooth, and the anal plate is undivided.

Similar snakes The ranges of Texas' four subspecies of milk snakes are difficult to define with precision because throughout their ranges, individuals typical of neigh-boring milk snake races can be found. For example, the Central Plains milk snake intergrades with the **Louisiana milk snake (79)** as far south as Fort Worth, where the latter is distinguished by its fewer, wider, and brighter red dorsolateral bands (an average of only 16.2) as well as by its pale midventral area. The **New Mexico milk snake (81)** also has fewer, wider, and redder body bands (averaging 22.1 in num-ber), whitish pale body bands and a light-hued midbelly. The **Texas longnose snake (86)** has black-speckled yellowish lower sides, rectangular red and black dorsal sad-dles, and an unmarked white belly with a single row of subcaudal scales.

Behavior Perhaps because so much of its habitat consists of open prairie, *L. t. gentilis* seldom risks emerging into the open; during cool weather, rather than bask-ing to elevate its temperature, it reportedly more often seeks warmth by coiling against the underside of sun-heated flat rocks.

83 Gray-banded Kingsnake
Lampropeltis alterna

Nonvenomous   In captivity, *Lampropeltis alterna* almost never bites, though when first picked up in the field it may give a single frightened nip.

Abundance   Widespread but uncommon. Because they are almost entirely fossorial during much of the year, gray-banded kingsnakes were for decades thought to be extremely rare, and this species was long protected by the state of Texas. *Lampropeltis alterna* is no longer regarded as threatened, however, largely because it is now known to be widely distributed, with over 90% of its habitat occurring either on private ranchland or within state and national parks (south of the Rio Grande, where two-thirds of the gray-banded kingsnake's range lies, it has even less contact with humans due to the mostly roadless terrain it inhabits).

While *L. alterna* remains at the center of environmental controversies—several magazine articles have suggested that this species is in danger—the prevailing scientific view is that neither the 50 to 100 gray-banded kingsnakes taken every year by collectors, nor those run over by local ranch traffic, is ecologically significant. (These losses are also unlikely to get much larger because *L. alterna* is entirely inaccessible to the public except where road cuts and canyon bluffs border the few back roads that cross thousands of square miles of its barren range.) As a result, *L. alterna* was denied federal designation as a threatened species in 1980 and is no longer protected in Texas.

Although the gray-banded kingsnake has recently become the object of intense scrutiny, it has been known for almost a century. The type specimen was collected during 1901 in the Davis Mountains by E. Meyenberg, then formally described by A. E. Brown, who named it *Ophibolus alternus* for its alternating broad and narrow dorsolateral bands. For the next forty-seven years this animal, re-renamed *Lampropeltis alterna* after its affinity with the kingsnakes became apparent, was known only from the Chisos, Davis, and Sierra Vieja mountains, from a single locality near Bakersfield in Pecos County, and from the Mexican State of Coahuila.

Then, in 1948, a much paler, broadly orange-banded kingsnake unlike any previously reported from the Trans-Pecos was discovered 9 miles west of Dryden. This animal was thought to be a new species, which was formally described by A. G. Flury and named *Lampropeltis blairi* after University of Texas herpetologist W. F. Blair. This nomenclature was in error, however, for some twenty years later Ernest Tanzer found both pale-and dark-hued gray-banded kingsnakes hatching from a single clutch of eggs laid by a wild-caught gravid female, demonstrating that "*L. alterna*" and "*L. blairi*" were really a single species. The older scientific name prevails, so *Lampropeltis alterna* is the proper term for all West Texas' gray-banded kingsnakes.*

In recent years, herpetoculturalists have bred thousands of gray-banded kingsnakes in captivity, but wild-caught specimens carry far more cache, and even the remote chance of capturing one attracts a cult-like following of enthusiasts who, from all over the world, seek out Trans-Pecos Texas during the breeding season in late April, May, and June. Hoping to intercept an adult male *L. alterna* on its nocturnal courtship for-

---

*For a time, West Texas' gray-banded kingsnake was also thought to be a subspecies of the wide-ranging Mexican kingsnake *L. mexicana*, and it was known as *Lampropeltis mexicana alterna* until 1982, when W. R. Garstka taxonomically separated Texas' gray-banded kingsnake from its Mexican relative.

ays, bands of enthusiasts sometimes crowd the best-known collecting sites. Yet, despite their sometimes gaudy colors, gray-banded kingsnakes are difficult to see at night because red looks gray in poor lighting, and the variegated dorsolateral patterning of *L. alterna* masks its serpentine shape against shadowy rock faces.

In contrast to these groups, serious collector/breeders such as Joe Forks, D. Craig McIntyre, and Gerry Salmon are primarily interested in preserving, by means of captive propagation, the distinct color/pattern types unique to particular regions of the Trans-Pecos. It is not uncommon for these researchers to spend nearly every night between the first of May and mid-July searching Trans-Pecos roads for new populations of distinctly marked or colored *Lampropeltis alterna,* mapping its regional variants, and expanding its known range, which now includes 15 Texas counties plus adjacent Eddy County in New Mexico.**

Size Adult gray-banded kingsnakes average 28 to 34 inches in length, with those from the Chisos and Davis Mountains averaging slightly smaller. The record is a 58-inch-long male "Blair's" from 17 miles west of Rocksprings in Edwards Co.

Habitat Throughout the Chihuahuan Desert, *L. alterna* inhabits rocky environments in terrain ranging from barren, lowlying desert flats (usually adjacent to bluffs or arroyos) to mountain slopes as high as 7,000 feet. This means it lives amid a huge variety of plant life: Both low altitude mesquite and creosote bush associations and montane pinyon-pine, juniper, and oak communities are occupied, while canyons, craggy ridges, talus slopes, and boulder piles are its preferred microenvironment; the limestone faces of road cuts are where these animals are most often seen.

In this arid country, conditions on the surface are harsh but, except for breeding forays by males, the gray-banded kingsnake seldom experiences them because it spends most of its life in a more sheltered world deep beneath the desert floor. Here, moving slowly through the maze of interconnecting crevices that underlie the region's broken limestone topography, *L. alterna* need never emerge from its chthonic warren because at night the lizards on which it feeds descend into its crenelated lair in search of shelter.†

Prey On the surface, where it sometimes hunts, *L. alterna* uses its prominent ventral scales to grip rough-surfaced stone, inching its way across nearly vertical rock faces while searching every crevice for the side-blotched and spiny lizards that sleep there (Salmon observed an adult male gray-band trying to pull a crevice spiny lizard from a crack in a roadside rock-cut where the lizard had wedged itself by expanding its lungs.) In captivity, *L. alterna*—which is a bit clumsy at conventional constriction—may engage in a specialized form of "constriction" by pressing mice against the walls of its enclosure. (Most wild-caught adults feed readily on small rodents, though the young are exclusively lizard eaters.) Lizard eggs, snake eggs, and canyon tree frogs have also been noted as food items among wild *L. alterna* (I found a desert sideblotched lizard in the stomach of a road-killed specimen), but ophiophagy, which is common among kingsnakes, is rare in gray-banded kings.

**Because endemic populations are often separated by geographic barriers, gene flow between groups is thought to be minimal. Like zoos engaged in endangered species breeding programs, committed herpetoculturalists therefore select their breeders on the proximity of their capture sites—even when that means driving from California or New York to find a mate for an animal taken from a particular stretch of West Texas dirt road.

†Fossil records indicate the presence of this reptile at Fowlkes Cave in Culberson Co. from the Late Pleistocene, while R. W. Van Devender has found *L. alterna* fossils up to 15,000 years old from both a packrat midden in Brewster Co. and Baker Cave in Val Verde Co.

Reproduction   Egg-laying. No reproductive behavior has been recorded for gray-bands in the wild, but the fascination of propagating regional variants of *Lampropeltis alterna* has led to the thorough documentation of its courtship and breeding.

Captive husbandry initially focused on building cages with false floors punctured by entrance holes leading to "underground" spaces filled with loose vermiculite. This attempt at recreating the gray-band's natural habitat proved unnecessary, but current techniques—successful propagation was first described by James Murphy of the Dallas Zoo—is equally exacting. Because winter dormancy is necessary for reproduction, the brief but cold Trans-Pecos winters are approximated by keeping breeders at about 55°F, without feeding, for a period of 10 to 12 weeks.

After brumation, males in the wild are likely to become territorial, because contests for dominance occur when two newly-warmed males are placed in the same cage. After a few minutes' struggle to attain the uppermost position, the combatants are separated, a female is introduced to the desired male's cage, and copulation occurs at once.

The clutches of 3 to 18 eggs, 1¼ to 1⅝ inches in length, are deposited from late May to July. After their 60- to 80-day incubation, the young pip through their leathery eggshells but remain coiled within the eggs for another couple of days, peaking out from time to time while adsorbing the last of their yolk sacs. Well-fed *L. alterna* reach reproductive maturity in their second or third year (wild females may become gravid at as small as 24 inches), and in captivity can live more than 20 years.

Coloring/scale form   The great variety of this species' color and patterning has made it the jewel of Texas herpetology among herpetoculturists, among whom it is said that, "no two *alterna* are exactly alike." This may not be entirely true, but gray-banded kingsnake populations are so highly polymorphic that wild specimens seem to present an almost infinite variety of color and patterning.

Ground color varies from black to light gray, although two principal color phases prevail. (The original terms "alterna" and "blairi" are still used to differentiate these types, although many specimens are intermediate between them). Individuals from the lower Pecos and Devil's River drainage are most often pale gray, for example, with orange dorsal saddles delineated by narrow, sometimes thinly white-bordered black edges, while among the more northerly and easterly specimens known as "alterna" morphs, heavier pigmentation is likely. Thin black bands, sometimes narrowly split with red, are separated by still thinner intermediate, or "alternating," dark bands or vertical rows of small black spots.

These differences are loosely tied to the hue of the background rocks on which these populations live. In the southern part of the range, where the paler "Blair's" form more often occurs, there is more chalky desert pavement than in the north and at higher elevation, where more moisture causes the lichen-encrusted granite to be darkly weathered. Here, more heavily pigmented "alterna" morphs prevail. Because both sorts of young are produced in the both regions, natural selection determines which color phase is best camouflaged against its local background rock and is thus most likely to survive there.

Ventral coloring varies almost as much as that of the dorsum, ranging from off-white to, in the Davis Mountains, almost entirely black (ventral scale counts range from 208 to 232 with an average of 221; supralabials range from 6 to 8, while infralabials usually number 10). The 25 midbody rows of dorsal scales are smooth and the anal plate is undivided.

The sites where these variable color morphs have been found include:

Brewster County

Five miles west of Alpine on US Hwy. 90; 6 to 28 miles south on US Hwy. 118. About 20 specimens are known from these two sites, mostly medium or dark phase "alterna" morphs with thin (or absent) orange splits in their crossbands. This type, characterized by profuse speckling and variegated patterns on a tan or ocher ground color, is found on the same dark red granite as are the similar-looking *L. alterna* that occur on the same granite formations near Fort Davis.

Black Gap: FM 2627. Black Gap Wildlife Management Area has an extremely variable population of gray-banded kingsnakes that may reflect the region's well-known diversity of terrain and vegetation. Both this area and that around Sanderson, just to the northeast, are famous for the bold colors and patterning of the resident *L. alterna,* and may be the part of the gray-band's range where the highest degree of color/pattern variation occurs. Both light and dark "Blair's" color phase animals are known—one such individual, collected on FM 2627 on June 10, at 12:10 a.m., is a light phase "Blair's" whose twelve large, bright orange saddles are separated by alternate markings. Still, "alterna" morphs are the more abundant color morph found here, a dark ground color is more common than light, and both heavily speckled and completely patternless specimens also occur.

Christmas Mountains: North of Study Butte on US Hwy. 118. Snakes from the Christmas Mountains are usually speckled "alterna" morphs, many with all their primary bands split by orange wedges. One of these, a male found here by Joe Forks on June 26, at 4:20 a.m., had 19 primary bands, the four anterior-most split with bright orange. Orange scales were speckled throughout the remaining bands, and both speckling and triple alternate bands were present in the neck. "Blair's" morphs have also been collected in the Christmas Mts., but seem to be uncommon there. Dennis Miller of the Chihuahuan Desert Research Institute reports black specimens in this area. Additional gray-bands are known from 17 miles east of Marathon on US Hwy. 90, Big Bend National Park, Pepper's Hill on FM 170, and Bee Mountain (Hwy. 118 just north of Study Butte).

Crane and Upton Counties

King Mountain. Only a handful of *L. alterna* are known from this locality. Most are light- or dark-phase "Blair's" with symmetrical patterns: one young male "Blair's" found by Forks on the east slope of King Mountain in Upton County during September is indistinguishable from specimens that occur far to the southeast in Val Verde County. One "alterna" morph has also been reported from this locality.

Crockett County

Iraan: US 190 East of Iraan. Suitable habitat extends some 20 miles east of Iraan on US 190. Both "Blair's" and "alterna" morphs occur here, most of them showing the symmetrical patterning typical of the easternmost reaches of the gray-band's range.

FM 2083 southwest of Ozona: Pandale Paved Road. The gray-banded kings seen here are predominantly "Blair's" morphs; as of 1996, only 8 live specimens were known from this area, none of them "alterna" morphs.

Sheffield and Fort Lancaster on US Hwy. 290. Few *L. alterna* have been recorded here, although both "alterna" and "Blair's" morphs are represented. An "alterna" phase found southwest of Fort Lancaster in May 1995 has a primary band count of 19, the first 7 of which are split by 3 horizontal rows of markings called triple alternates.

Other Crockett County Localities. There are few reports of *L. alterna* from FM 163 (Juno Road and I-10) in Crockett County. I saw two "alterna" morphs—one a heavily speckled adult male road-kill found in May, the other a smaller, typical "Blair's" phase male seen on June 19—just south of Sheffield, where FM 349 drops into a limestone canyon.

Culberson County

Guadalupe Mountains. Lampropeltis alterna has been reported from 3 miles south of Pine Springs on US 62/180, as well as on the east side of Guadalupe Peak. All are typical "alterna" morphs with few primary bands consisting of thin, white-edged black rings separated by wide gray patches and containing little or no orange. Another specimen found on the east side of Guadalupe Peak had 19 dark body blotches and lacked red pigment.

Beach Mountains. Toby Hibbitts found a single gray-band 3.3 miles north of Van Horn in the Beach Mountains. It is a light "alterna" morph male with 13 dark primary bands, most separated by alternate dark markings. There was very little orange except in its X-shaped nuchal blotch.

Edwards County

FM 674 south of Rocksprings. A single specimen—a dark "alterna" male with almost no orange—is known from this county. It was found 31.5 miles south of Rocksprings on FM 674 on June 19.

Other Edwards County localities. At different times, both Forks and I have found gray-banded kingsnakes in this county; Forks in Carta Valley, a cave in the Devil's Sinkhole, and I at a site 17 miles west of Rocksprings on Hwy. 377. Gehlbach & Baker (1962) report a specimen from Dunbar Cave, 21 miles southwest of Rocksprings. All were light "Blair's" morphs.

El Paso and Hudspeth Counties

Hueco Mountains: El Paso and Hudspeth counties. Few gray-banded kings have been found in this area, all being typical "alterna," with a low crossband count and little or no orange. A female collected on August 25, by Richard Worthington, on the Hueco-Gasline Road, had 15 body blotches, no more than 2 scale lengths wide, with 4 of the anterior blotches being laterally incomplete.

Eagle Mountains: Hudspeth County. A small male gray-band—a dark ground-colored "alterna" morph—was found on June 25 at 5,500 ft elevation on the Eagle Mountain Ranch. It had 16 dark body blotches, most of which contained scattered red scales.

Jeff Davis County

Fort Davis: FM 1832, Limpia Canyon, McDonald Observatory, Musquiz Canyon. Typical specimens from these localities are medium to dark phase "alterna" morphs with a tan or brownish-orange ground color. Both light phase *L. alterna* and individuals with heavy speckling are also known, and in both varieties the ventral scales are darkly pigmented. A male "alterna" collected by D. Craig McIntyre and Mark Brown at 10:10 p.m. on July 3 about 20 miles north of Fort Davis, had 26 primary bands on a brownish-gray ground color. Alternate markings were present between every primary crossband except the last four posterior bands, and there was orange pigment within 19 of the primary bands.

Kinney County

FM 674 north of Bracketville. One light-hued "Blair's" female with a black head was found 12 miles north of Bracketville.

FM 2523 in northwestern Kinney County. One live and one road-killed specimen are reported for this locality. The living specimen was a dark phase female found a mile south of the Edwards County line on FM 2523. She had narrow primary crossbands, of which only the first four anterior bands were split with orange; her ten perfectly symmetrical dorsal saddles were almost completely black. (Because there were no intermediate or "alternate" markings between her primary dorsolateral bands, this animal would be considered intermediate between the "alterna" and "Blair's" color phases due to the reduced width of her body bands.)

Pecos County

Glass Mountains on US Hwy. 385. The rocky outcrops favored by gray-banded kings lie far from the road in the Glass Mountains, which are private property, so very little *L. alterna* habitat is adjacent to US Hwy. 385. Nevertheless, Dennis Miller reported a single specimen from this locality.

West of Iraan on US Hwy. 190. Both "Blair's" and "alterna" color phases are represented along this stretch of very good habitat. Most individuals have the cleanly symmetrical patterning typical of individuals found far to the south in Val Verde County.

Other Pecos County Localities. *L. alterna* has been found by Forks and Salmon to the north and west of Sanderson just inside Pecos Co. Other specimens are known from an atypical habitat of creosote plains 14 miles southwest of Fort Stockton, 14 miles west of Bakersfield, and FM 305 northwest of Iraan.

Presidio County

FM 170, or the River Road. "Alterna" morphs occur more often than "Blair's" along this famous scenic drive, most of which is now part of Big Band Ranch, an extension of Big Bend National Park and therefore a wildlife refuge. The few "Blair's" morphs seen here have come from the vicinity of Mud Flats. A male "alterna" phase, found by Troy Hibbitts on June 4, 4.6 miles west of the Big Hill on FM 170, had 20 narrow primary bands split with orange, and laterally restricted dark "alternate" markings between most of them. Several totally speckled gray-bands have also been found in this locale.

Other Presidio County Localities. Very few *L. alterna* have been reported from Candelaria, Shafter, Pinto Canyon, and the Sierra Vieja Mountains.

Sutton County

US 277 south of Sonora. A single individual—a dark phase female "Blair's" with bright orange saddles—is recorded for Sutton Co., approximately 15 miles south of Sonora on US Hwy. 277.

Terrell County

Dryden, Palma Draw, and Lozier Canyon. Several hundred gray-banded kingsnakes are known from this area along US Hwy. 90, most of them dark "Blair's" phase individuals. An "alterna" type, possibly the only one seen between Dryden and Pumpville on US 90, was located by Forks on October 1 in a vertical crevice near the bottom of a roadside cut at 8:00 a.m., some 8 miles east of Dryden.

Sanderson: US Hwy. 285; US Hwy. 90. *Lampropeltis alterna* from this area are highly variable, sometimes with atypical patterning. Both "alterna" and "Blair's"

215

morphs are represented, with speckling appearing in the nuchal blotches of both types; the primary markings tend to be faded in the center. (Dark-hued "alternas" with thin, bright red slashes in their primary crossbands are also known to occur east of Sanderson.)

Other Terrell County Localities. A dark male "Blair's" with 15 bright orange saddles is noted from 54 miles northeast of Sanderson on FM 2400; another was located by Hibbitts nearby on US 349. Two "alternas" are also recorded from Myers Canyon 14 miles north of Dryden on US 349.

Val Verde County

FM 163, or Juno Road. This bleak little rural route is world-famous in the herpetological community as one of the few places that brightly colored "Blair's" graybanded kings occur more often than "alterna" morphs. A light phase adult male "Blair's" with a black head found by Forks at 1:20 a.m., June 11 about 5 miles south of Baker's crossing, had twelve big, bright orange saddles on a light gray ground color. Another male "alterna" morph located at 11:45 p.m. June 21 had 18 reduced primary crossbands, some split with bright red, on a dark gray ground color; there were almost no alternate markings, and wide white borders edged its primary bands.

Langtry: US Hwy. 90; Langtry Loop Road; Pandale Dirt Road. These equally well-known localities—the first a major highway sandwiched between high limestone road-cuts, the latter two, tiny desert tracks—have produced more sightings of *L. alterna* than any other locality. (Most have been "Blair's" color phase with medium to dark gray ground color). As a result, Comstock and Langtry have become headquarters for *L. alterna* fanciers, and because little else happens in this remote corner of the state, each summer every scruffy cafe and motel hangs out a "Welcome Snake Hunters" sign.

Loma Alta, or US Hwy. 277. "Blair's" color phase gray-bands are also often found here, and this road claims some of the most brightly colored, pale-hued "Blair's" with large orange saddles. One such snake, found 32 miles north of Del Rio at 4:20 a.m., July 3, had 14 vivid orange saddles; another pale female "Blair's" with a black head, also found by Forks from at the same site at 11:15 p.m. on July 16, had 11 big red saddles, each split by a dark "alternate" marking.

Similar snakes The light-hued color phase of the **mottled rock rattlesnake (104)** is almost identical in pigmentation to pale-phase gray-banded kingsnake. The heads of both species are somewhat triangular, but rattlesnakes have both a rattle and a dark, distinctly depressed heat-sensing pit midway between the nostril and the slit-pupilled eye (like other subterranean or nocturnal serpents, *L. alterna* has bulging eyes with prominent round pupils).

Behavior Gray-banded kingsnakes' movement on the surface fluctuates according to both season and weather: its infrequent forays usually occur on warm spring nights with low or falling barometric pressure, especially when rainfall has recently occurred and the humidity is higher than normal. (The summer of 1997, which followed the wettest spring in a decade, produced an exceptional number of sightings throughout its range, including individuals discovered in habitats as atypical of this species as the specimen found on the rolling plains 20 miles north of Marathon.) *Lampropeltis alterna* is encountered slightly more frequently in the very dry country near the Pecos and Devil's rivers, however, as well as in desert terrain near the Rio Grande, than in better-watered parts of its range.

Northern Scarlet Snake
Cemophora coccinea copei

Nonvenomous   Northern scarlet snakes seldom bite, even when first picked up.

Abundance   Fairly common. **Protected by the State of Texas.** Especially during May and June, *C. c. copei* is sometimes abundant on East Texas back roads.

Size   Most adult *C. c. copei* measure 14 to 20 inches in length.

Habitat   An inhabitant of the sandy soil of pine, hardwood, and mixed forest environments, the northern scarlet snake is also sometimes found in adjacent open, soft-earthed terrain. Here, it occurs both in agricultural fields and along the borders of swamps and stream banks. In the wetter southern part of its range too much water may be a problem, however, for Jim Ashcraft reports that in riparian forest near Beaumont *C. c. copei* is most often found on the white pine-wooded sandy ridges that rise a few feet above intervening boggy ground covered with baygall and magnolia.

Prey   Reptile eggs are evidently the preferred food, and to puncture the leathery shells of those too large to be swallowed whole, *C. c. copei* has developed enlarged teeth in the rear of its upper jaw.

Reproduction   Egg-laying. The 3 to 8 eggs, 1 to 1⅜ inches in length, are deposited during late June or July; the very slender young are 5½ to 6 inches long at hatching.

Coloring/scale form   Up to 32 broad red dorsal saddles prominently bordered with black line the northern scarlet snake's back. The lower sides are flecked with brown and the elongate snout is orange-red, as is the crown, which is sometimes capped by a circular marking edged with black.

In a process known as ontogenetic variation this reptile's coloring changes so much with age that hatchlings, adults, and very old individuals look like different species. Hatchlings' dorsal saddles are pink and extend, above black lateral flecks, only a short way down their whitish sides. As they grow older, these flecks become the dark lower borders of reddening dorsal blotches, which eventually develop a broad black lateral edging. Among very old *C. c. copei,* the colors dull, its once-carmine saddles fade to mahogany, and the formerly white spaces between them become tarnished with tan or gray. The unmarked venter is white, there are 19 midbody rows of smooth dorsal scales and the anal plate is undivided.

Similar snakes   The **Texas coral snake (91)** has red and yellow dorsolateral bands that border one another and extend across its belly; its stubby snout is jet black, its anal plate divided. The **Louisiana milk snake (79)** usually has a white-flecked black nose, dorsolateral bands that extend onto its red, white, and black ventral scales, and 21 rows of dorsal scales.

Behavior   *Cemophora coccinea copei* seldom appears in the open except on late spring and early summer nights—it is one of the most deeply subterranean serpents in East Texas. To escape by digging it presses its tapered snout into the ground at a shallow angle and wags its head from side to side to root up a pair of little earthen berms that soon collapse inward over its foreparts. Thus partially concealed, *C. c. copei* discontinues its sideways cephalic motions in favor of forcing its head almost straight down into the soil. No one knows if it continues, like a big earthworm, to move about in this way below ground or whether it follows existing underground tunnels and crevices, but during building excavation scarlet snakes have been uncovered as much as 6 feet beneath the surface.

217

85 Texas Scarlet Snake
Cemophora coccinea lineri

Nonvenomous   See **Northern Scarlet Snake (84).**

Abundance   Threatened. Protected by the State of Texas.
Named in honor of herpetologist Ernest A. Liner, *Cemophora coccinea lineri* is a very rare animal that is endemic to Texas.

Size   Texas scarlet snakes grow to a length of at least 26 inches.

Habitat   Almost the only habitat in which *C. c. lineri* has been observed is sand-floored baygall thicket adjacent to Texas' lower Gulf Coast.

Prey   Although evidently a sometime constrictor—small lizards and snakes are probably taken—*C. c. lineri* seems to feed largely on reptile eggs, which it punctures with the slightly enlarged teeth located in the rear of its upper jaw. One newly-captured individual brought to the Houston Zoo drank nearly a quarter of the contents of a hen's egg from a shallow dish and, over the next 8 days, consumed nine Texas spiny lizard eggs. Then for months it refused eggs and small snake and lizard prey; another captive *C. c. lineri* lived nearly a year in captivity, feeding solely on fresh hen's egg yolks while refusing both living and dead lacertillians and small serpents. Jim Ashcraft (who has elicited feeding responses among northern scarlet snakes that were reluctant to feed by providing them with deep soil in which to burrow) has suggested that exposure in an open cage may have inhibited the feeding of both these specimens.

Reproduction   Egg-laying. See **Northern Scarlet Snake (84).**

Coloring/scale form   Color, pattern, and scutellation are similar to those of the northern scarlet snake, *Cemophora coccinea copei,* from which this subspecies was formally distinguished in 1966 by Kenneth Williams, Bryce Brown, and L. D. Wilson. Both races have a grayish-white dorsolateral ground color, 17 to 24 heavily black-bordered carmine to mahogany-red vertebral saddles, and elongate orange-red snouts. Like its northeastern subspecies, the Texas scarlet snake exhibits ontogenetic variation, growing first redder and then darker and more brownish with age, but among Texas scarlet snakes the black border of its vertebral saddles does not join across their lower edges, as it does in the northern race, nor is its mid-crown marking as pronounced. Smooth and glossy, the dorsal scales occur in 19 rows at midbody, its venter is unmarked white, and its anal plate is undivided.

Similar snakes   The **Texas coral snake (91)** has a rounded black snout, adjacent red and bright yellow dorsolateral bands that cross its venter, and a divided anal plate. The **Mexican milk snake (80)** also has a black, sometimes white-speckled nose, a red, white, and black venter, and 21 midbody rows of dorsal scales. The **Texas longnose snake (86)** usually has rectangular black dorsolateral saddles, black-speckled yellowish lower sides, 23 rows of dorsal scales, and a single row of undertail scales (unlike the double row of every other harmless snake in the state).

Behavior   Few observations of Texas scarlet snakes have been made in the wild, but *C. c. lineri*'s activity cycle is probably similar to that of its northern subspecies. Captives ordinarily remain buried in the loose sand of their cage bottoms during the day, emerging to move about the surface only at night. At this time, it is thought that the Texas scarlet snake's bright colors, by visually breaking up its outline, may function primarily as nocturnal camouflage. See **Louisiana Milk Snake (79).**

Texas Longnose Snake
Rhinocheilus lecontei tessellatus

Nonvenomous   *Rhinocheilus lecontei tessellatus* does not bite, though if picked up suddenly individuals may defecate and writhe in agitation.

Abundance   Uncommon. Sparsely distributed in both Central Texas and the Stockton Plateau grasslands, the Texas longnose snake is more often found in the Trans-Pecos, and may be seasonally fairly numerous in the grasslands of the Panhandle as well as in thorn brush savannah of South Texas.

Size   Most adults are 16 to 30 inches long; the record is 41 inches.

Habitat   A burrower in the dry, gravelly soils of the western half of the state, *R. l. tessellatus* is most often found near the moisture of stock tanks and intermittently flowing streams.

Prey   McKinney and Ballinger (1966) found only lacertillian remains in 14 Texas longnose snakes from the Panhandle (much too swift to be captured by the slow-moving longnose during the day, lizards are vulnerable to scent-hunting snakes at night when they sleep wedged into crevices or buried beneath a layer of sand, and Abilene Zoo Director Jack Joy reports observing *R. l. tessellatus* root out racerunner lizards in this way after dark). Rodents are also taken by some populations, perhaps preferentially, because several captives from LaSalle and McMullen counties refused reptilian food but immediately recognized small mammals as prey. Although no more than a half-inch in diameter, these *R. l. tessellatus* had no difficulty in constricting adult mice with a loop of their slim but surprisingly muscular trunks.

Reproduction   Egg-laying. Four to 9 eggs are deposited in an underground nest. After 2 to 2½ months the 6½-to 9½-inch-long young emerge, pallidly marked with pink-dorsal saddles and whitish sides.

Coloring/scale form   Its elongated rostral scale is the source of both this creature's common and scientific names: *rhino* is Greek for "nose" and *cheil* means "lip." (*Lecontei* honors John Eatton Leconte, an army engineer who, after engineering the defense of Savannah during the War of 1812, devoted himself to herpetology. In reference to the longnose's mosaic-like dorsal pattern, *tessellatus* is Latin for "tiled.")

Although the coloring of all longnose snakes darkens and intensifies with age, Texas populations vary in hue and marking. South Texas specimens have rectangular vertebral patches of red and black, lightly black-speckled yellow sides, and white venters. In the northern Trans-Pecos, most Texas longnose snakes have larger red dorsal blocks separated by wide (sometimes hourglass-shaped) black dorsolateral bands. There is little yellow, and the venter is often dark-splotched. The 23 midbody rows of dorsal scales are smooth, the anal plate is undivided and, as in no other nonvenomous serpent in Texas, the scales beneath the banded tail usually occur in a single row.

Similar snakes   In Texas, every race of **milk snakes (79—82)** has narrow black dorsal crossbands and a double row of scales under the tail.

Behavior   In 1967, McCoy and Gehlbach established that some *R. l. tessellatus* employ defensive behavior in which bloody fluid mixed with anal gland musk is discharged through the cloaca; if more severely threatened, such an auto-hemorrhagic longnose may hang as limply as a moribund carcass. Alternatively, with its head buried in its coils for safety, the longnose may wave its curled tailtip in a threatening pose thought to evoke the similarly banded, about-to-strike head of the coral snake.

RED- AND BLACK-BANDED SNAKES

87 Texas Night Snake
Hypsiglena torquata jani

Mildly venomous   Although its mildly toxic saliva has a paralytic effect on its diminutive reptile, insect, and annelid prey, the Texas night snake does not bite larger creatures—despite threat behavior in which it engages in abrupt, strike-approximating movements of its slightly triangular head.

Abundance   Variable. This widespread though seldom seen little animal inhabits a variety of dry, terrestrial environments. Uncommon east of the Great Plains and Central Hill Country, *Hypsiglena torquata jani* is most common in oak/juniper savannah, South Texas' Tamaulipan thorn brush community, as well as in grassland throughout the Trans-Pecos.

Size   Most adults are 10 to 14 inches, but *H. t. jani* is recorded to 20 inches.

Habitat   The Texas night snake's favored microhabitat is sandy or gravelly ground broken by rocky bluffs or overlain by flat stones and fallen branches. In South Texas it is often found in the neighborhood of water sources such as stock tanks or irrigation ditches; in the Trans-Pecos it occurs in short-grass prairie.

Prey   Lizards, smaller snakes, worms, and insects have been reported.

Reproduction   Egg-laying. In northern Tom Green Co., Abilene Zoo Director Jack Joy observed a copulating pair of Texas night snakes on May 10. Other records report clutches of 4 to 6 proportionately large—up to 1⅛ inches in length and ½ inch in diameter—eggs found between early April and late June, beneath stones, decaying vegetation, or debris. John E. Werler (1951), reported an incubation period of 54 days, after which

> . . . one clutch of 5.7-inch to 6-inch young emerged and, 13 days after hatching
> . . . ate newly hatched rusty lizards but refused the small anole lizards that were
> offered from time to time. Most of the day the snakes remained hidden
> beneath the sand in their cage, coming to the surface to prowl only after dark.

Coloring scale/form   Dorsolateral ground color is beige, marked with 50 or more irregular brown vertebral blotches and numerous small dark lateral spots. Night snakes' most distinctive characteristic, however, are their large coppery eyes, slit by a vertical hairline pupil; the big brown blotches that mark the nape and sides of its neck are also definitive. The venter is white with a faint silvery sheen. Except for slightly ridged vertebral scales above the anal region of adult males, the 21 midbody rows of dorsal scales are smooth and the anal plate is divided. Along the Rio Grande from Big Bend to the Quitman Mountains in southern Hudspeth County, much paler night snakes occur as an intergrades with the more westerly spotted night snake, *H. t. ochrorhyncha*.

Similar snakes   Their tiny upturned snouts distinguish **western (64)** and **Mexican (65) hooknose snakes,** which have but 17 rows of dorsal scales, round-pupilled dark eyes, and lack large brown nuchal blotches.

Behavior   Active between April and late October, *H. t. jani* shares an elliptical pupil (whose vertical aperture protects the light-sensitive optic rods, yet allows for more radical expansion after dark than a circular pupil) only with the pitvipers and other rear-fanged colubrids. Ordinarily entirely terrestrial, the Texas night snake also sometimes forages in low vegetation: north of Sanderson, Connie McIntyre found an adult *H. t. jani* 4 feet off the ground in thorny roadcut shrubbery.

Black-striped Snake

Coniophanes imperialis imperialis

Mildly venomous   The longitudinally-grooved rear teeth for which *Coniophanes imperialis imperialis* is noted allow it to introduce salivary toxins into its small vertebrate prey. Yet its small size and calm temperament means that it is unlikely to bite a human being—in whom its saliva has produced no lasting effects. Baylor University herpetologist Bryce C. Brown (1939), who allowed a black-striped snake to bite him on the hand as an experiment, found that the sharp initial pain was similar to a bee sting but lasted much longer, because within an hour the discomfort had reached his elbow and his slightly swollen hand had grown temporarily numb.

Abundance   Threatened. Protected by the State of Texas. The black-striped snake is a predominantly Mexican reptile known in the U.S. only from Cameron, Hidalgo, and Willacy counties, where it was numerous before World War II. Today, because elimination of the Rio Grande Valley's native thorn woodland by agricultural clearing has devastated much of the area's wildlife, *C. i. imperialis* is seldom encountered.

Size   Most black-striped snakes are 12 to 18 inches; the record is 20 inches.

Habitat   The Tamaulipan thorn thicket—particularly its riparian arroyos and seasonally-filled watercourses and resacas—was the black-striped snake's original home. This tangle of catclaw acacia, paloverde, tamarisk, cenizo, and ocotillo, named for Mexico's most northeastern state, formerly covered the Gulf coastal plain from Port Mansfield to Tampico and was among Texas' richest biotic communities, harboring tropical fauna like *C. i. imperialis,* which ranged no farther north than the Rio Grande Valley.

In what is left of this thorn brush, the semi-fossorial black-striped snake's microhabitat on the surface consists of natural or man-made debris: on the outskirts of Harlingen, black-striped snakes are edificial, turning up around buildings beneath long-discarded trash and construction material.

Prey   Mostly small frogs and toads, lizards, and smaller snakes.

Reproduction   Egg-laying. In Chiapas, Mexico, clutches have been found to number up to 10 eggs, which typically take only about 40 days to hatch into 6½-inch-long young.

Coloring scale/form   This slender colubrid is notable for the three dark dorsolateral stripes—a single prominent black vertebral line and a wider dark longitudinal stripe low on each side—that run the length of its medium brown body. In contrast, the black-striped snake's venter shades from orange to pink, with a bright red undertail. There are 19 rows of smooth dorsal scales and the anal plate is divided.

Similar Snakes   None. No other serpent within its range is likely to be mistaken for the black-striped snake.

Behavior   This secretive serpent typically forages from late evening to early morning, avoiding daytime activity by burrowing into sandy soil or hiding under cacti, fallen palm fronds, or logs. Like other snakes with brightly hued undertails, *C. i. imperialis* typically everts this part of its belly when harassed. With its foreparts lowered, it may then wave its elevated tail tip back and forth in a gesture presumed to approximate the threatening head of a venomous reptile such as the coral snake.

89 Northern Cat-eyed Snake
Leptodeira septentrionalis septentrionalis

Mildly venomous   The longitudinal grooves of its pair of
slightly enlarged rear teeth enable *L. s. septentrionalis* to chan-
nel its mildly toxic saliva is into its small prey, which is slowly
immobilized by its narcotic effect.

Abundance   **Endangered. Protected by the State of Texas.** This tropical
serpent (it is "northern" only in comparison to its Mexican and Central American
relatives) enters the U.S. only at the southern end of the Rio Grande Valley, where
it is one of the rarest reptiles in Texas.

Size   Adults average 14 to 32 inches (females are slightly longer), with bodies no
thicker than a forefinger among even the largest individuals.

Habitat   Principally a Mexican species, the northern cat-eyed snake inhabits the
jungle of coastal thorn brush, known as Tamaulipan woodland, whose remnants
can still be found along the Gulf Coast from Tampico to Texas' Kleberg Co. At one
time this mass of catclaw acacia, paloverde, tamarisk, cenizo, and ocotillo harbored
an entire tropical—a biotic community comparable to East Texas' "Big Thicket" in
species diversity. But during the 1950s an agricultural boom leveled most of its
native vegetation, and the Mexican birds, mammals, and reptiles that historically
ranged only as far north as the Rio Grande floodplain remain only in isolated and
diminishing populations. In what remains of this tropical thicket, the northern cat-
eyed snake's favored microhabitat is dense vegetation bordering ponds and watercourses, where this semi-arboreal reptile's agility affords it an effective means of
flight from danger.

Prey   Predominantly pond and tree frogs. Given the feeding preferences of captives, smaller snakes, minnows, and mice are probably also taken.

Reproduction   Egg-laying. The incubation time of several clutches deposited by
Mexican females has varied from 79 to 90 days; except for their bolder dorsal patterning, the 9-inch-long young resemble adults.

Coloring scale/form   The northern cat-eyed snake's slender dorsum is alternate-
ly crossbarred with rectangular khaki and dark brown blocks; its light-hued crown
bears a distinctive darker ring with a rearward-pointing apex. But it is the bulging
golden eyes that are this animal's signature. Shared with other rear-fanged, mildly-
venomed colubrids, as well as with the pitvipers, they are slashed with the sharply-
defined, cat-like vertical pupils that are the source of this reptile's common name.

The pale underchin and throat shade to light orange at midbody and salmon
beneath the tail, while the outer ends of many of the belly scales, which have a
slightly darkened posterior border, are peppered with brown speckling. The 21 to
23 midbody rows of dorsal scales are predominantly smooth (some are pocked by
tiny apical pits) and the anal plate is divided.

Similar snakes   None. No other serpent within its range is likely to be mistaken
for the northern cat-eyed snake.

Behavior   The cat-eyed snake is an exclusively nocturnal reptile, whose toxins are
only as potent as needed to subdue its diminutive, mostly anuran prey, and it has a
slender, muscular body that both allows it to hide effectively in thick branches and
gives it the agility to evade predators.

Texas Lyre Snake
Trimorphodon biscutatus vilkinsonii

Mildly venomous   Vertically slit hairline pupils mark this as a mildly venomous serpent, whose posterior upper jaw carries a pair of slightly enlarged, grooved teeth. (This unusual opistho-glyphic dentition is the source of the Texas lyre snake's Latin genus name: *Trimorphodon* means "three forms of teeth.") *T. b. vilkinsonii* poses no danger to humans, because it cannot inject muscle-pressurized venom. Instead, after a bite the lyre snake must advance its jaws far enough to engage the rear fangs, down whose lengthwise furrows its toxic saliva is squeezed by contractions of the jaw—a process far too time-consuming to affect large mammals able to break free immediately.

Abundance   Threatened. Protected by the State of Texas. *Trimorphodon biscutatus vilkinsonii* is quite rare, yet seems to be broadly, if sparsely distributed throughout the Northern Chihuahuan Desert.

First described by E. D. Cope in 1886, the Texas race of *Trimorphodon biscutatus* was known from only three specimens at the time of L. M. Klauber's comprehensive review of the genus in 1940. A few of these secretive animals turn up every summer in widely separated locales across the Trans-Pecos, however, most often among the granite bluffs along the river road west of Big Bend. (A notable exception is the 29 road-killed specimens recorded by Jerry Davis in the Franklin Mts. during a single summer; why so many were found there is not known.)

Size   Adults are 24 to 36 inches in length; the record is 41 inches.

Habitat   This slender, saxicolous reptile is most often found in jumbles of fallen boulders or along fissured bluffs lining the River Road from Big Bend to the Franklin Mountains near El Paso. Like most chthonic, arid land-living serpents, only well after dark does this rare animal leave its creviced retreats, and field observations are few. In the Chisos Mts., Degenhardt and Steele (1957) found two Texas lyre snakes crawling in the open at night, while Earl Turner, who has spent decades hunting snakes in the Trans-Pecos, has only twice observed *T. b. vilkinsonii* on barren desert flats, in Presidio Co.'s Pinto Canyon, and at the mouth of Santa Elena Canyon on the Rio Grande, where he found a small female on a rock ledge overhanging the river.

Prey   The Texas lyre snake will probably feed on any small vertebrate, but it primary prey seems to be lacertillian: Dave Barker found only lizard remains in the feces of several newly-caught *T. b. vilkinsonii*. The way Texas lyre snakes capture this prey became evident only when Dallas herpetologists Dave Blody and James Murphy observed one large individual methodically searching a stony arroyo wall for the several species of lizards that had squeezed into its crevices for the night.

Reproduction   Egg-laying. Little is reported: On Pepper's Hill between Lajitas and Terlingua in Brewster Co., Damon Salceies found the only hatchling *T. b. vilkinsonii* ever seen in the wild. (Because of their great rarity, hatchling Texas lyre snakes may remain below ground for their first several seasons.) Mired in newly laid road tar late in October, this very thin 7 inch-long neonate—whose photograph is included here (90)—had widely separated, sharply defined chocolate dorsolateral saddles quite different from the duller pigmentation of adult *T. b. vilkinsonii*. This newborn also had a recent umbilical scar that showed it to have hatched in late

Sept. or early Oct. (Gus Renfro, who has bred a different subspecies in captivity, reports that a 28-inch-long female in his care deposited 6 adhesive-shelled eggs averaging 1⅛ inches in length and ⅝ inch in diameter in late June. After a 77-day incubation period these hatched into slim, 7½-to 8-inch-long young that were marked like their parents except that their three dark cephalic spots were joined by a distinct brown line.)

Coloring scale/form   The adult Texas lyre snake's ground color is medium brown, with 17 to 24 very widely spaced dorsolateral saddles (so widely spaced, in fact, that Hobart M. Smith has suggested some unique genetic suppression of what would be expected to be intervening markings between them). Broadest over the spine and outlined by an irregular yellowish border, each of these saddles has a paler, cinnamon-hued center and tapers to a point no more than a single scale in width at the belly line; across its tail the lyre snake's saddles become narrow brown bands. The wiry neck supports an oval head notable for the big, slit-pupilled eyes associated with the development of a rudimentary venom system.

Among more westerly subspecies of *Trimorphodon biscutatus,* the dark cephalic marking has a somewhat lyre-like shape that is the source of this reptile's common name, but the crowns of Texas specimens show little more than a trio of chocolate smudges. The anterior venter is yellowish or pinkish-brown, becoming buff on the posterior third. A small facial scale called a lorilabial is located between the loreal and upper labial scales, the dorsal scales are smooth, usually arranged in 23 rows at midbody, and the anal plate is divided.

Similar snakes   None. No other serpent in the Trans-Pecos shares the Texas lyre snake's slim configuration and brown-blotched dorsum (*Trimorphodon* also has a distinctive gait, typically moving along with its head held high off the ground; if restrained, these animals tend to thrash about wildly).

Behavior   Exclusively nocturnal in the wild, Texas lyre snakes may have less aversion to bright light than other nocturnal reptiles because, according to Barker, captives are willing to emerge in the evening to explore even a well-lit room. Blody and Murphy observed one *T. b. vilkinsonii* on a rainy night early in March, but Texas lyre snakes usually restrict their rare appearances in the open to later in the year, especially during periods of elevated humidity following summer rainfall. Because *T. b. vilkinsonii* is probably able to capture its lacertillian prey without leaving the creviced warrens where desert lizards retire for the night, it is thought that rather than foraging, most of the individuals found abroad—a majority of them adult males—are engaged in breeding forays initiated by the pheromonal scent of females intensified in still, humid air. (Females and young apparently seldom venture beyond the shelter of their residential canyons and rock piles.)

Elapidae

Coral Snakes

91 Texas Coral Snake
Micrurus fulvius tener

Venomous   Because its venom is made up mostly of neuro-toxically destructive peptides, *Micrurus fulvius* is (along with western populations of the Mojave rattlesnake) the most virulently-toxined snake in North America. The lethal venom dose for a human adult is estimated to be as little as 5 to 10 milligrams, approximately the same potency as the toxins of most cobras. Immediate pain usually accompanies a bite by *M. fulvius,* but nervous system impairment may not manifest symptoms for several hours; in any case of definite envenomation antivenin should therefore be ready before the onset of neurological problems, because once symptoms appear it may be difficult to prevent further decline.

Yet few people are harmed by coral snakes. If unmolested, coral snakes are so nonaggressive toward people that virtually everyone bitten by one has first touched or handled it, and only about 1% of North American venom poisonings involve *M. fulvius.* Many coral snake bites result in no envenomation, partly because at only about an ⅛ inch in length the coral's tiny, rigid fangs are too short to penetrate shoe leather or thick clothing. (As Francis Roze, the world's leading authority on coral snakes has pointed out, *Micrurus* typically also release a small additional amount of venom from glands located in the lower mandible, but the lower jaw's teeth are much smaller than the fangs, and would have to be worked repeatedly into human skin to deliver any toxins.) Nevertheless, *Micrurus fulvius* is adept at biting a large adversary. Its mouth can gape open to form a surprisingly wide biting surface and its strong jaws can easily pinch out a fold of skin anywhere on the human body. Moreover, as hollow hypodermic needles, coral snake fangs are designed to both puncture skin and rapidly inject venom. (A common myth is that *M. fulvius* must chew deliberately to slowly transmit its toxins. These little snakes do bite-and-chew, but an agitated coral snake can instantly deposit venom onto a pinning stick or handling glove.) In confined areas *Micrurus fulvius* can also move quickly, twisting its head to suddenly snap sideways. See **Venom Potency Table.**

Abundance   Common. Because the Texas coral snake is not averse to human habitation, it is likely to be encountered in suburban areas; the coral's seldom-seen nocturnal look-alikes, the milk snakes, prefer unaltered natural terrain.

Size   Texas coral snakes are larger than most people expect: 74 adult females averaged 26½ inches in length, 93 males just over 24 inches. The record is a 47¾-inch specimen from Brazoria Co.

Habitat   *Micrurus fulvius tener* occupies a variety of dry terrestrial milieus, generally at least partially wooded. These include the state's eastern pine forest, its central oak-juniper brakes, and the thorn brush woodland of the Rio Grande plain. Either rock-crevice cover or thick plant litter is important, both as a hiding place and as habitat for the semi-subterranean serpents on which coral snakes prey.

Prey   Coral snakes feed largely on other snakes. I have seen an adult specimen of *M. f. tener,* in the wild, envenomate, overpower, and swallow a young Texas rat snake nearly as long as itself. Lizards—especially slender, snake-like lizards such as skinks—are reportedly also taken. (Captive Texas coral snakes are so reluctant to feed that, lacking a maintainable specimen, one Texas zoo substituted a rubber replica for a real coral snake in its "Four Venomous Snakes" exhibit.) The food of hatchling coral snakes in the wild is unknown, but one captive brood fed on small earth and brown snakes.

Reproduction   Egg-laying. "No other North American snake has been reported to breed from late summer to late spring, then lay its eggs in midsummer," wrote Hugh Quinn (1979). The 3 to 5 white, sausage-shaped eggs—1⅛ in. in length by ⅜ in. in diameter—are laid during June and July, hatching 2 months later into 6½-to 7½-inch-long young. In the wild these neonates evidently lead almost entirely fossorial lives, perhaps for years, because they have only rarely been seen; one brood I cared for virtually never emerged from cage-bottom litter, even to feed.

Coloring/scale form   The coral snake is the only black-, red-, and yellow-banded serpent in Texas whose red and yellow bands touch. If "Red against yellow, kill a fellow" is usually too extreme a prognosis, it is still the best way to quickly identify *M. fulvius.*

The Texas coral snake's trunk is completely circled with 12 to 16 equally broad red and black bands separated by much narrower yellow rings. Both head and tail are banded only with black and yellow; the nape and posterior crown are marked with a wide yellow band. These dorsolateral bands continue across the coral snakes' venter, whose undertail has a double row of scales like that of most nonvenomous snakes. There are 15 midbody rows of smooth dorsal scales and the anal plate is divided.

Similar snakes   Among **milk snakes (79—82)** and **scarlet snakes (84—85)** red and yellow or white crossbands do not touch—black dorsolateral rings separate them. "Red against black, venom lack." Unlike coral snakes, whose tails are entirely black and yellow, milk and scarlet snakes' red crossbands occur all the way to their tail tips. The **Texas longnose snake (86)** may have a few red and creamy yellow scales that touch, but only in the speckled edging of its dorsal saddles. Its venter is mostly white, its protruding snout light brown or orange.

Behavior   To what degree the coral snake's bold patterning functions as a warning signal has long been an area of controversy. To realize their defensive potential, however, those bright body bands may need to be combined with the coral snake's distinctive threat behavior. In one study, opossums confronted with inert replicas or dead coral snakes were not frightened. Only when live *Micrurus fulvius* actively raised and slowly wagged their yellow- and black-banded tail tips (presumably in a threatening imitation of their similarly-patterned heads, which remained tucked under a body coil) did the opossums hesitate. See **Louisiana Milk Snake (79).**

CORAL SNAKES

Viperidae

Moccasins

Rattlesnakes

Southern Copperhead
Agkistrodon contortrix contortrix

Venomous   Only a few venomous snakebites occur in Texas every year, but when venom poisoning occurs in the eastern part of the state, the southern copperhead is the snake most likely to be involved. Yet, few of these bites are serious: While poisoning by *A. contortrix* could be fatal to a small child, records of the Antivenin Institute of America show that throughout the U.S., regardless of the kind (or lack) of treatment, over a 10-year period not a single death resulted from 308 copperhead bites.

This is largely because *A. contortrix* seldom strikes unless it is stepped on or handled, because it has short (⅜-in. maximum length) fangs, and because its toxins are only about half as destructive to tissue as those in an equal quantity of western diamondback rattlesnake venom. Even animals as small as cats—which are often bitten due to copperheads' prevalence in suburban neighborhoods near wooded creeks—usually survive envenomation by *A. contortrix,* though they typically experience tissue loss and skin-sloughing. See **Venom Potency Table.**

Abundance   Common. In much of the eastern third of Texas, broad-banded and southern copperheads are the most numerous venomous snake, and are invariably killed when found by the local human population. Yet, some three hundred miles to the east, the ecological value of the southern copperhead is recognized to the extent that in Florida it is a threatened animal afforded state protection.

Size   The largest of the copperhead subspecies, *A. c. contortrix* from the southeastern U.S. can measure over 50 inches in length. In Texas, most individuals are much smaller with most adults measuring 20 to 30 inches; the longest in the state are probably no more than 40 inches.

Habitat   Southern copperheads are almost always found in tree-shaded areas where fallen leaves, logs, and branches afford these cryptic ambush-foragers both a camouflage background and shelter for their small terrestrial prey (longleaf pine forest seems to be a less optimal habitat than mixed pasture and woodland, however).

In the richest natural environments as many as six or seven adult copperheads can live on as little as a single acre. In one such North Texas study plot, most *A. contortrix* marked and subsequently recovered were found within 100 yards of where they had been released a year earlier. Some had ranged no farther than 20 yards. Likewise, if they find enough food to survive, young copperheads do not disperse far from their birth site: After tracking radio transmitter-equipped northern copperheads in Kansas, Henry S. Fitch (1971) found that some females remained within an acre or two throughout their entire lives. Most of Fitch's population, however, occupied larger ranges of between 8 and 25 acres, with males maintaining the largest territories.

Prey   Copperheads ordinarily take whatever small prey is most seasonally available. Year in and year out, however, deer mice are probably its principal food source—followed, in damp weather when they are active on the forest floor, by anurans. Large insects such as cicadas are also taken. When excited by nearby prey young copperheads vibrate their yellowish- or grayish-green tailtips in an unconscious but tantalizing imitation of a wriggling caterpillar—a maneuver that may lure small frogs and toads within striking range.

Reproduction   Live-bearing. See **Broad-banded Copperhead (93).**

MOCCASINS

229

Coloring/scale form This large eastern subspecies' most distinctive characteristic is its pale beige, sometimes almost pinkish ground color. This is marked with 13 to 20 pale-centered, dark-bordered reddish brown dorsolateral bands, which are cinched or contorted into an hourglass configuration over the spine—a shape that has given rise to the Latin name *A. contortrix contortrix.*

The tan, wedge-shaped crown bears a pair of dark posterior spots, while the prominent supraocular plates are part of a sharply angled intersection between the crown and the flat, undercut cheeks. Behind the slit-pupilled, coppery-colored eyes the cheeks are marked with a pale, rearward-pointing V whose upper border is defined by a dark line leading from the eye to the rear of the jaw; just below and behind the nostril is the vipers' dark heat-sensing pit. The whitish venter is unmarked or only slightly mottled, and is distally marked with large brown ovals. The 23 to 25 midbody rows of dorsal scales are weakly keeled, there is a single row of ventral scales beneath the tailtip, and the anal plate is undivided.

Similar snakes Where the ranges of the southern and **broad-banded copperhead** (93) meet along a strip of Cross Timbers stretching from the Gulf Coast to Oklahoma—the light gray area on the map—individuals intermediate in pattern between these subspecies prevail. The western broad-banded race can be distinguished, however, by its more darkly mottled venter, the absence of dark borders on its reddish-tan dorsolateral bands, and the almost equal width of these bands at the belly line and along the spine. The nonvenomous serpent most commonly mistaken for the southern copperhead is the **eastern hognose snake (60)**, especially in its coppery color phases. Sometimes similarly patterned, these equally heavy-bodied serpents occur in the same tree-shaded suburban neighborhoods as copperheads, and like them show little fear of humans. The hognose's raised forehead, round-pupilled dark brown eyes, comparatively thick neck, and prominently upturned snout are distinctive, though, as is its divided anal plate and the double row of scales beneath its tail. As a juvenile, the **western cottonmouth (95)** resembles the young southern copperhead, but it is a dusky gray-brown with dark dorsolateral bands. Newborn *A. p. leucostoma* also have a dark band across their cheeks and are seldom found far from water in the copperhead's drier woodland habitat.

Behavior Most often abroad at dawn or dusk between March and October, copperheads are such low energy-budget predators, and feed at such a leisurely rate—often no more than a meal every three weeks even during the months in which they are most active—that *Agkistrodon contortrix* often lives virtually alongside small mammal populations. During late spring and summer snakes and rodents may be simultaneously residents of the sheltered microhabitats beneath logs and human debris such as sheets of plywood or metal siding: I have found nests of baby mice within a few feet of a coiled, quiescent copperhead whose lethargy had failed to excite the parent mouse into moving her brood.

Although normally entirely terrestrial, after floods southern copperheads have been seen on sloping boughs above high water; in Lee Co. bottomland I once discovered an intergrade *A. c. contortrix* within a dead stump some 3 feet above standing water.

Broad-banded Copperhead
Agkistrodon contortrix laticinctus

Venomous   See **Southern Copperhead (92).**

Abundance   Very common. Ideal microenvironments for *A. contortrix* consist of mesic woodland with plentiful ground cover, and because this description fits many tree-shaded suburban neighborhoods, copperheads are sometimes abundant there. Readily adapting to the presence of humans, *A. contortrix* often does well in wooded suburbs, where it is typically so un-aggressive toward humans that the shock of unexpectedly finding one in a woodpile or trash heap is usually the only harm that comes from the encounter.

Size   See **Southern Copperhead (92).**

Habitat   Almost everywhere in their range broad-banded copperheads occur in either riparian or upland woods on a carpet of fallen oak leaves or pine needles—against which their russet dorsal patterning makes them almost invisible. This reptile is also locally abundant in the live oak/cedar brake bottomland of the Edwards Plateau.

Prey   Primarily small rodents, nestling ground birds, spiny lizards, and large insects; newly-metamorphosed cicadas, which periodically emerge in swarms numbering thousands per acre, have been recorded as accounting for up to 20% of the total volume of prey.

Copperheads' success in feeding within a small area—thereby avoiding the exposure to danger that extensive foraging entails—is a result of pitvipers' superior predatory adaptations. Good night vision, heat-sensing facial pits, sophisticated venom, and delicately manipulable fangs requiring only a short striking jab enable these animals to kill a high percentage of the small prey animals that come within ambush range.

Reproduction   Live-bearing. Courtship begins with the male advancing to touch the female with his snout and, if she does not move away, rubbing her body with his chin. If she is receptive, the female will remain stationary, often flattening her body, waving or vibrating her tail, and eliminating waste from her cloaca as a preliminary to mating.

Copulation is initiated only when she gapes open the cloaca to receive the male's hemipene, after which the pair can remain linked for several hours. Although prior breeding by the female tends to deter subsequent mating attempts by other males, spring copulation by a female carrying sperm from a previous autumn pairing can presumably produce a litter sired by two males. Born during the latter part of July and all of August, the 4 to 8 neonates are 7-½ to 10 inches long, with paler pigmentation than their parents.

Coloring/scale form   *Agkistrodon contortrix laticinctus* is distinguished by its light brown ground color and its 11 to 17 reddish-tan dorsolateral bands—almost equally wide at the belly line and along the spine—that lack dark borders. To accommodate the large venom glands the rear of the skull broadens to more than 3 times the width of the narrow neck; ahead of the eyes and slightly below the level of the nostrils lie the copperheads' dark, heat-sensing pits. The pale venter is mottled with reddish brown. Arranged in 23 (occasionally 25) rows at midbody, the dorsal scales are weakly keeled, and under the tail the belly scales are arranged in a single row behind the vent; the anal plate is undivided.

MOCCASINS

Similar snakes   The hourglass-shaped, often chocolate-bordered dorsolateral bands of the **southern copperhead (92)** typically narrow to solid brown bars across its spine; its buff-colored venter is only distally splotched with large brown ovals. Intermediate forms are found with both the southern copperhead (the light gray area on the map to the east of the broad-banded's range), and with the **Trans-Pecos copperhead (94)** (the light gray area on the map to the west). The western race is distinguished by its chestnut to near-black belly, interrupted by pale lateral intrusions. Its dorsolateral crossbands often bear a pale central aura around a dark mahogany spot just above the belly line, as well as a whitish bordering wash, while the area between these bands may be almost white. On the average, there are more undertail scales (52 to 59 to the broad-banded's 40 to 54). Seen from above, **hognose snakes (60−62)** have a proportionately thicker neck than pitvipers, dark beady eyes with round pupils, a bulbous forehead, and a markedly upturned snout; they also lack the broad-banded copperhead's grayish tail tip. Hognose snakes also have a divided anal plate and a single row of undertail scales. Newborn *A. c. laticinctus* to some degree resemble the similarly-shaped young **western cottonmouth (95),** but copperheads' cheeks have a rearward-facing pale V in place of the blackish sides of the young cottonmouth's head. Both species are often abundant in riverbottom woodland, but unlike the copperhead, the darker-colored cottonmouth seeks shelter in water.

Behavior   Copperheads and cottonmouths are the only North American members of the genus *Agkistrodon,* which apparently originated in Asia during early Miocene times, then spread to the New World over the Bering land bridge. Here, *Agkistrodon* subsequently gave rise to the more highly evolved rattlesnakes.

Like most temperate zone reptiles, the copperhead's activity patterns vary considerably throughout the year. After early spring emergence from winter denning, these reptiles seek an optimal temperature of 78° to 84°F by basking during the sunniest hours and hiding beneath woodland debris in the morning and evening. As midday temperatures climb beyond this level, copperheads grow largely crepuscular, foraging mostly at dawn and at twilight except on overcast days or when soil and vegetation are damp; in the hottest weather of midsummer they are abroad mainly at night.

Among the least agile of snakes—its only capacity for rapid motion is in the darting jab of its strike—the copperhead's predatory forays characteristically involve little more than deliberate travel from one ambush site to the another, although sedentary prey such as nestling birds and rodents is sought by scent. If threatened, *Agkistrodon contortrix* may both emit musk from a pair of anal glands flanking its vent and vibrate its tail in agitation.

Trans-Pecos Copperhead
Agkistrodon contortrix pictigaster

Venomous   See **Southern Copperhead (92).**

Abundance   Uncommon. Because locating *A. c. pictigaster* in the field is difficult, most records are of individuals encountered at night on backroads crossing the canyon-laced region north of Langtry in Val Verde and Crockett counties.

Size   Most adults are 18 to 26 inches; the record is 32⅞ inches.

Habitat   Although in most of the U.S. copperheads are associated with moist bottomland, this species' westernmost race, *A. c. pictigaster,* is found throughout even arid parts of Trans-Pecos Texas. This is largely because the area's Northern Chihuahuan Desert is of more recent origin than much of the local wildlife—some of which, including *A. c. pictigaster,* remains in relict populations often found in the vicinity of the scattered permanent springs remaining from the more verdant climate of the late Pleistocene. These springs, as well as seasonally moist canyons and creekbeds are the Trans-Pecos copperhead's favored microhabitat. (Henry Fitch did the pioneering field work with this subspecies along Independence Creek; it is also found along creeks in the Davis Mts., near Lajitas, and north of Sanderson.) Yet *A. c. pictigaster* is also a shrub desert-living serpent—individuals have been found on the rolling, creosote-shrub plains of Terrell Co.

Prey   See **Broad-banded Copperhead (93).**

Reproduction   Live-bearing. See **Broad-banded Copperhead (93).**

Coloring/scale form   The Trans-Pecos copperhead's 13 to 19 dorsolateral bands vary from cinnamon-bay to seal brown, usually with a pale aura around a mahogany spot just above the belly line; juveniles are slightly lighter in color. The heavily mottled ventral pigmentation, typically mahogany to black interrupted with pale lateral intrusions, is both unique to this subspecies and the source of its scientific name: *picti* means "painted" and *gaster* is "stomach." The tail is grayish brown above, with thin white crossbands, while a single line of undertail scales lines its posterior tip. The 21 to 25 midbody rows of dorsal scales are weakly keeled; the anal plate is undivided.

Similar snakes   The **broad-banded copperhead (93)** is distinguished by its more uniformly-colored body bands, its less heavily mottled venter, and its lower average number of subcaudal scales (52 to 59 in *A. c. pictigaster,* 37 to 54 in *A. c. laticinctus*). In the field such distinctions are largely arbitrary, however, because across a roughly east-west sequence of clinal variation, Texas' three copperhead subspecies only gradually diverge into their respective forms.

Behavior   The ability of a mesic-adapted species such as the copperhead to thrive in a region now considerably drier than at any time during its recent history is due partly to the ophidian capacity for enduring long periods of hostile conditions—heat, drought, or cold—as long as some portion of the year allows active foraging. But other moist climate snakes are not found here, and in the harsh Chihuahuan biome copperheads' minimal energy expenditure, which lets them get by on as little as a single meal per month during their activity season, is a major factor in their survival.

MOCCASINS

95 Western Cottonmouth
Agkistrodon piscivorus leucostoma

Venomous   Despite the cottonmouth's formidable reputation, very few people are bitten by this reptile, and even fewer are seriously injured: Only about 7% of Texas' snakebites involve cottonmouths, and throughout the United States the mortality rate is less than one person per year. Envenomation by *Agkistrodon piscivorus* may result in substantial tissue destruction, however, because these big aquatic vipers have up to ⅝-inch-long fangs and venom-storage lumens that, from the largest individuals, can yield hundreds of mg, dry weight, of venom. While its toxins are less potent than those of most large *Crotalus*-genus rattlesnakes—Sherman Minton estimates the lethal dose for a healthy human adult as about 150 mg—the hemorrhagic effects of cottonmouth venom are pronounced. See **Venom Potency Table.**

Abundance   Locally very common. Although most presumed "cottonmouth" sightings are actually of *natricine* water snakes, western cottonmouths are extremely numerous in some places. This is especially true on the coastal plain. Near Sinton, as well as on ricefield levees north of Egypt, I have seen a basking cottonmouth every few hundred yards, while around woodland ponds in East Texas the musky scent of *Agkistrodon piscivorus* can sometimes be detected in the still air. (When John Prine sings, in *Muehlenberg County,* of the abandoned old farm "where the air smelled like snakes," he's probably talking about cottonmouths.)

Size   The record *A. p. leucostoma,* taken on the Neches River by George O. Miller, is a fraction of an inch over 5 feet in length. Most cottonmouths are much smaller: Of 306 recorded individuals, only a few males—which grow larger than females—were longer than 3 feet, and most measured between 20 and 30 inches.

Habitat   Although western cottonmouths are generally found within a half-mile of permanent water, they are not limited to aquatic environments Cottonmouths favor leutic microhabitats primarily because of the more plentiful prey and better cover available there, but they do quite well in entirely dry milieus.

Dry forest, grassland, and even cornfields are also occupied; in spring, flooded prairie is a prime foraging site. Salt marshes and the low-lying saline barrier islands bordering the Texas coast also constitute good cottonmouth habitat, yet the density of cottonmouth populations tends to vary widely, with large areas of apparently perfect wetland terrain being almost entirely devoid of these reptiles.

Prey   Cottonmouths may feed on any vertebrate small enough to swallow. Frogs are probably this viper's most frequent prey, but *Agkistrodon piscivorus* is an indiscriminate feeder whose diet alters with the availability of different food species. Water birds, smaller snakes—including copperheads and even other cottonmouths—are also reported, as are a variety of fish species, although game fish are generally too fast for cottonmouths to capture. Like other aquatic serpents, *A. piscivorus* also feeds on carrion and is consequently drawn to wounded and dying fish dangling from fishermen's stringers.

Reproduction   Live-bearing. Reproduction follows the usual viperid pattern of slow growth, delayed maturation, and low reproductive frequency. But the enhanced foraging opportunities afforded by their rich aquatic habitat give female cottonmouths a better chance than terrestrial vipers of acquiring the increased body fat necessary for successful pregnancy. (Unlike terrestrial viperids, many of which require two years' hunting to acquire enough fatty tissue to nourish their large, well-developed young, female *A. piscivorus* may breed every year).

During early spring courtship adult male cottonmouths typically follow a female's pheromone scent trail, sometimes even across lily pads. If they encounter another male engaged in the same pursuit, dominance behavior is likely to ensue, with each combatant attempting to force down the other's foreparts. Pairing initially involves tongue-flicking of the female's back by the male, followed by rubbing his chin along her spine, after which copulation may last several hours.

Because gestation among snakes is not as uniformly timed as among birds and mammals, fertilization may be delayed for weeks while viable sperm are retained in the cloaca; several months after copulation the 8- to 11-inch-long young are born during August, September, and early October. They are so stoutly proportioned that gravid females bear only 3 to 12 offspring per litter (while similarly-sized water snakes typically deposit dozens of much more slender young).

Newborn cottonmouths are both more brownish and more clearly patterned than adults, with dark dorsal bars and lateral blotches. Their tails have gray-green tips that, in a predatory technique shared with their relatives the copperheads, are instinctively flicked back and forth in the excitement of seeing prey, thus imitating the movements of a worm or caterpillar and luring small frogs and toads within striking range.

Coloring/scale form   Sometimes displayed in open-jawed threat, the creamy-white interior of this reptile's mouth is the source of its common name. In its scientific name, *Agkis* is a mistranslation of *ancil,* meaning "forward"; *odon* refers to its teeth or fangs; and *piscivorus* means "fish-eating." *Leuco* is "white" and *stoma* is "mouth," so the entire appellation accurately describes a forward-fanged, white-mouthed, fish-eating serpent.

Adult cottonmouths are dark gray-brown, with broad, dimly-defined lateral banding. (Some individuals' dull dorsal coloring results from a film of water-deposited sediment and algae: Clean water-living cottonmouths show more distinct patterning.) Very old cottonmouths may be entirely dark gray or black.

In daylight, the pupils of the large, grayish eyes are vertical black slits easily discernable from a safe distance; at night in the beam of a flashlight they are oval or rounded for the few moments it takes them to close against the glare. Definitive but less evident is the dark orifice of the heat-sensing pit located between the eye and nostril, and the pronounced taper from the thick posterior trunk to the cottonmouth's attenuated little tail that, especially among females (the male's tail contains its hemipene and is somewhat larger), seems out of proportion to the thickset trunk.

The keeled dorsal scales occur in 25 rows at midbody, while the subcaudal scutes display a unique pattern by which even from their shed skins *Agkistrodon* can be identified: Behind the undivided anal plate a single row of belly-wide scales occupies the under-tail tip.

Similar snakes   The dark, heavy bodies and aquatic habitat of Texas' large **water snakes (30–36)** often cause them to be mistaken for the cottonmouth. All water snakes lack the cottonmouth's heat-sensing pit between eye and nostril, however, and have clearly visible round pupils. *Agkistrodon piscivorus* also behaves differently from water snakes, which neither gape in threat nor vibrate their tails in agitation. Also unlike water snakes, the cottonmouth swims in a leisurely way, its whole body floating buoyantly, with the head held high. Water snakes are much more agile, and swim by squirming rapidly along, their bodies drooping below the surface when they stop. Juvenile **copperheads** (92–93) are lighter brown and have dark-edged beige cheeks unlike the cottonmouth's dark labial scales.

Behavior   The most widespread story about cottonmouths concerns the water-skier purportedly killed by a flurry of bites after tumbling into a "nest" of these reptiles. For years various re-tellings of this fictitious event have circulated in boating circles, and a river-crossing version involving a cowboy on horseback appeared in the television special *Lonesome Dove.*

All such episodes are untrue: No water-skier or river-fording horseman has ever suffered multiple *A. piscivorus* envenomation. These scary myths originate in people's observations of the large number of harmless water snakes that, during late summer, become concentrated in drying creeks and stock tanks, where they are mistaken for "nests" of cottonmouths.

Cottonmouths do not "nest," however, and packed groups would last no longer than the time it took the larger *A. piscivorus* to swallow their smaller relatives. Further, most cottonmouths flee when approached; although on land some hold their ground and gape open-mouthed, none attack en masse. In fact, the cottonmouth's notorious gape is actually a rather passive defense gesture, for wide-jawed *A. piscivorus* often fail to strike even when prodded with a boot.

Can a cottonmouth bite underwater? Of course, that's how they catch fish. But its *only* fish: In the water, cottonmouths normally swim away if approached by a human. Actually, contrary to popular opinion cottonmouths spend almost no time submerged. *Agkistrodon piscivorus* seldom forages underwater, and in observation tanks usually takes fish only by cornering them in the shallows. In the wild this pitviper hunts primarily along banks and shorelines, basks on floating aquatic vegetation, and swims slowly across the surface, but dives, briefly, only if it is attacked.

Western Pigmy Rattlesnake
Sistrurus miliarius streckeri

Venomous   Despite the fact that the pigmy rattlesnake is a
nervous, quick-to-strike little reptile, *S. miliarius* is far less dangerous than the state's larger rattlesnakes. This is partly because
its diminutive fangs measure no more than ⁵⁄₃₂ inch across their curve,
which limits *Sistrurus miliarius* to superficial penetration.

   Moreover, even when its venom glands are artificially milked to depletion, a
large *S. miliarius* yields no more than 35 milligrams (dry weight) of venom. This is
more than twice as much as the snake could expel on its own, but it is still less than
half the probable lethal dose for an adult human being. Even though its venom is
moderately potent, about the same toxicity as that of the southern copperhead,
poisoning by *S. m. streckeri* seldom causes the extensive tissue necrosis characteristic of envenomation by larger crotalids, but any venomous snakebite is potentially
dangerous to a small child. See **Venom Potency Table.**

Abundance   Uncommon. Spottily dispersed throughout its broad East Texas
range, the western pigmy rattlesnake is seldom encountered even by those working
in the heart of its range since it is an extremely cryptic animal which spends the day
hidden beneath ground cover. In biologically generous riverbottom and palmetto
flatland environments it can be one of the most numerous serpents, however.

Size   Adult S. m. streckeri usually measure 14 to 20 inches in length; the record is
25⅛ inches.

Habitat   Favored habitat includes both wet and dry areas—loblolly/longleaf pine
forest, riverbottom hardwoods, wet sawgrass prairie, and palmetto lowlands.
Sistrurus miliarius streckeri also occurs in the riparian corridor of sycamore,
pecan, black willow, and mustang grape that traces the Trinity and Red River systems northwestward, allowing this fundamentally eastern-forest animal to penetrate an extensive dry, upland area.

   Along the upper coast, *S. m. streckeri* was formerly found in most places where
there was both heavy vegetation and abundant surface water. Such sites recently
included lowlying woodland in the Alvin/Liverpool/Angleton section of Brazoria
Co., the overgrown banks of Sheldon Reservoir south of Lake Houston, and the
swampy portion of Matagorda Co. between Cedar Lane and the coast. Extensive
urbanization has eliminated most of this habitat, however, and only the latter area
retains enough natural cover to support pigmy rattlesnakes.

Prey   Much of the warm-blooded prey taken by larger vipers is too big for the
western pigmy rattlesnake, so small reptiles, amphibians, and insects—the typical
food of juvenile crotalids—constitute most of the diet of adult *S. miliarius*. Thirteen
dusky pigmy rattlesnakes from Georgia contained 4 large centipedes, 3 ground
skinks, 1 six-lined racerunner lizard, 1 ringneck snake, and 2 deer mice.

Reproduction   Live-bearing. Pitvipers tend to have slow growth and maturation
rates, as well as low levels of reproduction. In the southeastern U.S., only about
half the adult female pigmy rattlesnakes become gravid every summer, and the
Texas population is likely to follow the same alternate-year reproductive agenda.

   Primarily autumn breeders—males have been observed in combat at this season—
S. miliarius typically gives birth in early summer after winter-long sperm storage by
the female. A captive pair maintained at the Fort Worth Zoo bred repeatedly
throughout September, with the female giving birth some 8½ months later to three, 237

¹⁄₁₀ ounce, 5⅓-inch-long young with pale yellow tail tips. (In the wild, prior to parturition females cease feeding and move to the sunniest parts of their territories to bask, thereby elevating their body temperature and accelerating the development of their young.)

Like other pitvipers, *S. miliarius* has a large abdominal cavity compared to most snakes, but because its neonates are also large in comparison to the size of their mother, litters usually number no more than 6. (Because the size of the individual offspring is generally determined primarily by the minimal dimensions it needs to survive, smaller snake species typically give birth to fewer young than larger species.)

Coloring/scale form   At first glance the western pigmy rattlesnake's black-spotted back and agile movements do not suggest the heavy-bodied "rattlesnake" image of its larger *Crotalus* relatives, and indeed it is a quite different animal. The head is proportionately narrower than that of larger rattlesnakes, and boldly black-striped on both its crown and cheeks, where the large slit-pupilled eyes are obscured by a dark mask.

Sistrurus miliarius streckeri—Sistrurus was coined in 1883 by S. Garman from the Greek for "rattle" and "tail," while the subspecies name honors herpetologist John K. Strecker, for whom the Mexican hooknose snake, a chorus frog, and Baylor University's Strecker Museum are also named—also has unusual coloring for a rattlesnake. Its gray dorsum is widely spotted with black and marked with a russet-tan vertebral stripe, while its lower sides bear a double row of dark spots that may overlap onto the whitish, faintly stippled venter. The strongly keeled dorsal scales are arranged in 23 to 25 rows at midbody, the crown is capped with 9 large scale plates, and the anal plate is undivided.

Similar snakes   The related **western massasauga (97)** has larger, more closely spaced brown dorsolateral blotches; it lacks a distinct vertebral stripe and has 25 rows of dorsal scales at midbody. It is rarely found in the pigmy rattlesnake's woodland/wetland habitat. Except as a juvenile, the **timber rattlesnake (99)** is a larger serpent jaggedly crossbarred with dark brown chevrons. It has a uniformly blackish tail and very small scales cover the center of its broad crown.

Behavior   Entirely terrestrial, *S. m. streckeri* may rattle its tail from beneath ground cover or fallen palmetto fronds, although its rattle is so minuscule that the sound is not easy to distinguish from insect buzzing like that of a cicada. (No longer than the width of its head, the western pigmy's inconspicuous little rattle has given rise to the myth of the rattle-less ground rattler.)

If exposed in its hiding place, the pigmy rattlesnake does not raise its forebody into the defensive posture that enables *Crotalus*-genus rattlesnakes to strike up to half their body length. Instead, threatened pigmy rattlesnakes tend to flatten their trunks and if touched, snap without coiling—though the strike never spans more than a few inches.

Western Massasauga
Sistrurus catenatus tergeminus

Venomous   Few envenomations by *Sistrurus catenatus tergeminus* occur in the wild (the great majority of all snake venom poisonings occur as a result of handling captives), because western massasaugas are retiring animals that avoid human-inhabited areas. In addition, this snake's nocturnal habits—out of 60 recorded field observations, not a single instance of daytime activity was noted—further restrict its chances of encounters with humans.

Massasauga envenomation itself is seldom serious because this reptile's fangs are no more than ⅜ inch long, which limits its bite to superficial penetration, while its venom capacity is comparatively low. Because only 15 to 45 milligrams (dry weight) can be obtained even by artificial milking, a bite lethal to a healthy human adult (for whom a probable lethal dose would be 30 to 40 mg) is unlikely; most envenomations are similar to those suffered by Rick Pratt, former director of the Armand Bayou Nature Center, and to Jack Joy of the Abilene Zoo, both of which caused no permanent damage.

Abundance   Uncommon. Western massasaugas have probably always occurred primarily in localized populations, where they were formerly sometimes numerous. According to John E. Werler (1978):

> This reptile was very abundant in some parts of the state more more than 50 years ago. In the early 1900s one Armstrong Co. farmer . . . killed 50 or 60 during one wheat season.

Even as late as the mid-1970s, it was not unusual to find concentrations of western massasaugas. Jonathan Campbell of the University of Texas at Arlington saw as many as 40 of these animals in a night's road cruising on the prairie west of Fort Worth. Yet this localization of its colonies has made *S. c. tergeminus* vulnerable to human expansion. Intensive crop cultivation has heavily impacted Panhandle populations, while residential real estate development and the destruction of their wintering dens has all but eliminated the western massasaugas living between Fort Worth and Weatherford, a place where they were once common; this is also true of most other groups of *Sistrurus catenatus* living near urban areas.

Size   Most adult *S. c. tergeminus* are about 2 feet in length; the record is 34¾ inches.

Habitat   The western massasauga is primarily an animal of Great Plains grasslands. In Texas, that habitat once meant a 200-mile-wide band of tall-grass prairie running from the Gulf to the northeastern Panhandle. (In the westernmost part of this now-fragmented band of prairie, *S. c. tergeminus* intergrades with its paler, arid-country subspecies, the desert massasauga, which inhabits two widely separated grassland milieus: Short-grass prairie in the southern Panhandle and mesquite savannah in South Texas.) Little of Texas' original tall-grass ecosystem has escaped human alteration, but where the big bluestem and Indian grass remain in non-agricultural parts of the eastern Panhandle, *S. c. tergeminus* is still present, spending the daylight hours hidden either below ground or in dense clumps of prickly pear or bunchgrass.

Prey   Western massasaugas are opportunistic predators on a variety of small vertebrates: 18 stomachs contained 9 pocket and harvest mice, 3 whiptail and fence lizards, 2 ground snakes, 1 lined snake, 2 leopard frogs, and a shrew.

Reproduction   Live-bearing. Breeding occurs both spring and fall, with a courtship that begins, as Joseph Collins (1974) writes, when:

239

The male crawls along beside the female with quick, jerking movements of his body. His tail bends beneath her until their cloacal openings meet and copulation occurs.

Viable sperm from autumn pairings remain in the female's cloaca during the winter, with fertilization occurring in spring. Pregnancy lasts 15 to 16 weeks, with litters of 5 to 13 young, 7 to 9 inches long, being born during July and August.

Coloring/scale form   *Sistrurus*-genus rattlers are thought to be similar to the first rattlesnakes to branch from their moccasin-like ancestors, for they retain the 9 large forecrown scale plates of the copperheads and cottonmouths. The western massasauga's 38 or more big brown vertebral splotches are closely-spaced along its gray-brown dorsum, while below its oval, brown-striped crown, a white-edged chocolate-brown mask hides its pale, vertically-pupilled eyes and extends posteriorly across its cheeks. The venter is mottled with gray. Arranged in 25 rows at midbody, the dorsal scales are keeled, the anal plate is undivided.

Similar snakes   The **desert massasauga (98)** is a slightly smaller, paler, arid-land race formally distinguished—though these distinctions do not hold true for many individuals of intermediate parentage living in areas where the ranges of these two races overlap—by its fewer (35 to 37) dorsal blotches on a creamy ground color, its uniformly white venter, and its 23 midbody rows of dorsolateral scales. Texas' other *Sistrurus* rattler, the **western pigmy rattlesnake (96),** is found in eastern woodland and along the Gulf Coast and is distinguished by its gray dorsolateral ground color, its widely spaced blackish dorsal blotches, and its russet-tan vertebral stripe. It has but 21 rows of dorsal scales and a diminutive rattle.

All other rattlesnakes within the western massasauga's range have crowns covered with small scales. The **timber rattlesnake (99)** is a woodland reptile with a black tail; no broad stripes line its wide, triangular crown. Both the **western diamondback rattlesnake (100)** and the **prairie rattlesnake (102)** have broad, unstriped, small-scaled crowns and the diamondback has a black-and-white ringed tail.

Behavior   In cool weather this nocturnal reptile sometimes thermoregulates by seeking the heart-retaining asphalt of little-traveled roads. Here, unlike more active serpents intercepted as they cross pavement on hunting or breeding forays, *S. c. tergeminus* typically coils quietly at the edge of the asphalt, soaking up its warmth. Yet western massasaugas are also very sensitive to elevated temperatures: Dmi'el (1972) reports diminished activity above 93°F, and few are massasaugas are seen on the roads after hot weather begins. By July, even in areas where it was abundant in late spring, *S. c. tergeminus* seems to be almost nonexistent, but the first cool, damp autumn weather sometimes draws a few individuals back to the sun-warmed pavement before they enter winter dormancy.

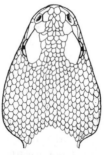

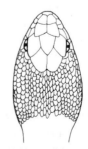

Crotalus *rattlesnake*   Sistrurus *rattlesnake*

8 Desert Massasauga
Sistrurus catenatus edwardsii

Venomous   No record exists of human envenomation by this retiring little rattlesnake, but the potency of its toxins is almost certainly the same as those of its subspecies, the western massasauga, *S. c. tergeminus.*

Abundance   Very uncommon. Although it is distributed over a large range, the desert massasauga is unevenly dispersed and is extremely difficult to find even during its late spring activity period.

Size   Adult desert massasaugas average less than 18 inches in length, with the record specimen measuring only 20½ inches.

Habitat   This misleadingly-named reptile is not a true desert-dweller and is only rarely found in the Trans-Pecos' arid Northern Chihuahuan biotic province. This unusual little pitviper is an inhabitant of dry, short-grass prairie in both the Panhandle and the Trans-Pecos. In South Texas, it is found in mesquite/prickly pear savannah near Norias in Kenedy Co., as well as along the inland side of the Laguna Madre in grass-covered sand dunes. (Along the eastern margin of both areas, the desert massasauga intergrades with its tall-grass prairie-living subspecies, the western massasauga.)

Prey   *Sistrurus catenatus edwardsii* captured in the thorn brush savannah of the lower coastal plain typically choose laboratory mice as prey over small reptiles or amphibians, but 2 adults taken in Presidio Co. grassland would feed only on whiptail lizards.

Reproduction   Live-bearing. See **Western Massasauga (97).**

Coloring/scale form   *Sistrurus catenatus edwardsii* is a xeric conditions-adapted race of the western massasauga, which it resembles except for its paler dorsal coloring, its fewer (35 to 37) dorsal blotches on a creamy ground color, its uniformly whitish venter, and its 23 midbody rows of dorsal scales. See **Western Massasauga (97).**

Similar snakes   The desert massasauga is the only rattlesnake within its range whose head is capped with the 9 large scale plates typical of its *Sistrurus* genus. The **western diamondback rattlesnake (100)** has a mottled grayish back patterned with white-edged vertebral diamonds, a distinctly black-and-white-ringed tail, and 25 to 27 dorsal scale rows at midbody. The **prairie rattlesnake (102)** is browner in ground color and also has 25 to 27 rows of dorsal scales at midbody, as well as numerous small cephalic scales between the large supraocular scales that flank its broad, triangular crown.

Exhibiting similar dorsolateral coloring, size, and body shape as the desert massasauga is the **Mexican hognose snake (63)**; at night, in the beam of a flashlight it takes a second look, checking for the viper's rattle, to be sure which animal is at hand. (This is an interesting case of parallel existence—in configuration, coloring, and habitat-selection—among unrelated snakes, for the Mexican hognose snake shares both of the desert massasauga's geographically separated ranges, favoring short-grass prairie in northwest Texas and mesquite savannah in south Texas.)

Behavior   Entirely nocturnal, *S. c. edwardsii* is usually seen shortly after dark during its late spring/early summer activity period, when individuals often appear coiled along the edges of roads.

RATTLESNAKES

99 Timber Rattlesnake
Crotalus horridus

Venomous In general, the timber rattlesnake's venom is less destructive to local tissue than that of the western diamondback rattler, although its most significant attribute is its great variability. This variability was established more than 20 years ago by Sherman Minton, who took from a pair of gravid female timber rattlers captured on the same day on a single hilltop venom samples, one of which was 5 times as powerful as the other. From 100 to 400 mg of venom has been obtained from the largest *Crotalus horridus* (the snake might inject some 30% of that amount on its own), while an average lethal dose for a human adult is estimated by Minton to be about 100 mg. See **Venom Potency Table.**

Abundance **Threatened. Protected by the State of Texas.** Timber rattlesnakes occur throughout the eastern third of the state, where they favor wooded, usually lowlying terrain, but they are unevenly distributed there. In areas with sparse human populations these animals may be abundant, however.

Size Most adult *Crotalus horridus* measure between 30 and 48 inches in length; the record is just over 74 inches.

Habitat In the central and northeastern U.S., the timber rattlesnake is an animal of upland woods and rocky ridges. Within its East Texas range, however, as well as in most southeastern states *C. horridus* does not characteristically occupy either elevated ridges or open pine forest. Here, it is known as the canebrake rattlesnake for its historic prevalence in the impenetrable cane reed thickets, or brakes, which before the turn of the century matted every damp clearing in East Texas. Almost all the old cane brakes are gone now, but the timber rattlesnake's preferred habitat is still dense undergrowth in deciduous riparian woodland.

Prey Small *Crotalus horridus* probably take mostly white-footed mice, but in the stomachs of 30 large individuals collected in Louisiana were 10 rabbits, 8 mice, 6 rats, and 1 fox squirrel.

This sample does not indicate an exclusive preference for endothermic prey, however, because woodland-living spiny lizards are readily taken by captive timber rattlesnakes and cannibalism has also been observed. A different prey orientation was exhibited by a 3-foot-long *C. horridus* captured by D. Craig McIntyre: After this individual had refused small mammal prey for weeks, McIntyre was about to release it for fear it would starve when he accidentally discovered its sole food requirement was birds—a diet on which it then thrived for years. (Research suggests that pitvipers can acquire prey preferences by successfully killing a particular food animal early in life.)

Reproduction Live-bearing. In his study of 51 gravid female *Crotalus horridus*, L. M. Klauber (1972) recorded a range of 5 to 17 unborn young, with an average brood numbering just over 10. Born in late summer, neonates range in size from 10½ to 13½ in. in length.

Coloring/scale form The timber rattlesnake's black tail, cinnamon vertebral stripe, and dark dorsolateral chevrons are definitive. Its crown is much paler than its dorsum and on the sides of its head its big, slit-pupilled eyes are hidden in the pitvipers' characteristic dark mask. Both ontogenetic variation and sexual dimorphism, the latter rare among snakes, occur in *Crotalus horridus*, for as this viper ages its body darkens, obscuring the contrast between its creamy youthful ground color, black dorsolateral chevrons, and rusty vertebral stripe. Males are grayer than females, so the oldest and largest males—one of which is pictured here—are much less vividly marked than young females.

Northern and western timber rattlesnakes—which include Texas' residents—have 23 mid-body rows of keeled dorsal scales (among southeastern timber rattlers, more individuals have 25 rows), the yellowish venter is smudged along its edges with darker pigment, and the anal plate is undivided.

Similar snakes Herpetological opinion is divided over whether the southern form of the timber rattlesnake (pictured here) constitutes a subspecies, the **canebrake rattlesnake**, *C. h. atricaudatus*. One view is that the canebrake is merely a variant color phase, although in other serpents a geographically specific color phase often defines a subspecies. Both "canebrake" and "northern-form" timber rattlesnakes—the latter have solid blackish forebodies—occur together in eastern Kansas and Missouri, however, but those who define the canebrake as a separate subspecies do so on the basis of its overall paler ground color, its 25 rows of dorsal scales and, in the South, its distinctly different microhabitat.

In Texas' Cross Timbers, the **western diamondback rattlesnake (100)** share the western part of the timber rattlesnake's range, but the diamondback inhabits upland pastures and mesquite shrubland, while the timber rattlesnake occupies moist forest. The diamondback is distinguished by its white-edged vertebral diamonds, its black- and white-banded tail, and its white-bordered brown postocular stripe.

The **western massasauga (97)** and the **western pigmy rattler (96)** are smaller animals whose proportionately narrower crowns are striped with chocolate and, unlike the small-scaled forecrown of the timber rattlesnake, capped with 9 large scale plates.

Behavior As a sedentary, nocturnal forager, the timber rattlesnake is not often seen even in areas where a substantial population survives; in early spring, however, an occasional individual can be found basking in a patch of sunlight at the base of a tree or next to a fallen log. This propensity for coiling next to logs has been noted since 1900, but only recently have studies shown the behavior to be part of an active hunting strategy. Because *C. horridus* feeds on alert, highly mobile prey, it must maximize its contact with these creatures beyond chance encounters on the forest floor, and because fallen logs are important byways for both lizards and small mammals, timber rattlers have been observed investigating these elevated pathways by repeated tongue-flicking along their upper surfaces.

Quickly passing over trunks lacking active scent trails, *Crotalus horridus* selected only the most-traveled logs for ambush sites, then, coiling next to such a well-used avenue, the rattlers typically rested their chins on the trunk's upper surface. Here, the overlapping sensory fields of these vipers' eyes and heat-sensing pits are directed in both directions along the log, while its throat and lower jaw are thought to be able to detect the slight vibrations of an approaching spiny lizard or white-footed mouse. (Confirmation that this chin-on-log posture is an active hunting technique comes from the fact that only males and non-gravid females engage in this behavior; pregnant females, which have no interest in feeding, do not seek out such ambush sites.)

100 Western Diamondback Rattlesnake
Crotalus atrox

Venomous   Nearly all of the most serious cases of snakebite treated in Texas hospitals are inflicted by *Crotalus atrox,* the largest and statistically the most dangerous (*atrox* is Latin for "frightful") serpent in the state. Its venom contains roughly 17% neurotoxically active peptide components, 30% tissue-digestive proteases, and 53% blood-targeted toxic enzymes, the injection of which is characterized by immediate severe pain, swelling, weakness, sweating and chills, faintness or dizziness, elevation or depression of pulse, nausea, vomiting, and swelling of the regional lymph nodes.

Yet few people die from diamondback rattlesnake bites. Widely available care at hospital facilities accustomed to combating hypovolemic shock has cut the fatality rate to less than 10% of even severely envenomated patients; those who succumb are mostly children, whose body fluid volume is too small to accommodate the plasma leakage brought about by the venom toxins' perforation of their capillaries. Peripheral morbidity, including the loss of digits and even limbs, is still fairly high, however, in cases of deep envenomation, and may be aggravated by ill-advised first-aid procedures. See **Venom Potency Table.**

Abundance   Very common. *Crotalus atrox* is by far the most numerous and widespread venomous snake in the western two thirds of the state. Because of its bold temperament and frequently diurnal foraging pattern, it is also one of the most likely to be noticed, especially around farm buildings that shelter rats and mice.

Size   Adults average 3 to 4 feet in length. In observations of more than 200 western diamondbacks in the Trans-Pecos, Gerry Salmon recorded only one individual longer than 40 inches; much larger diamondbacks are found in South Texas, but because newborns are so numerous in early autumn, most *C. atrox* encountered are less than 20 inches long. Huge western diamondbacks–always males, because among pitvipers males are the larger gender–have measured nearly 7½ feet in length. (Because such animals have invariably been radically stretched after death by being hung up for photographs, which can add 20% to their length, their true size is difficult to determine, however.)

Nevertheless, many western diamondback rattlesnakes have spent long lives–the record is nearly 26 years–in confinement without reaching remarkable size. Therefore, these extremely large specimens are not simply very old snakes (aged rattlesnakes cannot be told by the size of their rattle strings, because old rattles break off periodically like a too-long fingernail), but true genetic giants.

Almost all of these record-sized *Crotalus atrox*–whose heads can be wider than a man's spread hand and whose maximum diameter may exceed 6 inches–come from Starr, Hidalgo, and Willacy counties in the Rio Grande Valley. Among this population, where western diamondbacks over 5 feet in length are not unusual, naturalist Greg Lasley observed a copulating pair, both of which were more than five feet long.

Habitat   At one time or another *Crotalus atrox* resides in nearly every terrestrial habitat within its range (it is especially abundant on the coastal barrier islands, in South Texas' Tamaulipan thorn woodland, and in the northern part of Big Bend National Park).

Compared to most rattlesnakes in Texas, which are to a greater degree oriented toward specific habitat niche divisions, *Crotalus atrox* is typically the generalist—an animal whose microhabitat overlaps, to the east, that of the mesic-bottomland, dense cover-preferring timber and pigmy rattlesnakes. To the northwest, the western diamondback inhabits large portions of the prairie and massasauga rattlesnakes' grassland range; to the west, it occurs throughout much of the rock and blacktail rattlesnakes' mountainous and/or saxicolous environs; to the southwest, the western diamondback simultaneously occupies the creosote desert and mesquite-tarbush zone typical of the arid-adapted Mojave rattlesnake.

Prey *Crotalus atrox* feeds mostly on mammals. Newborns take mice while, among the largest adults, squirrels, prairie dogs, cottontails, and even young jackrabbits are suitably-sized prey; ground-living birds are also taken.

Reproduction Live-bearing. Litter size among *Crotalus atrox* averages 9 to 14, with most newborns measuring between 9 and 13½ inches in length. Shortly after their birth in September and early October, small western diamondbacks are commonly encountered by humans because they are often locally abundant, are naively unwary, and are engaged in dispersing across unfamiliar terrain.

Coloring/scale form Dorsolateral coloring is dark-speckled gray-brown, marked with the big, light- and dark-edged vertebral "diamonds" for which the species is named. On the posterior back these markings become obscure, but dorsal pigmentation is less helpful in quickly identifying *Crotalus atrox* than is its boldly black-and white-banded "coon tail." (Dorsal coloring varies considerable among *C. atrox,* in part because this species' population is so large; I have seen one nearly all-black individual, an almost patternless specimen, and several rusty-hued individuals from near Monahans.)

A chocolate-gray mask, its anterior and posterior edges lined with white, diagonally marks each cheek, obscuring the slit-pupilled eye. The pale forward border of this band intersects the upper lip midway along its length, while the white posterior edge of this dark cheek stripe runs from behind the eye straight to the rear corner of the mouth. The venter is unmarked yellowish white, the heavily keeled dorsal

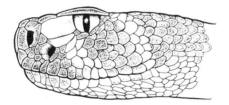

Western diamondback rattler

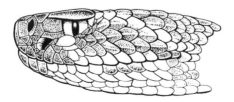

Prairie and Mojave rattlers

245

scales are arranged in 25 to 27 rows at midbody, and only 2 internasal scales intersect the rostral. Like that of all pitvipers, the anal plate is undivided.

Similar snakes   The **prairie rattlesnake (102)** has rounded brown vertebral blotches, which on its posterior trunk elongate into narrow crossbands. More than 2 internasal scales intersect its rostral, while the white posterior border of its dark subocular cheek band curves backward *above* the corner of its mouth. The **Mojave rattlesnake (103)**, found only in the central and southwestern Trans-Pecos, has only 2 or 3 longitudinal rows of large, slightly roughened cephalic scales between the supraocular plates of its anterior crown. See **Mojave Rattlesnake** for illustration. The Mojave rattler also has white tail bands much wider than its black caudal rings, its brownish vertebral diamonds elongate on the posterior third of its back into crossbands like those of the prairie rattler, and it has a white postocular line that curves backward above the posterior corner of its mouth.

The **timber (99) rattlesnake** has an entirely dark, sooty tail, a russet vertebral line, and black, crossdorsal chevron-shaped bands. **Rock rattlesnakes (104 & 105)** lack the diamond-shaped vertebral markings and have only 23 midbody rows of dorsal scales. The crowns of both Texas' **massasaugas (97 & 98)** are dark-striped and capped with 9 large scale plates.

Behavior   Most western diamondback rattlesnakes typically follow structured seasonal activity patterns. By late May or June this reptile's predatory forays have split into early morning and evening periods, while during July and August, high temperatures limit its foraging to the coolest part of the day, long after dark.

In winter, most *C. atrox* seek shelter in communal dens, even if for relatively brief periods: On the Rio Grande plain and coastal islands many individuals become fully active during spells of warm midwinter weather. Even in cooler parts of the state western diamondbacks may be abroad for a short time at midday during winter, although they remain in the vicinity of their dens from the late November through March.

In spring, this grouping enhances the chance of males to mate with emerging females before they disperse—*C. atrox* may move as far as 3 miles to summer ranges—but it renders western diamondbacks very vulnerable to predation by humans. Barred by most states for their ecologically-destructive pumping of gasoline fumes into rock and earthen crevices in an attempt to flush wintering *Crotalus atrox* from their brumation dens, participants in Texas' "rattlesnake roundups" inadvertently kill hundreds of other wildlife species as well.

The western diamondback rattlesnake is certainly in no danger of extinction here. Most roundups' organizers buy their snakes from suppliers who capture them as much as six months prior to the shows and truck them from city to city on the rattlesnake roundup circuit. But Texas' grisly springtime carnivals—based on the derring-do of handling, then killing dangerous animals—are as out of place today as cock-fighting or bear-baiting.

Blacktail Rattlesnake
Crotalus molossus molossus

Venomous   Because *C. m. molossus* inhabits relatively unpopulated and inaccessible terrain where it is unlikely to be accidentally walked over, few bites are recorded. As a partial result, the specific pathology of its venom was little known until recently, when its primary toxic effect was found to be as an anticoagulant with a lethal potency—some 79% that of the venom of the western diamondback rattlesnake.

Abundance   Uncommon. Found only occasionally on the western Edwards Plateau, blacktail rattlesnakes are much more numerous in the deserts, mountains, and canyons of the Trans-Pecos.

Size   Although adult *C. m. molossus* are generally less than 32 inches in length, the largest blacktail on record is the 53-inch-long male I captured and measured on the edge of a rocky Davis Mts. arroyo in September 1995.

Habitat   On the western edge of the Hill Country *C. m. molossus* lives in well-foliaged limestone canyons; west of the Pecos River it occurs in both upland pine-oak forests and, at lower elevation, in desert terrain broken by rocky bluffs and canyons.

Prey   Adult blacktail rattlesnakes probably take mostly small mammals; the young may take lizard prey. Because recent captives are sometimes disinclined to feed on either lizards or mice, maintaining them in captivity can be difficult.

Reproduction   Live-bearing. Two Brewster Co. females found while gravid deposited litters of 7 and 8 young (all of which measured between 8 and 10¼ inches in length) in late July.

Coloring/scale form   Calling to mind the jagged light-dark patterning of Navajo blankets, the blacktail rattlesnake's dark vertebral band inlaid with patches of pale scales is distinctive—as is its uniformly dark tail and forecrown. In Texas, this reptile's ground color ranges from brownish- to silver-gray, with boldly contrasting patches of off-white, tan, or faintly olive vertebral scales. (Blacktails from the Chiricahua and Huachuca mts. in southern Arizona often have beautiful lemon-hued dorsal patches and nearly golden lower sides.) The posterior crown is speckled and spotted, the forecrown covered by a wide black band that hides both the heat-sensing viperid pit and the slit-pupilled eyes and tapers rearward to a point just above the posterior corner of the jaw.

Most Texas' blacktail rattlesnakes have 27 midbody rows of keeled dorsal scales, but individuals vary between 25 and 29 rows. The pale venter may have a yellowish cast, clouded and mottled in places with gray; the anal plate is undivided.

Similar snakes   No other rattlesnake in the state has a black forecrown and tail and creamy vertebral scales enclosed by dark pigment.

Behavior   *Crotalus molossus molossus* seldom emerges from shelter until evening, and may forage in comparatively cool weather. Despite temperatures near 60°, three Kerr County individuals were abroad as late as December 12; other blacktails have been found in the Trans-Pecos as early as mid-February.

RATTLESNAKES

Prairie Rattlesnake
Crotalus viridis viridis

Venomous   Findlay E. Russell's work with the toxins of
Crotalus viridis (1980) indicates that prairie rattler toxins have
only about half the tissue-necrotizing effect, and less than a third
the blood-destroying potency of diamondback venom. But, due to its
large complement of neurotoxically active peptide components, the
prairie rattlesnake's overall venom potency is slightly greater than that of the
western diamondback rattler.

Yet the small stature of most *C. viridis* means that this species' average venom
capacity ranges from only 35 to a maximum of 110 mg, dry weight, compared to
the largest diamondbacks' 175 to 600 mg capacity, and as a result this species'
potential threat to humans is considerably less than that of the western diamondback. See **Venom Potency Table.**

Abundance   Along gully and canyon drop-offs, or in places where agriculture has
not plowed under the Great Plains' native grassland, *C. v. viridis* may be locally
abundant. On the western Stockton Plateau and in the Trans-Pecos prairie rattlesnakes are uncommon, but a population of these animals resides in the short-
grass pastureland southwest of the Davis Mts.; they have also been found, in a
sparse, short-grass milieu, to the north of Marathon, while *C. v. viridis* is abundant
in much of the Panhandle.

Size   Although this slender pitviper reaches a maximum of 4-½ feet, most adults
are between 2 and 3 feet long.

Habitat   Prairie rattlesnakes, like massasaugas, are grassland animals. Although
the Texas portion of its range occupies only the southern tip of the Great Plains,
one race or another of *Crotalus viridis* occupies this long sweep of open country
from southeastern Alberta and Saskatchewan to northern Chihuahua. Because this
environment offers little cover, *C. v. viridis* probably spends more time beneath
the surface than any other Texas pitviper; on these western grasslands the primary
shelter available to prairie rattlesnakes is small mammal burrows, which are shared
at times with not only the resident rodents but with burrowing owls, toads, and a
host of invertebrates.

Prey   An ambush specialist like most pitvipers, *Crotalus viridis* is adept at making
the most of the few ambush sites its rangeland habitat provides, coiling inconspicu-
ously beside any small, outline-masking bush or rock shadow. Yet it is a more active
forager than strictly sit-and-wait predators like the blacktail and rock rattlesnakes,
and has been described by Crotalid authority Harry Greene as a "mobile ambush-
er." This means that *Crotalus viridis* maximizes its chances of encountering prey by
seeking out and patroling sites, such as gopher colonies and prairie dog towns,
where food animals are most concentrated. Other prey includes baby rabbits,
ground-nesting birds, and lizards.

Reproduction   Live-bearing. The prairie rattlesnake's interrupted reproductive
schedule is an example of the adaptations employed by pitvipers living in northern
ranges. Here, the foraging season is too brief for females to build up in a single year
the reserves of body fat necessary to give birth, so that alternate-year parturition is
often the case.

In combination with Crotalids' characteristically slow growth and delayed maturation, this lack of fecundity makes it imperative for as many as possible of the only

,)eriodically reproductively-receptive female prairie rattlesnakes to be found by males during their bi-annual fertile periods. This is the reason communal denning is an important part of this animal's reproductive strategy: As the denning group simultaneously emerges from winter brumation all the sexually-receptive females available in any particular year find themselves surrounded by a host of males ready to breed.

In the northern environments where most prairie rattlesnakes live it is also important for gestating females to observe an energy-conserving regimen of midday basking and nocturnal sheltering beneath the earth or beside sun-warmed stones. Devoting all their hard-won reserves of body fat to the final development of their young, gravid female *Crotalus viridis* move about very little and feed rarely if at all during their final weeks of gestation; birth of the 8½- to 11-inch-long offspring occurs in late August, September, and early October.

Coloring/scale form   Thirty-five to 55 oval brown blotches line the center of the prairie rattlesnake's tan dorsum. Frequently narrowed over the spine anteriorly, these blotches elongate into crossbands on the posterior third of the trunk. *Crotalus viridis* is also unique among Texas rattlesnakes in having more than 2 internasal scales touching its rostral scale, while along its cheeks a pair of thin white seams—the higher of which curves backward above the corner of the mouth—border a dark postocular band. Arranged in 25 to 27 rows at midbody, the dorsal scales are keeled, the unmarked venter is yellowish white, and the anal plate is undivided.

Similar snakes   The **western diamondback rattlesnake (100)** has wide black and white bands around its tail, diamond-shaped, dimly white-edged anterior vertebral blotches, 2 internasal scales intersecting its rostral, and a white upper cheek stripe that runs straight to the posterior corner of its mouth. The **Mojave rattlesnake (103)** has wide white and narrower black tail bands and the same white-edged anterior vertebral diamonds as the diamondback. Two internasal scales touch its rostral and a unique double or triple row of large, rough scales lines the center of its crown (here, the prairie rattler has 4 or more rows of much smaller scales). The **rock rattlesnakes (104—105)** lack the prairie rattlesnake's brown vertebral ovals as well as its white cheek stripes. These little reptiles have 23 rows of dorsal scales and only 2 internasal scales touch the rostral.

Behavior   Prairie rattlers are most likely to forage abroad between 80 and 90°F. In the northern portion of their range this makes for a short annual activity period, yet this snake's adaptation to life below ground (including months-long winter denning) combined with its ability to exploit the rich bird and small mammal life of the Great Plains, enable it to range farther into Canada than any other serpent except the bullsnake and garter snakes.

103 Mojave Rattlesnake
Crotalus scutulatus scutulatus

Venomous   *Crotalus scutulatus* is probably the most dangerous serpent north of Mexico due to its combination of quick-striking defensive behavior and great venom potency. This is certainly true of the population living in California's Mojave Desert, and perhaps those in Arizona, whose great venom (referred to as Type A Mojave) approaches that of the cobras. This venom's lethal dosage for a human adult is reportedly no more than 10 to 15 mg, dry weight, and a large specimen can be milked of up to 90 mg (pitvipers can typically deliver about a third of this milked volume). New Mexico and West Texas' *C. s. scutulatus* populations (Venom Type B) may have less virulent toxins, however. See **Venom Potency Table.**

Abundance   In Texas *C. scutulatus* has been found predominantly in Brewster, Presidio, and Jeff Davis counties. Yet, because so much of the Trans-Pecos is private ranchland, huge areas have never been biologically surveyed. Several small *C. scutulatus* recently turned up near stock tanks and in moist areas on the lower slopes of Elephant Mountain south of Alpine.

Size   Mojave rattlesnakes are relatively slender, with most adults measuring less than 32 inches. The record is just over 54 inches.

Habitat   Most of the range of *Crotalus scutulatus scutulatus* is windswept Mexican tableland at 2,000-to 6,800-foot elevations. Along the U.S./Mexican border, according to Frederick Gehlbach (1981):

> The Mojave rattlesnake prefers the shortest grass and fewest shrubs at lowest elevations . . . Overlap between the diamondback and Mojave in the mesquite-tarbush zone is (perhaps a result of) an invasion by the Mojave over the last hundred years . . . The most logical scenario . . . evokes the all-too-familiar theme of desertification. As grassland is degraded into shrubland, (then desert), the (dry-adapted) Mojave rattler moves in . . .

In Texas this desert biome includes creosote bush flats along the Rio Grande west of Big Bend, as well as parts of the arid Christmas Mts. *C. s. scutulatus* is also present, but uncommon, in the rolling grasslands around Marfa for here, according to Van Devender and Lowe (1977) it finds strong competitive interaction with the prairie rattlesnake, *C. viridis:*

> Mojave rattlesnakes do not enter into more than the southwestern fringes of the Great Plains communities occupied by the prairie rattlesnake [although in] the absence of *C. viridis,* (the Mojave) inhabits both plains grassland and oak woodland communities.

The latter community includes the evergreen-wooded Davis Mts., where this species is also found.

Prey   Little is reported, but the Mojave rattlesnake's prey probably consists primarily of rodents.

Reproduction   Live-bearing. The only documented litter of Texas *C. s. scutulatus* is the brood conceived, after copulation on October 2, at the Fort Worth Zoo. The young were born more than 9 months later on July 23 and measured 9½ to just over 10 inches in length.

Coloring/scale form   Between and forward of the big supraocular plates that cap its eyes, a unique double (occasionally triple) row of enlarged, roughened scales (or scutes) occupies the midsection of the Mojave rattlesnake's crown. This distinctive scutellation distinguishes this species, and is the characteristic for which it receives its Latin name *C. scutulatus*. This attribute is much less evident among Mojaves from the eastern part of the range, which includes the Texas population. In Brewster County's Black Gap area these animals are so aberrant from typical Mojaves, and so closely resemble western diamondback rattlesnakes, that hybridization between *C. s. scutulatus* and *C. atrox* must be considered.

The anterior section of the Mojave's back resembles that of the western diamondback rattlesnake, with distinctly dark- and light-edged brown vertebral diamonds; its posterior section is often marked like a prairie rattlesnake's with brown dorsolateral crossbands. Narrow black and wider white bands encircle its tail, the pale venter may be darkly-smudged along its edges, and the lower half of the basal rattle segment may have a yellowish hue. The diagonal white line bordering the rear of the mouth Mojave rattlesnake's brown subocular band usually passes above the posterior corner of the mouth. Arranged in 25 rows at midbody, the dorsal scales are keeled and the anal plate is undivided.

Similar snakes   The very similar-looking **western diamondback rattlesnake (100)** is distinguished by less sharply defined vertebral diamonds that fade posteriorly. It has nearly equally wide black and white tail bands, its upper postocular white line directly intersects the posterior corner of its mouth, and 4 or more rows of very small scales cover its forecrown.

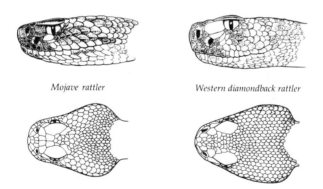

Mojave rattler   *Western diamondback rattler*

The **prairie rattlesnake (102)** is unique in that more than 2 of its internasal scales touch its rostral. The center of its forecrown, unlike the Mojave's, is evenly covered with 4 or more rows of little scales, and along the spine its dorsal foreparts are patterned with rounded brown blotches unlike the Mojave's angular, white-edged vertebral diamonds. **Rock rattlesnakes (104 & 105)** have heavy dorsolateral speckling, irregular dark crossbands, and lack the Mojave rattler's characteristic row of enlarged fore-crown-scales.

Behavior   When threatened, adult Mojave rattlesnakes may lower their heads, raise their tails, and employ a slow and—in light of their extremely toxic venom—particularly menacing gesture, deliberately flicking their rattles from side to side like a metronome.

104 Mottled Rock Rattlesnake
Crotalus lepidus lepidus

Venomous   Because deep penetration is not necessary to kill its diminutive prey, *Crotalus lepidus* has very small fangs generally, according to L. M. Klauber (1956), no more than ¼ inch measured across the curve. Its venom, however, contains a high percentage of very potent neurotoxic peptide components. The danger of being bitten is largely limited to reptile fanciers and zoo personnel, though, because the rock rattlesnakes' inaccessible mountain and desert habitat, as well as its inclination to withdraw into crevices at the first vibration of human footsteps makes accidental encounters unlikely.

Abundance   Moderately common in areas of suitable habitat. Mottled rock rattlesnakes are thinly distributed over much of the southwestern quarter of the state, but in their favored Davis Mountain canyons these animals are fairly abundant.

Size   The smallest of West Texas' rattlesnakes, *C. l. lepidus* averages under 2 feet in length; the record length is 32½ inches.

Habitat   Mottled rock rattlesnakes occupy a wide range of environments, but two quite different primary habitats prevail. In the northern part of its range this primarily rock-dwelling animal inhabits canyon ledges and bluffs and in evergreen mountain woodland at altitudes above 2,500 feet. To the south, in a somewhat less saxicolous milieu, another population of much paler individuals lives on the barren sandy mesas and shallow limestone canyons of Terrell, Crockett, and Val Verde counties.

Prey   *Crotalus lepidus lepidus* feeds mostly on lacertilian prey: There are reports of desert side-blotched and spiny lizards being taken in the wild. Smaller snakes, mice, and occasional amphibians are also probably eaten.

Reproduction   Live-bearing. Its small litters and probable alternate-year reproductive agenda mean that *Crotalus lepidus* has one of the lowest reproductive rates of any indigenous viper. The 2 to 4 young are born in mid- to late summer, 8 or 10 months after mating. The earliest account of parturition came from John Werler (1951):

> A 20.15-inch-long female [taken on] the Blackstone Ranch in Terrell County . . . gave birth to three young on July 21. The newborns averaged 8½ inches in length and differed from their pale, indistinctly banded parent in being more vividly colored, with dark gray crossbands. Food taken includes young rusty lizards . . . and newborn mice.

Coloring/scale form   *Crotalus lepidus lepidus* is folklore's celebrated "pink" and "little blue" rattlesnake. While not ever really blue (although certainly sometimes quite pink), by matching its background coloring the mottled rock rattlesnake's highly variable dorsal hues offer camouflage from both its lizard quarry and its similarly color-visioned avian predators. For example, *C. l. lepidus* from the Davis Mountains, where brownish-maroon volcanic rock is prevalent, have numerous dark primary blotches on a mottled dark russet—or, less often, pinkish buff—ground color. In contrast, mottled rock rattlesnakes living along the Rio Grande, as well as on the Stockton and western Edwards plateaus, live on pale limestone and have ground colors of chalk to faintly bluish gray. Their dark cross-dorsal bars occur mostly on the posterior body, where there is also considerable dark speckling. The wedge-shaped head, much wider than the wiry neck, is crowned with small scales. It has large, slit-pupilled eyes often masked by a dark stripe, the viperid heat-sensing pit posterior to the nostril, and 2 internasal scales that touch the rostral. The 23 midbody rows of dorsal scales are keeled and the anal plate is undivided.

Similar snakes   Against a predominantly pale, un-speckled ground color, the **banded rock rattlesnake (105)** has distinct blackish crossbands that occur throughout its length. Adult *C. l. klauberi* also usually lack a dark postocular stripe, while the rear of the crown is likely to be marked with a pair of large brown spots absent in *C. l. lepidus*. The **desert massasauga (98)**, a grassland serpent, is distinguished by its 9 large cephalic scale plates and the pair of brown stripes which band its crown. The **northern blacktail rattlesnake (101)** has a blackish tail and dark vertebral pigmentation patched with groups of pale scales. The **western diamondback rattlesnake (100)** has white-edged anterior vertebral diamonds. The **mojave rattlesnake (103)** is also distinguished by anterior vertebral diamonds edged with light and dark scales and by the double or triple row of enlarged, roughened scales that lines the middle of its forecrown.

Behavior   Walking across Davis Mt. talus slopes it is sometimes possible to hear these little reptiles buzzing their rattles from hiding beneath the rocks. Yet, in spite of this wariness, *Crotalus lepidus* may have a characteristic curiosity, because individuals will withdraw into stony crevices less deeply than they might for their own protection in order to watch—and rattle at—an intruder. During spring and fall, as well as on overcast days, rock rattlesnakes engage in extensive diurnal foraging, especially after thunderstorms when individuals emerge onto the still-moist rocks.

At these times *Crotalus lepidus* is often abroad in early morning and around sunset, avoiding the midday heat by coiling against tree trunks (in the Guadalupe and Davis Mountain highlands) or under rock overhangs or low bushes in the low desert of Val Verde and Terrell counties. Although seemingly inactive at these times, these little pitvipers are fully alert and poised to strike any lizard that darts through their patch of shade.

105 Banded Rock Rattlesnake
Crotalus lepidus klauberi

Venomous   See **Mottled Rock Rattlesnake (104)**.

Abundance   Uncommon. *C. l. klauberi* is almost unknown as
a pure race in Texas, for this predominantly Mexican subspecies' genetic influence occurs only in the state's two most western counties.

Size   See **Mottled Rock Rattlesnake (104)**.

Habitat   *Crotalus lepidus klauberi* inhabits saxicolous montane terrain from
3,500- to over 7,000-ft. elevations. In Texas, this range is evidently limited to the
Franklin Mts. north of El Paso (where the male pictured here was found).

Prey   See **Mottled Rock Rattlesnake (104)**.

Reproduction   Live-bearing. Among *C. l. klauberi* observed in Chihuahua during
Sept., Armstrong and Murphy (1979) note that courtship began as "The male
directed rapid head bobs onto the dorsum of the female. Tongue-flicking occurred
at the same speed." (Unlike most autumn-breeding snakes, which simply retain the
living spermatozoa throughout the winter to permit springtime fertilization shortly
after emergence from denning, female *Crotalus lepidus* evidently become gravid
immediately after fall copulation and experience a 9- to 10-month gestation period
protracted by winter dormancy.) First bred in captivity in 1975 by Dave Barker of
the Dallas Zoo, breeding pairs of banded rock rattlesnakes were initially only
cooled to simulate the dormancy of winter brumation.

But San Antonio Zoo Reptile Supervisor the late Jozsef Laszlo and Alan Kardon
found that *C. l. klauberi* did best in captivity if kept year-round at lower temperatures—76° to 80°F during the day, 67° or 68°F at night—than those preferred by
lowland serpents. The problem was that at these temperatures the reproductively
delicate gravid females tended to give birth to either malformed offspring or unde-
veloped ovum called slugs.

Finally, it was discovered that, in addition to maintenance at cool temperatures,
after copulation a long winter period of even greater cooling—up to 14 weeks—was
desirable, but only if the gravid female had access to electrically heated "hot rocks"
on which to bask, just as she would have done by seeking the radiated heat of sun-
warmed rocks and ledges on warm winter days in her high-desert habitat. The
result of this technique was healthy, 7½-inch-long neonates weighing just over a
quarter ounce at birth, with bright yellowish tail tips.

Coloring/scale form   In Texas *C. l. klauberi* from north of El Paso have been
found with silvery dorsums patterned solely by sawtooth-edged black crossbands.
A few males from Arizona have a beautiful lichen green ground color (the "green
rattler" of Southwestern folklore is a *C. l. klauberi*) while females are grayish—a
type of sexual dimorphism charactertistic of birds but almost unknown among reptiles.

Similar snakes   See **Mottled Rock Rattlesnake (104)**.

Behavior   See **Mottled Rock Rattlesnake (104)**.

Glossary

Adhesive-shelled eggs   Eggs with a sticky surface that causes them to adhere in a cluster when laid (the shells soon dry out, but the eggs remain stuck together).

Aestivation   The hot weather-induced dormancy of many reptiles and amphibians.

Allopatric   Having a separate or discrete range.

Amelanistic   Color phase almost entirely lacking black pigment.

Amphiuma   Large, eel-like aquatic salamander with small legs and no external gills.

Anal plate   Scale covering the cloacal vent.

Anaphylaxis   Antigen-antibody reaction caused by sensitivity to a foreign protein such as antivenin; capable in extreme cases of producing severe shock, respiratory impairment, coma, and death.

Anchor coil   The lowermost loop of the body of a coiled snake; this serves the animal as a foundation from which to strike.

Anerythristic   Color phase almost entirely lacking red pigment.

Annelid   Segmented worm or leech; most commonly the earthworm.

Anterior   Toward the head.

Antibody   A globulin produced in reaction to the introduction of a foreign protein.

Antiserum   The fluid portion of the blood of an animal previously infused with a reactive foreign protein.

Antivenin   Crystallized serum produced from the antibodies of animals infused with venom; able to partly neutralize venom's effects on the victim's tissue by blocking the toxic enzymes' access to their target cells.

Antivenin Index   A compendium of antivenins is available in the United States (including those for non-indigenous snakes) from the Arizona Poison Center at the University of Arizona Medical School in Tucson. Antivenin for indigenous North American pitviper and coral snake venoms is produced by Wyeth Laboratories in Philadelphia.

Anuran   Frog or toad.

Aposematic   Warning signal: sound, posture, coloration, etc.

Arachnid   Eight-legged invertebrate—spiders, scorpions, mites, and ticks.

Arthropod   Segmented invertebrate with jointed legs—insects, arachnids, and crustaceans.

Azygous scale   A single scale, that is, not one of a bilateral pair.

Belly line   The horizontal line of intersection between the venter, or belly, and the lower sides of the body.

Brumation   The winter dormancy of reptiles and amphibians.

Caudal   Pertaining to the tail.

Cephalic   Pertaining to the head or crown.

Chemoreception   The perception of chemical signals such as scent particles by the smell/taste mechanism of olfactory and veromonasal glands.   See **Jacobson's organ.**

Chin shields   The central scales on the underside of the lower jaw.

Chthonic   Below or within the earth.

Cloaca   Lower chamber of the digestive, urinary, and reproductive systems of birds, reptiles, and amphibians, which opens to the outside through the anus, or vent

Colubrid   A member of the largest worldwide family of snakes, *Colubridae*; most North American species are harmless.

Compartment syndrome   The pressure of extreme edema, which after severe envenomation may rarely cut off blood flow to a limb, causing the death of its tissue. Some authorities believe this to be a cause of local necrosis that warrants surgical alleviation by fasciotomy; most maintain that necrosis is due almost exclusively to the enzymatic, digestive action of the venom itself.

Congeneric   Within the same genus; species belonging to the same genus are congeneric.

Conspecific   Within the same species; subspecies, or races, of a single species are conspecific.

Corticosteroid   Steroid often used to treat venom poisoning; it originates in the adrenal cortex and whose effects include the enhancement of protein replacement, the reduction of inflammation, and the suppression of the body's immune responses.

Crepuscular   Active at dusk or dawn.

Crossband   Among snakes, a pigmented strip running from side to side across the back.

Crotalid   A pitviper; a member of the family *Viperidae*, subfamily *Crotalinae*; in the United States: rattlesnakes, cottonmouths, and copperheads.

Cryotherapy   Treatment of an injury with cold. Dangerous when a snakebitten extremity is radically chilled, since this can cause tissue death. (A cold pack on the wound may slightly reduce pain; another on the forehead may help to offset the nausea that often accompanies pitviper poisoning.)

Cryptic   Serving to conceal or camouflage.

Debridement   The surgical removal of (venom-saturated) tissue.

Depauperate   Diminished in species diversity.

Dichromatism   The presence of two or more color phases within a species or subspecies.

Diel   Daily or daytime.

Disjunct   Geographically separate.

Distally   Toward the periphery, or sides, of the body.

Diurnal   Active during the day.

DOR   Initials of Dead On Road, an abbreviation for vehicle-slain wildlife, originally coined by rattlesnake authority L. M. Klauber. It is now in general use for all kinds of animals and offers a rough but useful indicator of the presence of fauna in an area.

Dorsal   Pertaining to the back.

Dorsolateral   Pertaining to the back and sides, usually the entirety of the back and sides.

Dorsum   The back and upper sides.

Duvernoy's gland   A gland that produces some of the venom of rear-fanged colubrid snakes; named for the French anatomist D. M. Duvernoy, who first described it.

Ecdysis   The shedding of a reptile's outer skin. See **Exuviation.**

Ecotone   Transition zone between differing biological communities, such as the border between forest and meadow.

Ectotherm   Animal whose temperature is almost entirely determined by its environment.

Edema   Swelling of tissue due to the release of fluids (primarily from the vascular and lymphatic systems) into the interstitial tissue spaces.

Elapid   A rigidly front-fanged, venomous serpent of the family *Elapidae,* such as the coral snake. Elapids are characterized by a large proportion of neurotoxically active peptide venom fractions.

Endemic   Only found in a particular area.

Endotherm   Internally heat-regulating animal.

Envenomation   Infusion of venom.

Enzyme   Organic agent capable of producing the metabolic breakdown of tissue into its component proteins.

Exuviation   A shed; the sloughing of the entire outer covering, or *stratum corneum,* of a snake's body. This process first occurs soon after birth, then occurs every few weeks to months (more often if the snake has been injured; less often as the snake grows older) throughout the animal's annual foraging period. This process can occupy from ten minutes to several hours. Rattlesnakes add a new basal rattle segment with each exuviation; the terminal segments are periodically broken off.

Fasciotomy   Surgical incision into the fascial band enclosing a muscular compartment. This is usually done in an attempt to prevent tissue destruction from excessive hydraulic pressure caused by the fluid released by the venom's perforation of the capillary walls and pumped into the tissues by the heart. Fasciotomy is of questionable value except as an emergency measure to save a limb in immediate danger of general necrosis due to vascular constriction.

Form   Subspecies or race.

Fossorial   Adapted to burrowing; subterranean.

Frontal scale(s)   Scale(s) located on the crown, or top of the head between the eyes.

Genotype   Genetic makeup of an individual.

Gravid   Pregnant.

Hemotoxic   Destructive to blood, blood cells, or the vascular system.

Hemipene   The bi-lobed, therefore Y-shaped, penis of serpents and lizards.

Herpetoculture   The husbandry and breeding of reptiles in captivity.

Hibernation   Dormancy during winter.

Holotype   The specimen from which the description of a species or subspecies is derived.

Hydric   Well watered.

Hydrophytic   Plant life adapted to living in standing fresh water.

Hypovolemic shock   Shock due to a loss of fluid from the circulatory system. In snakebite, this occurs when the arteriole and venule walls are perforated by venom enzymes.

Infralabial scales   The scales that line the lower jaw.

Indigenous   Native to an area; not introduced.

Infrared perception   Apprehension of the infrared band of the light spectrum.

Intergradation   The gradual genetic alteration of one subspecies into another across a geographical continuum.

Intergrade   Intermediate individual or population which often exhibits some combination of the characteristics of two or more species or subspecies.

Internasal scales   Scales just posterior to the rostral scale on top of the snout, anterior to the prefrontals.

Jacobson's organ   Double-sided sensory organ located in the roof of the mouth of serpents and some lizards into which the tips of their forked tongues are pressed. When a snake flicks it tongue, molecules that adhere to its sticky surface are carried into the mouth when the tongue returns to its sheath, then placed in ducts in the roof of the mouth. These ducts lead to veromonasal epithelia containing the chemosensory neurons which have evolved highly specific, inherited selective recognition of the chemical signature of appropriate prey species.

Keel   Small longitudinal ridge creasing the centerline of a dorsal scale.

Labial scales   Large scales lining the outer edges of the upper and lower jaws (**supralabial scales** line the upper jaw; **infralabial scales** line the lower jaw).

Lacertilian   Pertaining to lizards.

Lateral   Pertaining to the sides.

Lecithotrophy   Yolk-nourished embryos.

Leucistiphosis   The nourishment of embryos by means of an egg yolk.

Leutic   Still, non-flowing water.

Linear constriction   Pressing a prey animal against a stationary object such as the side of a burrow or rock crevice to immobilize it.

Ligature   Binding a limb with a circulation-impairing band such as a tourniquet.

Littoral   Pertaining to the margins of bodies of water; shoreline.

Live-bearing   Reproduction by means of fully-formed young born in membranous sheaths, which are immediately discarded.

Loreal scale   Scale between the preocular and nasal scales.

Lumen   Venom-generating and storing gland.

Lysis   The breakdown or metabolism of cells or tissue by a peptide or enzyme.

Matrotrophy   Nourishment of embryos by nutrient exchange from the mother's blood.

Maxillary bones   Paired bones at the front of the upper jaw that in anterior-fanged venomous snakes carry the fangs. Among pitvipers the maxillary bones are able to rotate outward separately, swinging each the fang tip forward independent of the other.

Mesic   Moderately watered; moist.

Midventral   The center of the belly.

Milieu   Environment or habitat.

Morph   Short for morphological; of variant appearance. For example, a color phase.

Morphological   Pertaining to an animal's appearance (as opposed to its genetic make-up).

Natricine   Large water snakes of the genus *Nerodia*.

Nasal scales   Scales through which the nostrils open.

Necrosis   Death of bone or soft tissue.

Neonate   A newborn, offspring.

Noetenic   Retention of the juvenile form or coloring into adulthood.

Non-indigenous   Not native to an area: therefore, introduced.

Neurotoxic   Destructive primarily by impairing neuromuscular function. Among the most dangerous effects of ophidian neurotoxins is the blockage of acetylcholine receptor sites in the upper spinal ganglia.

Nuchal   Pertaining to the neck.

Ocular   Pertaining to the eye.

Ocular scale   Scale covering the eye.

Ontogenetic   A change in morphology due to aging.

Ophidian   Pertaining to snakes.

Ophiophagous   Feeding on snakes.

Oviparous   Egg-bearing or laying: producing young by means of eggs that hatch outside the body.

Oviposition   Egg-laying.

Ovoviviparous   Live-bearing. Producing young by means of membranous eggs, whose membrane-encased embryos remain within the mother's body until hatching, at which time they are deposited as fully developed offspring.

Paraphyletic   Genus or species-level groups of organisms which, due to significantly-differing habits, morphology or physiology, have emerged from their ancestral families and, rather than replacing them, now exist alongside their progenitors in slightly different niches.

Parietal scales   Pair of large scales located on the rear of the crown.

Parotid gland   Organ that secretes saliva in mammals and most of the venom in pitvipers and elapids.

Parthenogensis   Reproduction by the development of an unfertilized egg.

Parturition   The process of giving birth.

Phenotype   Physical characteristics of an organism.

Pheromone   Primarily hormone-derived chemical substance released by an animal that influences the behavior of others of the same species. Ophidian pheromones include both general scents used for locating the retreats, hiding places, or microhabitat of other individuals of the same species and male-attracting scents excreted by breeding-condition females.

Placentophosis   Nourishment of embryos by nutrient exchange from the mother's blood.

Plate   Large scales covering the crown, or top of the head, as well as the venter, or belly.

Polyvalent antivenin   An antivenin produced from a combination of antibodies and therefore useful against the venom of a genus or related group of venomous snakes. Wyeth's polyvalent antivenin is a single crystallized serum developed to treat the bites of all North American pitvipers: rattlesnakes, copperheads, and cottonmouths.

Posterior   Toward the tail.

Postocular scales   Scales bordering the posterior edge of the eye.

Preocular scales   Scales bordering the anterior edge of the eye.

Primary band   A snake's more distinct and complete dorsolateral crossbands (as opposed to the irregular, broken markings which may occur between them).

Proteinase   Proteolytic, or tissue-dissolving, enzyme.

Proteolysis   Destruction of tissue due to the inability of venom-weakened cell walls to withstand their internal fluid pressures.

Race   Subspecies.

Range   The area thought to be the entire geographic distribution of an organism.

Relict population   Contemporary remnant group of a species formerly found over a broader range.

Riparian   The banks or bottomland along streams or rivers.

Rostral scale   Scale covering the tip of the snout, frequently enlarged among burrowing species.

Ruderal   Agricultural.

Saxicolous   Inhabiting or growing among rocks.

Scute   Scale plate.

Scutellation   Scalation; the arrangement of scales.

Serosanguinous   Swollen with blood.

Sexual dimorphism   A morphological difference (in coloring, pattern, size, configuration, or other trait) according to gender.

Siren   Large aquatic salamander shaped like an eel but possessing forelegs and external gills.

Spermatogenesis   Generation of spermatozoa.

Squamata   The order of classification comprising snakes and lizards.

Subcaudal scales   The scales lining the undersurface of the tail posterior to the cloacal opening.

Subocular scales   Small scales separating the lower edge of the eye from the supralabial scales.

Subspecies   A group or cluster of local populations that, to a significant degree, differs taxonomically from adjacent groups or clusters.

Supralabial scales   The scales that line the upper jaw.

Supraocular scales   The scales on the sides of the crown above the eyes.

Sympatric   Overlapping or corresponding ranges; occurring in the same area.

Syntopic   Overlapping or corresponding microhabitats; occurring in the same pond or beneath the same log.

Temporal scales   Scales along the side of the head behind the postocular scale(s) and between the parietal scales and the supralabial scales.

Terminal segment   Among *Sistrurus* and *Crotalus,* the last, or posteriormost rattle segment. Because rattles break off periodically, there are rarely more than 8 or 10 segments in a series no matter how old the snake. See **Exuviation.**

Thermoregulation   Control of body temperature—usually by an ectotherm—by moving toward or away from warmer or cooler areas.

Variant   Individual or population difference—most often in color or pattern—not judged to be of sufficient genetic magnitude to warrant recognition as a subspecies or race.

Venom fractions   The approximately three dozen discrete toxic proteins—principally peptides and enzymes—that make up reptile venoms. Most of these fractions can be isolated from the venom mix by electrophoresis and dialysis.

Vent   The posterior opening of the cloaca.

Venter   The belly.

Ventral   Pertaining to the belly.

Ventral scales   The transversely elongate scale plates, or scutes, that line the underbody of most snakes.

Ventrolateral   On the outer edge of the venter and the lower sides of the body.

Vertebral   Along the spine.

Vitellogenesis   Generation of ova.

Viviparous   Live-bearing. Among snakes this means retaining the developing young (in their membranous egg-sacs) within the body cavity of the mother until their birth/hatching, which occur simultaneously.

Vomeronasal organ   The primary chemical sense that snakes use to orient themselves in their environment and to detect prey is vomerolfaction, which is the perception of scent particle carried into the mouth by the tongue, then placed in the vomeronasal, or Jacobson's organ, located in the roof of the mouth. See **Jacobson's organ.**

262 **Xeric**   Arid.

Bibliography

Abell, Joseph M., Jr., M.D. 1974. Snakebite: Current treatment concepts. *University of Michigan Medical Center Journal* 1 (40):29–31.

Allen, Frederick M., M.D. 1938. Mechanical treatment of venomous bites and wounds. *Southern Medical Journal* 31 (12):1248–1253.

_____. 1939. Observations on local measures in the treatment of snake bite. *American Journal of Tropical Medicine* 19:393–404.

Anderson, Paul K. 1961. Variation in populations of brown snakes, genus *Storeria*, bordering the Gulf of Mexico. *American Midland Naturalist* 66 (1):235–247.

Armstrong, Barry L. and James B. Murphy. 1979. *The Natural History of Mexican Rattlesnakes*. Lawrence, Kansas: University of Kansas Press.

Ashton, Ray E., Jr., Stephen R. Edwards, and George R. Pisani. 1976. *Endangered and Threatened Amphibians and Reptiles in the United States*. Lawrence, Kansas: Society for the Study of Amphibians and Reptiles, Herpetological Circular No. 5.

Assetto, R., Jr. 1978. Reproduction of the graybanded kingsnake, *Lampropeltis mexicana alterna*. *Herp. Review*, 9 (2): 56–57.

Axtell, R. W. 1951. An Additional Specimen of *Lampropeltis blairi* from Texas. *Copeia* 4: 313, pl. 1.

_____. 1959. Amphibians and reptiles of the Black Gap Wildlife Management Area, Brewster County, Texas. *Southwest. Natur.*, 4 (2): 88–109.

_____. 1978. Ancient playas and their influence on the recent herpetofauna of the northern Chihuahuan Desert. In: R. W. Wauer & D. H. Riskind: Transactions of the symposium on the biological resources of the Chihuahua Desert Region, United States and Mexico. Natl. Park Service Trans. Proc. Ser. 3: 493–512.

Bartlett, Richard D. 1988. *In Search of Reptiles and Amphibians*. New York: E. J. Brill.

_____. 1993. Herping Texas: The Guadalupe River and Langtry. Parts 1 & 2. *Notes from Noah*, 20 (4):7–10.

Bechtel, Bernard H. 1978. Color and pattern in snakes. *Journal of Herpetology*. April 1978:521–532.

_____. 1995. *Reptile and Amphibian Variants: Colors, Patterns, and Scales*. Malabar, Florida: Krieger Publishing Company.

Behler, John L., and F. Wayne King. 1979. *The Audubon Society Field Guide to North American Reptiles and Amphibians*. New York: Alfred A. Knopf Inc.

Bellairs, Angus. 1970 *The Life of Reptiles*. 2 vols. New York: Universe Books.

_____ and John Attridge. 1975. *Reptiles*. London: Hutchinson.

_____ and C. B. Cox (eds.) 1976. *Morphology and Biology of Reptiles*. London: Academic Press.

_____ and Garth Underwood. 1951. The origin of snakes. *Biological Reviews of the Cambridge Philosophical Society* 26:193–237.

Blair, W. F. 1949. The Biotic Provinces of Texas. *Texas J. Sci.* 2 (1): 93–117.

Blanchard, F. N. 1920. Three new snakes of the genus *Lampropeltis*. Occ. Papers Mus. Zool. Univ. Michigan (81): 1–10.

_____. 1920. A synopsis of the Kingsnakes, genus *Lampropeltis* Fitzinger. Occ. Papers Mus. Zool. Univ. Michigan 87: 17.

_____. 1921. A Revision of the Kingsnakes, genus *Lampropeltis*. Bull. United States Nat. Mus. 114: 1–260.

_____. 1924. The snakes of the genus *Virginia*. Papers of the Michigan Academy of Arts, Science, and Letters 3 (3):343–365.

_____. 1938. Snakes of the genus *Tantilla* in the United States, Field Museum of Natural History (Zoology) 20 (28):369–376.

_____. 1942. The ring-neck snakes, genus *Diadophis*. Bulletin of the Chicago Academy of Science 7 (1):1–142.

Blaney, R. M. 1973. *Lampropeltis* Fitzinger, Kingsnakes. *Cat. Amer. Amphib. Rept.*: 150.1–150.2.

Bloom, F. E. 1981. Neuropeptides. *Scientific American* 245 (October 1981):148–168.

Bogert, C. M. 1949. Thermoregulation in reptiles, a factor in evolution. *Evolution* 3:195–211.

_____ and V. D. Roth. 1966. Ritualistic combat of male gopher snakes, *Pituophis melanoleucus affinis*. American Museum Novitiates 2245:1–27.

Bonilla, C. A. and M. K. Fiero. 1971. Comparative biochemistry and pharmacology of salivary gland secretions. II.: Chromatographic separation of the basic proteins from North American rattlesnake venoms. *Journal of Chromatography* 56:253.

Boulenger, G. A. 1973. *Contributions to American Herpetology: Collected papers.* Facsimile Reprints. (Index 1977). New York: Society for the Study of Amphibians and Reptiles.

Bowler, J. Kevin. 1977. Longevity of reptiles and amphibians in North American collections. Society for the Study of Amphibians and Reptiles, Herpetological Circular No. 6.

Boxall, J. 1982. Pressure/immobilization first aid treatment of snake bite. *Medical Journal of Australia* 1:155.

Bragg, A. N. 1960. Is *Heterodon* venomous? *Herpetologica* 16:121–123.

Braswell, A. L. and W. M. Palmer. 1984. *Cemophora coccinea copei. Herpetological Review* 15(2):49.

Brattstrom, B. H. 1955. The coral snake "mimic" problem and protective coloration. *Evolution* 9:217–219.

_____. 1964. Evolution of the pitvipers. Transactions of the San Diego Society of Natural History 13:185–265.

_____. 1965. Body temperature of reptiles. *American Midland Naturalist* 1965:376–422.

Brinton, D. G. 1968. *Myths of the New World.* 3rd ed. New York: Haskell House.

Brisbin, I. L. and C. Bagshaw. 1993. Survival, weight changes, and shedding frequencies of captive scarlet snakes, *Cemophora coccinea,* maintained on an artificial liquid diet. *Herpetological Review* 24(1):27–29.

Brodie, E. D., III and Peter K. Ducey. 1989. Allocation of reproductive investment in the redbelly snake *Storeria occipitomaculata. The American Midland Naturalist.* 122(1):51–58.

Brown, A. E. 1901. A New Species of *Ophibolus* from Western Texas. Proc. Acad. Nat. Sci. Philadelphia, 53: 612–613, pl. 34.

Brown, B. C. 1950. *An Annotated Check List of the Reptiles and Amphibians of Texas.* Waco: Baylor Univ. Studies.

Brown, William S. 1993. *Biology, Status, and Management of the Timber Rattlesnake (Crotalus horridus):* A Guide for Conservation.

Burghardt, G. M. 1970. Chemical perception in reptiles. In: *Advances in Chemoreception Communication by Chemical Signals,* p. 241–308. Johnson, J. W., Jr., Moulton, D. G., Turk, A. (eds.) New York: Appleton-Century-Crofts.

Burkett, Ray. O. 1966. Natural history of the cottonmouth moccasin, *Agkistrodon piscivorus.* University of Kansas. Publications of the Museum of Natural History 17 (9):435–491.

Calhoun, G. 1995. The Gray-banded Kingsnake. *The Forked Tongue,* 20 (7–8): 5.

Campbell, Jonathan A. and Edmund D. Brodie, Jr. (eds.) 1992. *Biology of the Pitvipers.* Tyler, Texas: Selva.

Carpenter, Charles C. 1979. A combat ritual between two male pigmy rattlesnakes (*Sistrurus miliarius*). *Copeia* 1979 (4):638–642.

Carr, Archie F. 1963. *The Reptiles.* Life Nature Library. New York: Time-Life.

Chenowith, W. L. 1948. Birth and behavior of young copperheads. *Herpetologica* 4:162.

Chiszar, David, Charles W. Radcliffe, and Roy Overstreet. 1985. Duration of strike-induced chemosensory searching in cottonmouths (*Agkistrodon piscivorus*) and a test of the hypothesis that striking prey creates a specific search image. *Canadian Journal of Herpetology* 63:1057–1061.

Clark, Donald R., Jr. and Robert R. Fleet. 1976. The rough earth snake (*Virginia striatula*): Ecology of a Texas population. *Southwestern Naturalist* 20 (4):467–478.

Clausen, H. J. 1936. Observations on the brown snake, *Storeria dekayi,* with especial reference to habits and birth of young. *Copeia* 1936:98–102.

Cloudsley-Thompson, J. L. 1971. *The Temperature and Water Relations of Reptiles.* London: Merrow Publishing.

Cohen, P., W. H. Berkley, and E. B. Seligmann, Jr. 1971. Coral snake venoms: In vitro relation of neutralizing and precipitating antibodies. *American Journal of Tropical Medical Hygiene* 20:646–649.

Cohen, Wayne R., Warren Wetzel, and Anna Kadish. 1992. Local heat and cold application after eastern cottonmouth moccasin (*Agkistrodon piscivorus*) envenomation in the rat: Effect on tissue injury. *Toxicon* 30(11):1383:1386.

Cole, Charles J. and Lawrence M. Hardy. 1981. Systematics of North American Colubrids related to *Tantilla planiceps* (Blaineville). Bulletin of the American Museum of Natural History, vol. 171; (3) p. 201–284. New York.

Collins, Joseph T. 1990. *Standard Common and Current Scientific names for North American Amphibians & Reptiles.* 3rd. ed. Lawrence, Kansas: University of Kansas, Museum of Natural History.

_____. 1993. *Amphibians and Reptiles in Kansas.* 3rd. ed. Lawrence, Kansas: University of Kansas Museum of Natural History.

Conant, Roger and A. Downs, Jr. 1940. Miscellaneous notes on the eggs and young of reptiles. *Zoologica* 25:33–48.

_____. 1956. A review of two rare pine snakes from the Gulf coastal plain. American Museum Novitiates 1781:17–21.

_____. 1975. *A Field Guide to Amphibians and Reptiles of Eastern and Central North America*. 2nd ed. Boston: Houghton Mifflin Co.

_____ and J. T. Collins. 1991. *A Field Guide to Amphibians and Reptiles of Eastern and Central North America*. 3rd ed. Boston: Houghton Mifflin Co.

Cook, D. G. and F. J. Aldridge. 1984. *Coluber constrictor priapus*. *Herpetological Review*. 15(2):49.

Cook, F. R. 1964. Communal egg laying in the smooth green snake. *Herpetologica* 20:206.

Cooper Jr., William E., Donald G. Buth and Laurie J. Vitt. 1990. Prey odor discrimination by ingestively naive coachwhip snakes (*Masticophis flagellum*). *Chemoecology* 1:86–89.

Coote, J. 1978. Spotlight on a species. The grayband kingsnake (*Lampropeltis mexicana alterna*). *Herptile*, 3 (2): 67.

_____ and R. J. Riches. 1978. Captive reproduction in North American Colubrids of the genera *Lampropeltis* and *Elaphe*. Rep. Cotswold Herp. Symp. 1978: 6–15.

Coulter, A. R., J. C. Cox, S. K. Sutherland, and C. J. Waddell. 1978. A new solid-phase sandwich radioimmunoassay and its application to the detection of snake venom. *Journal of Immunological Methodology* 23:241–252.

Cowles, R. B. and R. L. Phelan. 1958. Olfaction in rattlesnakes. *Copeia* 1958:77–83.

Clark, Donald R. 1974. The western ribbon snake (*Thamnophis proximus*): Ecology of a Texas population. *Herpetologica* 30:372–379.

Crews, David and William R. Gartska. 1982. The ecological physiology of a garter snake. *Scientific American* 247 (5):158–168.

Cunningham, E. R., et al. 1979. Snakebite: Role of corticosteroids as immediate therapy in an animal model. *American Surgery* 45 (12):757–759.

Curtis, Lawrence. 1952. Cannibalism in the Texas coral snake. *Herpetologica* 8:27.

Danzig, L. E. and G. H. Abels. 1961. Hemodialysis of acute renal failure following rattlesnake bite, with recovery. *Journal of the American Medical Association* 175:136.

Degenhardt, William G. and G. E. Steele. 1957. Additional specimens of *Trimorphodon vilkinsonii* from Texas. *Copeia* 1957:309–310.

_____. Charles W. Painter, and Andrew H. Price. 1996. *Amphibians and Reptiles of New Mexico.* Albuquerque: University of New Mexico Press, p. 1–431.

Ditmars, R. L. 1936. *The Reptiles of North America.* Garden City, New York: Doubleday and Co., Inc.

Dixon, J. R. 1987. *Amphibians and Reptiles of Texas. With Keys, Taxonomic Synopses, Bibliography, and Distribution Maps.* Texas A&M University Press, College Station: 1–434.

Drummond, H. 1983. Aquatic foraging in garter snakes: A comparison of specialists and generalists. *Behaviour* 86:1–30.

_____. 1985. The role of vision in the predatory behavior of natricine snakes. *Animal Behavior* 33:206–215.

Dundee, Harold A., and M. Clinton Miller, III. 1968. Aggregative behavior and habitat conditioning by the prairie ringneck snake, *Diadophis punctatus arnyi.* Tulane Studies in Zoology and Botany 15 (2):41–58.

_____ and Douglas A. Rossman. 1989. *The Amphibians and Reptiles of Louisiana.* Baton Rouge: Louisiana State University Press.

Dunn, E. R. 1954. The coral snake mimic problem. *Evolution* 2:97–102.

Dyrkacz, S. 1982. Striped pattern morphism in the prairie kingsnake, *Lampropeltis c. calligaster. Herpetological Review* 13(3):70–71.

Edgren, Richard A. 1948. Notes on a litter of young timber rattlesnakes. *Copeia* 1948:132.

_____. 1955. The natural history of the hognosed snakes, genus *Heterodon:* A review. *Herpetologica* 11:105–117.

_____. 1957. Melanism in hog-nosed snakes. *Herpetologica* 13:131–135.

Eichholz, M. W. and W. D. Koenig. 1992. Gopher snake attraction to birds' nests. *The Southwestern Naturalist* 37(3):293–298.

Emery, J. A. and F. E. Russell. 1961. Studies with cooling measures following injection of *Crotalus* venom. *Copeia* 1961:322–326.

Ernst, Carl H. 1992. *Venomous Reptiles of North America.* Washington: Smithsonian Institution Press.

Fearn, H. J., C. Smith, and G. B. West. 1964. Capillary permeability responses to snake venom. *Journal of Pharmaceutical Pharmacology* 16:79–84.

Fitch, Henry S., 1960. Autecology of the copperhead. University of Kansas Publications, Museum of Natural History 3 (4):85–288.

_____. 1963. Natural history of the racer *Coluber constrictor*. University of Kansas Museum of Natural History Publication 5 (8):351–468.

_____. 1970. Reproductive cycles of lizards and snakes. University of Kansas Museum of Natural History Miscellaneous Publication 42:1–247.

_____ and H. W. Shirer. 1971. Radio telemetry studies of spatial relations in some common snakes. *Copeia* (1) 118–128.

_____. 1975. A demographic study of the ringneck snake (*Diadophis punctatus*) in Kansas. University of Kansas Museum of Natural History Miscellaneous Publication No. 62.

_____. 1982. Resources of a snake community in prairie-woodland habitat of northeastern Kansas. N. J. Scott, Jr., (ed.) Herpetological communities. U.S. Fish and Wildlife Service, Wildlife Resources Report No. 13.

_____. 1985. Variation in clutch and litter size in New World reptiles. University of Kansas Museum of Natural History Miscellaneous Publication No. 76.

_____ and R. R. Fleet. 1970. Natural history of the milk snake *Lampropeltis triangulum* in northeastern Kansas. *Herpetologica* 26:387–395.

Flury, A. 1950. A new kingsnake from Trans-Pecos, Texas. *Copeia* (3): 215–217.

Foley, George W. 1971. Perennial communal nesting in the black racer (*Coluber constrictor*). *Herpetological Review* 3:41.

Force, Edith R. 1935. A local study of the opisthoglyph snake *Tantilla gracilis*. Papers of the Michigan Academy of Arts and Letters 20:645–659.

Ford, Neil B. 1979. Aspects of pheromone trailing in garter snakes. Ph.D. dissertation, Miami University (Ohio).

_____. 1981. Seasonality of pheromone trailing in two species of garter snakes. *Southwestern Naturalist* 26 (4):385–388.

Fox, W. and H. C. Dessauer. 1962. The single right oviduct and other urogenital structures of female *Typhlops* and *Leptotyphlops*. *Copeia* 1962:590–597.

Frank, N. and Erica Ramus. 1996. *A Complete Guide to Scientific and Common Names of Reptiles and Amphibians of the World*. Pottsville, Pa.: N G Publishing.

Frazer, James G. 1892. *The Golden Bough*. New York: Macmillan.

Gamow, R. I. and John F. Harris. 1973. The infrared receptors of snakes. *Scientific American* 228 (5):94–102.

Gans, Carl. 1970. How snakes move. *Scientific American* 222 (6):82–96.

_____ T. Krakauer, and C. V. Paganelli. 1968. Water loss in snakes: Interspecific and intraspecific variability. *Comparative Biochemical Physiology* 27:757–761.

_____ and F. Billet (eds.) 1970–present. *Biology of the Reptilia*. New York: John Wiley & Sons.

Garfin, S. R., et al. 1979. Role of surgical decompression in the treatment of rattlesnake bites. *Surgical Forum* 30:502–504.

Garstka, W. R. 1982. Systematics of the *mexicana* species group of the Colubrid genus *Lampropeltis*, with an hypothesis of mimicry. *Breviora*, Mus. Compl. Zool. 466: 1–35.

Garton, S. G., E. W. Harris, and R. A. Brandon. 1970. Descriptive and ecological notes on *Natrix cyclopion* in Illinois. *Herpetologica* 26:24–34.

Gehlbach, Frederick. R. 1967. *Lampropeltis mexicana*. Cat. Amer. Amphib. Rept.: 55.1–55.2.

_____ and F. R. and J. K. Baker. 1962. Kingsnakes allied with *Lampropeltis mexicana:* Taxonomy and natural history. *Copeia* 2: 291–300.

_____ and R. and C. J. McCoy, Jr. 1965. Additional observations on variation and distribution of the gray-banded kingsnake, *Lampropeltis mexicana* (Garman). *Herpetologica,* 21 (1): 35–38.

_____. 1970. Death-feigning and erratic behavior in leptotyphlopid, colubrid, and elapid snakes. *Herpetologica* 26:24–34.

_____ Julian F. Watkins II, and James C. Kroll. 1971. Pheromone trail-following studies of typhlopid, leptotyphlopid, and colubrid snakes. *Behavior* 40 (pts. 3–5) 282–294.

_____. 1972. Coral snake mimicry reconsidered: The strategy of self-mimicry. *Forma et Functio* 5:311–320.

_____. 1981. *Mountain Islands and Desert Seas: A Natural History of the U.S.- Mexican Borderland*. College Station, Tex.: Texas A&M University Press.

Geiser, S.W. 1948. *Naturalists of the Frontier*. Dallas: Southern Methodist University Press.

Gill, K. A., Jr. 1970. The evaluation of cryotherapy in the treatment of snake envenomation. *Southern Medical Journal* 63:552–556.

Gingrich, W. C. and J. C. Hohenadel. 1956. Standardization of polyvalent antivenin. In E. E. Buckley and N. Proges (eds.), *Venoms*. 381–385. Amer. Assoc. Advanc. Sci., Washington, D.C.

Githens, T. S. and N. O'C. Wolff. 1939. The polyvalency of crotalid antivenins. III. Mice as test animals for study of antivenins. *Journal of Immunology* 37:47–51.

Glass, Thomas G., Jr. 1969. Cortisone and immediate fasciotomy in the treatment of severe rattlesnake bite. *Texas Medicine* 65:41.

_____. 1976. Early debridement in pitviper bites. *Journal of the American Medical Association* 235:2513.

Glenn, James L. and Richard C. Straight. 1978. Mojave rattlesnake (*Crotalus scutulatus scutulatus*) venom: Variation in toxicity with geographic origin. *Toxicon* 16:81–84.

_____. 1982. *Rattlesnake Venoms: Their Action and Treatment.* New York: Marcel Dekker.

Gloyd, Howard K. and Roger Conant. 1934. Taxonomic status, range, & natural history of Schott's racer. Occasional Papers of the Museum of Zoology, University of Michigan. p. 1–17.

_____. 1944. Texas Snakes. *Texas Geogr,* 8: 1–18.

_____ and Roger Conant. 1990. *Snakes of the Agkistrodon Complex.* Oxford, Ohio: Society for the Study of Amphibians and Reptiles.

Goldstein, R. C. 1941. Notes on the mud snake in Florida. *Copeia* (1941):49–50.

Greene, Harry W. 1973. The food habitats and breeding behavior of New World coral snakes. Master's thesis, University of Texas at Arlington.

_____ and Roy W. McDiarmid. 1981. Coral snake mimicry: Does it occur? *Science* (213):1207–1212.

_____. 1992. The ecological and behavioral context for pitviper evolution. In *Biology of the Pitvipers.* J. A. Campbell and E. D. Brodie, Jr. (eds.) Tyler, Texas: Selva.

Grobman, Arnold B. 1950. The problem of the natural range of a species. *Copeia* (3):231–232.

_____. 1978. An alternative solution to the coral snake mimic problem. *Journal of Herpetology* 12 (1):1–11.

Grudzien, Thaddeus A. and Paul J. Owens. 1991. Genetic similarity in the gray and brown color morphs of the snake *Storeria occipitomaculata. Journal of Herpetology* 25(1):90–92.

Hahn, D. E., T. E. Megers, and J. W. Goetz. 1972. The status of *Elaphe guttata* (Serpentes: Colubridae) in central and northwestern Louisiana. *Southwestern Naturalist* 17(2): 208–209.

Hakkila, M. 1994. An assessment of potential habitat and distribution of the gray-banded kingsnake (*Lampropeltis alterna*) in New Mexico. Unpubl. Rept. submitted to NM Dept. Gam & Fish. Santa Fe, NM. 12 pp + 3 maps.

Hall, H. P. and J. F. Gennaro. 1961. The relative toxicities of rattlesnake (*Crotalus adamanteus*) and cottonmouth (*Agkistrodon piscivorus*) venom for mice and frogs. *Anat. Rec.* 139:305–306.

Hall, P.M. 1993. Reproduction and behavior of western mud snakes (*Farancia abacura reinwardtii*) in American alligator nests. *Copeia* (1):210–222.

Haller, R. 1971. The diamondback rattlesnakes. *Journal of Herpetology* 5 (3):141–146.

Hamilton, W. J., Jr. and J. A. Pollack. 1955. The food of some crotalid snakes from Fort Benning. Georgia Natural History Miscellanies, No. 140.

Hardy, David L. 1981. *Rattlesnake Envenomation in Southern Arizona.* Tucson, Ariz.: Arizona Poison Control System, University of Arizona Health Sciences Center.

_____. 1982. Overview of rattlesnake bite treatment. Address given November 5–6, 1982, at the Second Annual Southwestern Poison Symposium, Scottsdale, Arizona.

Heatwole, H. 1977. Habitat selection in reptiles. In C. Gans and D. W. Tinkle (eds.) *Biology of the Reptilia*, vol. 7, pp. 137–155. New York: Academic Press.

Heckman, C. W. 1960. Melanism in *Storeria dekayi. Herpetologica* 16:213.

Hillis, David M. and Stephen L. Campbell. 1982. New localities for *Tantilla rubra cucullata* (Colubridae) and the distribution of its two morphotypes. *Southwestern Naturalist* 27 (2):220–221.

Holman, J. A. 1962. A Texas Pleistocene herpetofauna. *Copeia* (1962):255–162.

_____. 1964. Pleistocene amphibians and reptiles from Texas. *Herpetologica* 20:73–83.

Huheey, J. E. 1959. Distribution and variation in the glossy water snake, *Natrix rigida. Copeia* (1959):303–311.

Jackson, Dudley. 1929. Treatment of snake bite. *Southern Medical Journal* 22:605–608.

_____. 1931. First-aid treatment for snake bite. *Texas State Journal of Medicine* 23:203–209.

Jameson, D. L. and A. G. Flury. 1949. The Reptiles and Amphibians of the Sierra Vieja Range of Southwestern Texas. *Texas J. Sci.* 1 (2): 54–77.

Jayne, Bruce C. and J. D. Davis. 1991. Kinematics and performance capacity for the concertina locomotion of a snake (*Coluber constrictor*). *The Journal of Experimental Biology* 1991(156):539–556.

Jones, J. M., and P. M. Burchfield. 1971. Relationship of specimen size to venom extracted from the copperhead, *Agkistrodon contortrix*. *Copeia* (1971):162–163.

Jones, K. B. and W. G. Whitford. 1989. Feeding behavior of free-roaming *Masticophis flagellum*: An efficient ambush predator. *Southwestern Naturalist* 34:460–467.

Kapus, Edward J. 1964. Anatomical evidence for *Heterodon* being poisonous. *Herpetologica* 20:137–138.

Kardong, Kenneth V. 1975. Prey capture in the cottonmouth snake. *Journal of Herpetology* 9(2):169–175.

Keenlyne, K. D. 1972. Sexual differences in feeding habits of *Crotalus horridus horridus*. *Journal of Herpetology* 6(3–4):234–237.

Kennedy, J. P. 1959. A minimum egg complement for the western mud snake, *Farancia abacura reinwardtii*. *Copeia* 1959:71.

_____. 1965. Territorial behavior in the eastern coachwhip, *Masticophis flagellum*. *Anatomical Record* 1965:151–499.

Kiester, A. R. 1971. Species density of North American amphibians and reptiles. *Systematic Zoology*. 20:127–137.

King, Richard B. 1993. Determinants of offspring number and size in the brown snake, *Storeria dekayi*. *Journal of Herpetology* 27(2):175–185.

Klauber, L. M. 1940a. The rattlesnakes, genera *Sistrurus* and *Crotalus*. Chicago Academy of Science Special Publication 4:1–266.

_____. 1956. *Rattlesnakes: Their Habits, Life Histories and Influence on Mankind*. 2 vols. Los Angeles: University of California Press.

_____. 1972. *Rattlesnakes: Their Habits, Life Histories and Influence on Mankind*. 2 vols. Revised edition. Berkeley: University of California Press.

Knight, R. L. and A. W. Erickson, 1976. High incidence of snakes in the diet of red-tailed hawks. *Raptor Res.* 10:108–111.

Kofron, C. P. 1978. Foods and habitats of aquatic snakes (Reptilia, Serpentes) in a Louisiana swamp. *Journal of Herpetology* 12:543–554.

_____. 1979a. Female reproductive biology of the brown snake, *Storeria dekayi*, in Louisiana. *Copeia* 1979:463–466.

_____ and J. R. Dixon. 1980. Observations on aquatic colubrid snakes in Texas. *Southwestern Naturalist* 25:107–109.

Kroll, James C. 1976. Feeding adaptations of hognose snakes. *Southwestern Naturalist* 20 (4):537–557.

Laszlo, Jozsef. 1977a. Notes on thermal requirement of reptiles and amphibians in captivity. Proceedings from the American Association of Zoological Parks and Aquariums Regional Conference, 1977, Wheeling, West Virginia.

Lawson, Robin, Albert J. Meier, Philip G. Frank, and Paul E. Moler. 1991. Allozyme variation and systematics of the *Nerodia fasciata-Nerodia clarkii* complex of water snakes (Serpentes–Colubridae). *Copeia* (3):638–659.

Levell, John P. 1995. *A Field Guide to Reptiles and the Law.* Excelsior, MN: Serpent's Tale Natural History Book Distributors.

Lipske, Michael. 1995. Observations on scarlet snakes, *Cemophora coccinea. Tropical Fish Hobbyist* 43(7):128.

Markel, R. G. 1990. *Kingsnakes and Milk Snakes.* T.F.H. Publications, Inc., Neptune City: 1–144.

_____ and R. D. Bartlett. 1995. *Kingsnakes and Milk Snakes.* Barron's Educational Series, Inc., Hauppauge, NY: 1–94.

Martin, William F. and R. B. Huey. 1971. The function of the epiglottis in sound production (hissing) of *Pituophis melanoleucus. Copeia* 1971:752–754.

Marvel, Bill. 1972. A feeding observation on the yellow-bellied water snake–*Nerodia erythrogaster flavigaster.* Bulletin of the Maryland Herpetological Society 8 (2):52.

McAdoo, J. 1995. Why keep locality *alternas? SEOSH News,* 2 (2): 2.

McCollough, N. E. and J. R. Gennaro, Jr. 1963. Evaluation of venomous snake bite in the southern United States. *Journal of the Florida Medical Association* 49:959–972.

McIntyre, D. Craig. 1977a. Reproductive habits of captive Trans-Pecos rat snakes *Elaphe subocularis. Journal of the Northern Ohio Association of Herpetology* 3(1):20–22.

_____. 1977b. First report of double embryos in *Elaphe subocularis. Journal of the Northern Ohio Association of Herpetology* 3(2):29.

_____. 1978. The NOAH Breeder's Corner. Notes from NOAH 6(2):9.

McKinney, Charles and R. E. Ballinger. 1966. Snake predators of lizards in Texas. *Southwestern Naturalist* Vol. 11 (2) 410–42.

Meade, George O. 1940a. Maternal care of eggs by *Farancia. Herpetologica* 2:15.

_____. 1941. The natural history of the mud snake. *Science Monthly* 63 (1):21–29.

Mecham, J. S. 1979. The biographical relationships of the amphibians and reptiles of the Guadalupe Mountains. Natl. Park Serv. Trans Proc. Ser., (4): 169–179.

_____ and W. W. Milstead. 1949. *Lampropeltis alterna* from Pecos County, Texas. *Herpetologica,* 5 (6): 140.

Mehrtens, J. M. 1987. *Living Snakes of the World.* Sterling Publishing Co., Inc. New York: 1–480.

Merker, G. and W. Broda, Jr. 1993. Poster: Geographic Variation in the Graybanded Kingsnake, *Lampropeltis alterna.* BrodaMerker Enterprises, Pacific Grove.

_____ and C. Merker. 1996. The mystical gray-banded: Gem of North American kingsnakes. *Reptiles,* 4 (7): 60–8.

Mertens, Robert. 1960. *The World of Amphibians and Reptiles.* London: George C. Harrap & Co. New York: McGraw Hill.

Miller, D. J. 1979. A Life History Study of the Gray-banded Kingsnake, *Lampropeltis mexicana alterna* in Texas. M. Sc. Thesis at the Sul Ross State University, Chihuahuan Desert Res. Inst. Cont., Alpine, (87): 1–48.

Milstead, W. W., J. S. Mecham and H. McClintock. 1950. The amphibians and reptiles of the Stockton Plateau in northern Terrell County, Texas. *Texas J. Sci.,* 2 (4): 543–562.

Minton, Jr., Sherman A., 1953. Variation in venom samples from copperheads (*Agkistrodon contortrix mokeson*) and timber rattlesnakes (*Crotalus horridus horridus*). *Copeia* 1953:212–215.

_____. 1954. Polyvalent antivenin in the treatment of experimental snake venom poisoning. *American Journal of Tropical Medicine and Hygiene* 3:1077–1082.

_____. 1957. Snakebite. *Scientific American* 196 (1):114–122.

_____. 1959. Observations on amphibians and reptiles of the Big Bend Region of Texas. *Southwest. Naturalist,* 3: 28–54.

_____. 1974. *Venom Diseases.* Springfield, Illinois: Thomas.

_____ and M. R. Minton. 1969. *Venomous Reptiles.* New York: Charles Scribner's Sons.

Morafka, D. J. 1977. A biogeographical analysis of the Chihuahuan Desert through its herpetofauna. *Biogeographica,* 9: 1–313.

Murphy, James B., W. Tryon, and B. J. Brecke. 1978. An inventory of reproduction and social behavior in captive gray-banded kingsnakes, *Lampropeltis mexicana alterna* (Brown). *Herpetologica,* 34 (1): 84–93.

_____ and Barry L. Armstrong. 1978. *Maintenance of Rattlesnakes in Captivity.* Lawrence, Kansas: University of Kansas Press.

_____ L. A. Mitchell, and J. A. Campbell. 1979. Miscellaneous notes on the reproductive biology of reptiles. *Journal of Herpetology* 13 (3):373–374.

Murray, L. T. 1939. Annotated list of amphibians and reptiles from Chisos Mountains. Contr. Baylor Mus., 24: 416.

Newman, Eric A., and Peter H. Hartline. 1982. The infrared "vision" of snakes. *Scientific American* 246 (3):116–127.

Owen, J. E. and J. R. Dixon. 1989. An ecogeographic analysis of the herpetofauna of Texas. *Southwest Naturalist,* 34(2): 165–180.

Oxer, H. F. 1982. Australian work in first-aid of poisonous snakebite. *Annals of Emergency Medicine* 11:228.

Painter, C. W., P. W. Hyder, and G. Swinford. 1992. Three species new to the herpetofauna of New Mexico. *Herp. Review,* 23 (2): 64.

Palmer, William M. 1971. Distribution and variation of the Carolina pigmy rattlesnake, *Sistrurus miliarius miliarius. North Carolina Journal of Herpetology* 5 (1):39–44.

Parker, H. Wildman and A. G. C. Grandison. 1977. *Snakes: A Natural History.* London: British Museum of Natural History; Ithaca, N.Y.: Cornell University Press.

Parker, W. S., and W. S. Brown. 1980. Comparative ecology of two colubrid snakes, *Masticophis t. taeniatus* and *Pituophis melanoleucus deserticola,* in north Utah. Milwaukee Public Museum Publication, *Biological Geology* 7. 104pp.

Parmley, D. 1990. Late Pleistocene Snakes from Fowlkes Cave, Culberson County, Texas. *Journal of Herpetology,* 24 (3): 266–274.

Parrish, Henry M. 1963. Analysis of 460 fatalities from venomous animals in the United States. *American Journal of Medical Science* 245 (2):35–47.

_____. 1966. Incidence of treated snakebites in the United States. Public Health Reports 81:269–276.

_____. 1980. *Poisonous Snakes in the United States.* New York: Vantage Press.

_____ and M. S. Khan. 1967. Bites by coral snakes: Report of eleven representative cases. *American Journal of Medical Science* 253:561–568.

Peam, J., J. Morrison, N. Charles, and V. Muir. 1981. First-aid for snakebite. *Medical Journal of Australia* 2:293–295.

Peters, James A. 1964. *Dictionary of Herpetology.* New York: Hafner Publishing.

Pisani, G. R., J. T. Collins, and S. R. Edwards. 1973. A re-evaluation of the subspecies of *Crotalus horridus.* Kansas Academy of Sciences 75 (3):255–263.

Platt, Dwight R. 1969. Natural history of the eastern and western hognose snakes *Heterodon platyrhinos* and *Heterodon nasicus.* University of Kansas, Publications of the Museum of Natural History 18 (4):253–420.

Plummer, Michael V. 1981. Habitat utilization, diet, and movements of a temperate arboreal snake (*Opheodrys aestivus*). *Journal of Herpetology* 15(4):425–432.

_____. 1983. Annual variation in stored lipids and reproduction in green snakes (*Opheodrys aestivus*). *Copeia* 1983(3):741–745.

_____. 1990. Nesting movements, nesting behavior, and nest sites of green snakes (*Opheodrys aestivus*) revealed by radiotelemetry. *Herpetologica* 46:190–195.

_____ and Howard L. Snell. 1988. Nest site selection and water relations of eggs in the snake, (*Opheodrys aestivus*). *Copeia* 1988(1):58–64.

_____ and Justin D. Congdon. 1994. Radiotelemetric study of activity and movements of racers (*Coluber constrictor*) associated with a Carolina Bay in South Carolina. *Copeia* 1994(1):20–26.

Porras, L. 1992. Gray-banded kingsnake, *Lampropeltis alterna*, predation. *Intermontanus*, 1 (4): 3.

Porter, K. R. 1972. *Herpetology*. Philadelphia: W. B. Saunders Co.

Pough, F. H. 1964. A coral snake "mimic" eaten by a bird. *Copeia* 1964:223.

Quinn, Hugh R. 1979. Reproduction and growth of the Texas coral snake (*Micrurus fulvius tenere*). *Copeia* 1979:453–463

Raun, G. G. 1965. *A Guide to Texas Snakes*. Texas Memorial Museum, Univ. Texas, Austin, Museum Notes No. 9: 1–85.

Rawat, Sophia, Gavin Laing, Damon C. Smith, David Theakston, and John Landon. 1993. A new antivenom to treat eastern coral snake (*Micrurus fulvius fulvius*) envenoming. *Toxicon* 32(2):185–190.

Raymond, L. R. and L. M. Hardy. 1983. Taxonomic status of the corn snake, *Elaphe guttata* (Linnaeus) (Colubridae), in Louisiana and eastern Texas. *Southwest Naturalist*, 28(1): 105–107.

Reddell, J. R. 1971. A Checklist of the Cave Fauna of Texas. 6. Additional Records of Vertebrata. *Texas J. Sci.*, 22 (23): 139–158.

Redi, Francesco. 1664. *Osservazioni Intorno alle Vipere*. Florence.

Reichling, Steven B. 1995. The taxonomic status of the Louisiana pine snake (*Pituophis melanoleucus ruthveni*) and its relevance to the evolutionary species concept. *Journal of Herpetology* 20(2):186–198.

Riches, Robert J. 1976. *Breeding Snakes in Captivity*. St. Petersburg, Fla.: Palmetto Publishing.

Riemer, W. J. 1957. The snake *Farancia abacura*: An attended nest. *Herpetologica* 13:31–32.

Robertshaw, D. 1974. *Environmental Physiology*. Baltimore: University Park Press.

Rogers, James S. 1976. Species density and taxonomic diversity of Texas amphibians and reptiles. *Systematic Zoology* 25:26–40.

Rosenberg, Martin J. 1981. *Medical Treatment of Venomous Snakebite*. Cleveland: Cleveland Museum of Natural History.

Rossi, John V. 1992. *Snakes of the United States and Canada, Keeping Them Healthy in Captivity*. Vol. 1: Eastern Area. Malabar, Florida: Krieger Publishing Company.

_____. 1995. *Snakes of the United States and Canada, Keeping Them Healthy in Captivity*. Vol. 2: Western Area. Malabar, Florida: Krieger Publishing Company.

Rossman, Douglas A. 1962. *Thamnophis proximus:* A valid species of garter snake. *Copeia* 1962: 741–748.

_____. 1963b. The colubrid snake genus *Thamnophis:* A revision of the *sauritus* group. Bulletin of the Florida State Museum of Biological Sciences 7 (3):99–178.

_____ and Robert L. Erwin. 1980. Geographic variation in the snake *Storeria occipitomaculata* (Serpentes: Colubridae) in southeastern United States. *Brimleyana* 4:95–102.

_____ Neil B. Ford, and Richard Seigel. 1996. *Garter Snakes: Evolution and Ecology*. University of Oklahoma Press. Norman, Okla. p. 1–322.

Roze, Janis A. 1996. *Coral Snakes of the Americas: Biology, Identification, and Venoms*. Malabar, Florida: Krieger Publishing Company.

Russell, Findlay E. 1961. Injuries by venomous animals in the United States. *Journal of the American Medical Association* 177:903–907.

_____. 1966. Shock following snakebite. *Journal of the American Medical Association* 198:171.

_____. 1967. Pharmacology of animal venoms. *Clinical Pharmacology Therapy*. 8:849–873.

_____. 1969. Treatment of rattlesnake bite. *Journal of the American Medical Association* 207:159.

_____. 1980. *Snake Venom Poisoning*. Philadelphia: J. B. Lippincott.

_____ R. W. Carlson, J. Wainschel, and A. H. Osborne. 1975. Snake venom poisoning in the United States: Experiences with 550 cases. *Journal of the American Medical Association* 233:341.

Salmon, Gerard T., William F. Holmstrom, Jr., Bern W. Tryon, and Gerold P. Merker. 1977. Longevity Records for *Lampropeltis alterna*. Bull. Chicago Herp. Soc. 32 (7); 152–153.

Schmidt, Karl P. and D. D. Davis. 1941. *Field Book of Snakes of the United States and Canada*. New York: G. P. Putnam's Sons.

_____ 1953. *A Check List of North American Amphibians and Reptiles*. Chicago. University of Chicago Press.

_____ and D. D. Davis. 1941. *Field Book of Snakes of the United States and Canada*. New York: G. P. Putnam's Sons.

_____ and D. W. Owens. 1944. Amphibians and Reptiles of Northern Coahuila, Mexico. Zool. Ser. Field Mus. Nat. Hist., 26 (6): 97–115.

Scudday, J. F. 1965. Another *Lampropeltis alterna* in Brewster County, Texas. *Southwestern Naturalist,* 10 (1): 77–78.

Secor, S. M. 1990. Reproductive and Combat Behavior of the Mexican Kingsnake, *Lampropeltis mexicana. J. Herp.,* 24 (2): 217–221.

Seigel, Richard A. and H. S. Fitch. 1984. Ecological patterns of relative clutch mass in snakes. *Oecologia* 61:293–301.

_____ and Joseph T. Collins. eds. 1993. *Snakes: Ecology and Behavior.* New York: McGraw-Hill, Inc.

Semlitsch, R. D. and Gary B. Moran. 1984. Ecology of the redbelly snake (*Storeria occipitomaculata*) using mesic habitats in South Carolina. *The American Midland Naturalist* 111:33–40.

_____ J. H. K. Pechmann, and J. W. Gibbons. 1988. Annual emergence of juvenile mud snakes (*Farancia abacura*) at aquatic habitats. *Copeia* 1988:243–245.

Sexton, Owen J., Peter Jacobson, and Judy E. Bramble. 1992. Geographic variation in some activities associated with nearctic pitvipers. In *Biology of the Pitvipers.* (eds.) Jonathan A. Campbell and Edmund D. Brodie. Tyler, Texas: Selva Press.

Shaw, C. E. and S. Campbell. 1974. *Snakes of the American West.* New York, Alfred A. Knopf Publishing.

Slavens, Frank L. 1980. *Inventory of Live Reptiles and Amphibians in North American Collections*. Seattle, Wash.: Frank L. Slavens.

Smith, Hobart M. 1941a. *Lampropeltis alterna* from Mexico. *Copeia,* (2): 112.

_____. 1941b. A review of the subspecies of the indigo snake (*Drymarchon corais*). *Journal of the Washington Academy of Sciences* 31 (11):466–481.

_____. 1944. Snakes of the Hoogstraal Expedition to northern Mexico. Zool. Ser. Field Mus. Nat. Hist., 29 (8): 135–152.

_____ and W. L. Buechner. 1947. The influence of the Balcones Escarpment on the distribution of amphibians and reptiles in Texas. Bull. Chicago Acad. Sci., 8 (1): 1–16.

_____ and E. H. Taylor. 1950. Type localities of Mexican reptiles and amphibians. Univ. Kansas Sci. Bull., 33: 313–379.

_____ and Fred N. White. 1955. Adrenal enlargement and its significance in the hognose snakes (*Heterodon*). *Herpetologica* 11:137–144.

_____ D. Chizar, J. R. Staley, II and K. Tepedelen. 1994. Populational relationships in the corn snake *Elaphe guttata* (Reptilia: Serpentes). *Texas J. Sci.*, 46(3): 259–292.

Smith, N. G. 1969. Avian predation of coral snakes. *Copeia* 1969:402–404.

Smith, R. L. 1977. *Elements of Ecology and Field Biology.* New York: Harper & Row.

Smith, S. M. 1975. Innate recognition of coral snake pattern by a possible avian predator. *Science* 187:759–760.

Snyder, C. C., J. E. Pickins, R. P. Knowles, et al. 1968. A definitive study of snakebite. *Journal of the Florida Medical Association* 55:330–338.

Stewart, James R. 1989. Facultative placentotrophy and the evolution of squamate placentation: Quality of eggs and neonates in Virginia striatula. *The American Naturalist.* 133(1):111–137.

Stinner, J. N. and D. L. Ely. 1993. Blood pressure during routine activity, stress, and feeding in black racer snakes (*Coluber constrictor*). *American Journal of Physiology* 1993(264).

Strecker, John K. 1915. *Reptiles and Amphibians of Texas.* Baylor University Bulletin 18 (4):82.

_____. 1926. On the habits of some southern snakes. Contributions of the Baylor University Museum, No. 4.

_____. 1927. Chapters from the life history of Texas and amphibians. Contributions of the Baylor University Museum, No. 10.

Sutherland, Struan K. 1980. Venom and antivenom research. *Medical Journal of Australia* 2:246–250.

_____. 1981. When do you remove first-aid measures from an envenomed limb? *Medical Journal of Australia* 1:542–544.

_____ Alan R. Coulter, and R. D. Harris. 1979. Rationalization of first-aid measures for elapid snakebite. *Lancet* 1:183–186.

Switak, K. H. 1984. *The Life of Desert Reptiles and Amphibians.* Produced by Karl H. Switak, P.O. Box 27141, San Francisco, Calif. 94127: 1–32.

Tanzer, E. C. 1970. Polymorphism in the *mexicana* complex of kingsnakes, with notes on their natural history. *Herpetologica*, 26 (4): 419–428.

Telford, S. R., Jr. 1955. A description of the eggs of the coral snake, *Micrurus f. fulvius. Copeia* 1955:258.

Tennant, Alan. 1984. *The Snakes of Texas.* Austin: Texas Monthly Press, Inc.

_____. 1997. *A Field Guide to Snakes of Florida.* Houston: Gulf Publishing Co.

Thomas, R. G. and F. H. Pough. 1979. Effects of rattlesnake venom on digestion of prey. *Toxicon* 17 (3):221–228.

Thompson, Stith. 1936. *Index of Folk Literature.* Bloomington, Ind.: Indiana University Press.

Tinkle, Donald W. 1957. Ecology, maturation and reproduction of *Thamnophis sauritus proximus. Ecology* 38 (1):69–77.

_____. 1960. A population of *Opheodrys aestivus. Copeia* 1960:29–34.

Trapido, H. 1940. Mating time and sperm viability in Storeria. *Copeia* 1940:107–109.

Tryon, B. W. 1979. An unusually patterned specimen of the gray-banded kingsnake, *Lampropeltis mexicana alterna* (Brown). *Herp. Review,* 10 (1): 4–5.

_____ and J. B. Murphy. 1982. Miscellaneous notes on the reproductive biology of reptiles. 5. Thirteen varieties of the genus *Lampropeltis*, Species *mexicana, triangulum* and *zonata.* Trans Kansas Acad. Sci., 85 (2): 96–119.

_____ and R. K. Guese. 1984. Death-feigning in the gray-banded kingsnake *Lampropeltis alterna. Herp. Review,* 15 (4): 108–109.

Turner, Earl H. 1977. Colorful kingsnake of the Trans-Pecos. *Texas Parks and Wildlife,* 35 (1): 10–11.

Van Devender, Thomas R. and R. D. Worthington. 1977. The Herpetofauna of Howell's Ridge Cave and the Paleoecology of the Northwestern Chihuahuan Desert. In R. H. Waver and D. H. Riskind (eds.), Trans. Symp. Resources Chihuahuan Desert, U.S. & Mexico, pp. 16–41. U.S. Natl. Park Serv. Trans. Proc. Ser. No. 13. Washington, D.C.

_____ and C. H. Lowe, Jr. 1977. Amphibians and reptiles of Yepomera, Chihuahua, Mexico. *Journal of Herpetology* 11 (1): 41–50.

_____ and J. I. Mead. 1978. Early Holocene and Late Pleistocene amphibians and reptiles in Sonoran Desert Packrat Middens. *Copeia* 1978(3):464–475.

Van Mierop, L.H.S. 1976. Poisonous snakebite: A review. *Journal of the Florida Medical Association* 63:191–209.

Vaughan, K. R., J. R. Dixon, and R. A. Thomas. 1996. A re-evaluation of populations of the corn snake *Elaphe guttata* (Reptilia: Serpentes: Colubridae) in Texas. *Texas J. Sci.* 48(3): 175–190.

Visser, John and David S. Chapman. 1978. *Snakes and Snakebite*. London: Purnell & Son.

Ward, R., F. G. Zimmerman, and T. L. King. 1994. Environmental correlates to terrestrial reptilian distributions in Texas. *Texas J. Sci.* 46(1): 21–26.

Watt, Charles H., Jr. 1978. Poisonous snakebite treatment in the United States. *Journal of the American Medical Association* 240:654.

Webb, R. 1961. A new kingsnake from Mexico, with remarks on the *mexicana* group of the genus *Lampropeltis*. *Copeia*, (3): 326–333.

_____. 1970. *Reptiles of Oklahoma*. Norman, Okla.: University of Oklahoma Press.

Weinstein, Scott, Clement DeWitt, and Leonard A. Smith. 1992. Variability of venom-neutralizing properties of serum from snakes of the colubrid genus *Lampropeltis*. *Journal of Herpetology* 26(4):452–461.

Werler, John E. 1948. *Natrix cyclopion cyclopion* in Texas. *Herpetologica* 4:148.

Wharton, C. H. 1960. Birth and behavior of a brood of the cottonmouth, *Agkistrodon piscivorus leucostoma,* with notes on tail-luring. *Herpetologica* 16:125–129.

Williams, Kenneth L., Bryce C. Brown, and Larry David Wilson. 1966. A new subspecies of the Colubrid snake *Cemophora coccinea* (Blumenbach) from southern Texas. *Texas Journal of Science* 18 (1):85–88.

_____ and Larry David Wilson. 1967. A review of the colubrid snake genus Cemophora. *Tulane Studies in Zoology and Botany* 13 (4):103–124.

_____. 1970b. The racer, *Coluber constrictor,* in Louisiana and eastern Texas. *Texas Journal of Science* 22 (1):67–85.

_____. 1978. Systematics and Natural History of the American Milksnake, *Lampropeltis triangulum*. Milwaukee Public Museum, Publications in Biology and Geology, (2): 1–258.

Williamson, M. A., P. W. Hyder, and J. S. Applegarth. 1994. *Snakes, Lizards, Turtles, Frogs, Toads and Salamanders of New Mexico*. A Field Guide. Sunstone Press, Santa Fe: 1–176.

Wingert, W. A., T. R. Pattabhiraman, R. Cleland, P. Meyer, R. Pattabhiraman, and F. E. Russell. 1980. Distribution and pathology of copperhead *Agkistrodon contortrix* venom. *Toxicon* 18:591–601.

Winstel, A. 1996. Experience with a difficult feeder—*Lampropeltis alterna. The Forked Tongue,* 21 (4): 3.

Wolfenden, R. Norris. 1886. On the nature and action of the venom of poisonous snakes. *Journal of Physiology* 7:327.

Worthington, R. D. 1976. Herpetofauna of the Franklin Mountains, El Paso County, Texas. In: D. V. LeMone and E. M. P. Lovejoy: El Paso Geological Society Symposium on the Franklin Mountains. El Paso Geol. Soc. Quinn Mem. Vol.: 205–212.

_____ and E. R. Arvizo. 1974. Western records of the Davis Mountains kingsnake, *Lampropeltis mexicana alterna,* in Texas. *Southwestern Naturalist,* 19 (3): 330–331.

Wright, Albert Hazen and Anna Allen Wright. 1957. *Handbook of Snakes of the United States and Canada.* 2 vols: 1–1105. Ithaca, N.Y.: Comstock Publishing.

_____. 1979. *Handbook of Snakes of the United States and Canada.* Vol. 3: Bibliography. Ithaca, N.Y.: Comstock Publishing.

Ya, P. M., T. Guzman, and J. F. Perry, Jr. 1961. Treatment of bites of North American pitvipers. *Southern Medical Journal* 52 (2):134–136.

Young, Robert A. 1992. Effects of Duvernoy's gland secretions from the eastern hognose snake, *heterodon platirhinos,* on smooth muscle and neuromuscular junction. *Toxicon* 30(7):775–779.

Zug, D. A. and W. A. Dunson. 1979. Salinity preference in fresh water and estuarine snakes (*Nerodia sipedon* and *N. fasciata*). *Florida Sci.* 42:1–8.

Zug, George R. 1993. *Herpetology, and Introductory Biology of Amphibians and Reptiles.* London: Academic Press.

Zweifel, Richard G., G. R. Zug, C. J. McCoy, D. A. Rossman, and J. D. Anderson, eds. 1963–present. *Catalogue of American Amphibians and Reptiles.* New York: Society for the Study of Amphibians and Reptiles.

Index